The
PO

TOBIAS JONES is the author of eight previous books, including *The Dark Heart of Italy*, *A Place of Refuge* and the prize-winning *Ultra*. He is a regular contributor to the British, American and Italian press and has written and presented documentaries for the BBC and, in Italy, for RAI. The co-founder of two woodland charities in the UK, he has recently launched a new project, Common Home, in Parma.

www.tobias-jones.com

@Tobias_Italia

ALSO BY TOBIAS JONES

The Dark Heart of Italy

Utopian Dreams

The Salati Case

White Death

Blood on the Altar

Death of a Showgirl

A Place of Refuge

Ultra

The PO

AN ELEGY FOR
ITALY'S LONGEST RIVER

TOBIAS JONES

An Apollo Book

First published in the UK in 2022 by Head of Zeus Ltd,
part of Bloomsbury Publishing Plc

9 7 5 3 1 2 4 6 8

A catalogue record for this book is available from the British Library.

ISBN (HB): 9781786697394
ISBN (E): 9781786697387

Typeset by Ben Cracknell Studios
Maps by Jamie Whyte

Image credits: View of Mantova, 1575 courtesy of
Wikimedia Commons. All photographs © Tobias Jones.

The author is grateful for permission to quote from *Four Quartets*
by T. S. Eliot (Faber and Faber Ltd)

Every effort has been made to trace copyright holders and to obtain their permission
for the use of copyright material. The publisher apologizes for any errors or omissions
in the above list and would be grateful if notified of any corrections that should be
incorporated in future reprints or editions of this book.

Printed and bound in Great Britain by
CPI Group (UK) Ltd, Croydon CR0 4YY

Head of Zeus Ltd
First Floor East
5–8 Hardwick Street
London EC1R 4RG

www.headofzeus.com

For Matteo Galloni ("il Gallo")

"La vita moderna ha un ritmo falso.
I nostri tassametri continuano a salire e
tutti abbiamo paura di non poter pagare."

Bruno Barilli, 1963

Modern life has a false rhythm.
Our fares keep rising and all of us fear we
won't be able to pay.

Contents

Glossary

ACQUA DOLCE: Freshwater

ALPI COZIE: The Cottian Alps, the south-western section of the Alps whose symbol is MONVISO

ARCHIBUGIO: The arquebus gun

ARGINE (pl. ARGINI): Riverbank

ARGINE MAESTRO: The main riverbank (there is often a secondary one on the other side of the designated floodplain actually next to the water)

BASSA: Low-lying land/lowlands. Always accompanied by the definite article: LA BASSA

BODRIO (pl. BODRI): Floodplain lakes and ponds (aka BUGNO/I)

BONDINCUS: Synonym of River Po

BONIFICA (pl. BONIFICHE): Land reclamation

BUCO DI VISO: A tunnel excavated through MONVISO (c.1478–80), also known in French as "le pertuis du Viso" or "le tunnel de la Traversette"

BURATTINO: A glove puppet

CANNABIS SATIVA: The cannabis plant from which hemp is derived

CONDOTTIERO: A mercenary

DAUPHINÉ: A former province in south-eastern France under the control, until 1349, of the Counts of Albon (later called the Dauphins of Viennois due to the presence of a dolphin on their coat of arms)

DELIZIE: The "delights" of the Estensi dynasty

ERIDANO: A river of Greek mythology (Eridanos/Eridanus in English). Also the ancient Greek word for the River Po

ESCARTO[U]NS: A republic or federation straddling the Italo-French border in the Cottian Alps (c.1244–1713/1798)

ESTE (pl. ESTENSI): The SIGNORIA of Ferrara (1240–1597)

EUTROPHICATION: The enrichment of water by nutrients and minerals (very often agricultural fertilisers) leading to algal blooms

FARNESE: The SIGNORIA of Parma (1545–1731)

FOJONCO: One of the mythological beasts of the lowlands

FOSSA: A ditch

GOLENA (pl. GOLENE): Floodplain

GONZAGA: The SIGNORIA of Mantova (1328–1708)

IDROVORA: A pump station

LANZICHENECCHI: The Italianisation of *Landsknechte*, the Germanic foot soldiers of the Holy Roman Empire's Imperial Army

LATIFUNDISMO: A system of great landed estates

LEFT BANK: Looking downstream, the bank on the left (usually the northern side of the Po)

MATAF: Abbreviation of "Mediterranean Allied Tactical Air Force" in the Second World War

MENTHA PIPERITA: Peppermint

MONDINA (pl. MONDINE): A female rice paddy worker (*mondare* = to clean, peel or prune)

MONVISO: The mountain (3,842 metres) in whose "Plain of the King" the Po is born. Nicknamed *Re di Pietra*, "Stone King"

NUTRIA: *Myocastor coypus* (coypu)

PADUS: Synonym of River Po

PEDOCLIMATE: A microclimate within soil

PELLAGRA: A disease characterised by dermatitis, gastrointestinal disorders and mental disturbances associated with a diet deficient in niacin

PERCHED: A perched river has a bed higher than the surrounding ground elevation and is therefore not the lowest point in the valley

PIAN DEL RE: "The Plain of the King", site of the source of the Po

PIANURA PADANA: The plain of the Po

PIENA: "Full" (used to describe the river when it's almost flooding)

ROGGIA: An irrigation ditch

ROTTA: A breach in the riverbank

RIGHT BANK: Looking downstream, the bank on the right (usually the southern side of the Po)

RISAIA (pl. RISAIE): A rice paddy field

RISORGIMENTO: The movement for Italian unity in the nineteenth century

SICYOS ANGULATUS: Star-cucumber, aka ZUCCA PAZZA, the "mad pumpkin"

SIGNORIA: The governing dynasty of a city state

SINKHOLE: A hollow place or depression in which drainage collects; often connected to groundwater through cavities and swallets

TAGLIO: A cut (i.e. to divert the river)

TERRAMARE: Middle/Late Bronze Age settlements along the plain of the Po

VALDESI: the Waldensians, followers of Peter Valdo/Waldo of Lyon (*c.*1140–*c.*1205). Aka Vaudois or Waldenses

Spellings, Languages, Translations etc.

I've maintained the Italian spellings of all place names (although for geographical adjectives – like Lombard or Emilian – I have obviously kept the English). I have also maintained the Italian spellings of personal names to avoid mangling Vittorio into Victor and so on. Both place names and personal names should, however, be easily recognisable. A lot of writing about the river is either archaic or in dialect: the words are so rich and resonant that I have frequently quoted them in full (complete with unusual spellings) with translations alongside. Unless otherwise stated, translations (and challenging rhymes) are mine.

ONE

Pialassa

'm bobbing along in a small boat trying to work my way in but there's nothing to offer any bearings. In this eerie space, which is neither quite open sea nor solid land, it feels as if you're in a spacious maze of low-lying bars, islands and spits. All is flat. The sky is wide and the distant land is nothing more than blue-grey mould on the water.

Any ground here seems unsolid: the *scanni*, long sandbanks, are constantly dented or stretched by the slap of waves and the gusting winds. Little islands called *bonelli* emerge, moulded by the meeting of the tide and the river's slow flow. Then, days or years later, they go under again. This is what they call, in dialect, *pialassa* – the "give and take" of sea and river, of water and land.

It's no longer a place where humans belong. A ruined building stands in the water, its brick walls half gone, like a smashed-up Lego project. On every other spit there are abandoned churches, smokehouses and shacks. Absent windows and doors create dark, rectangular sockets.

Birds are in charge here. The executioner's cap of a sandwich tern looks down on you from a post. Stilts, with their bubble-gum-pink legs, wade in the mud and algae alongside the avocets and redshanks. Every minute another grey heron or little egret leaps into the air, squawking annoyance at your invasion.

It's peaceful but busy. There are sudden splashes as fish surface or birds dive. A couple of coots sprint across the water, black necks like wooden spoons straining forward as they flap for lift-off. There are shrieks and quacks. Distant human noises – an outboard motor or the metallic clank of farm machinery – are drowned out by the incessant hiss of reeds in the wind.

The closer you get to that blue-grey horizon, the more there are flashes of colour. It's early autumn, and the wispy tamarisks are green and purple. The marsh samphire is flowering a pinky-red. Pigweed and false indigo give these strips of land a violet and russet vibrance. Virgil – in one of his passages about the River

Po – called this the river's *mare purpureum*, its "crimson sea".

The colours are buttery, too. Amid the tangles of rinsed driftwood, yellow evening primroses loom tall. The shiny slime on the mud – called *velme* – is yellow-green. The more quietly you drift, the more colours you glimpse: the yellow dot on the end of the sandwich tern's black beak or the bright orange bill, like a tapering Pinocchio nose, on an oystercatcher.

I'm beginning at the delta end of the river so that I can work my way, against the current, to the source. But in this vast delta there is no singular end, only dozens of different ones. You write about a river expecting a clear line, assuming that strong banks and boundaries will give you direction. It's supposed to be, structurally, a cinch. But here, in the first hours of the long ride-and-paddle upstream, everything is smudged. The slow ribbon of the Po, whose whereabouts hasn't been in doubt for the previous 652 kilometres, is suddenly frayed 40 kilometres wide. Italy's longest river has the largest delta in the Mediterranean after the Nile.

The distances in this delta are so great that it seems like you're on infinite tin foil, glinting and crackling. Silhouetted punts have silent figures squatting over fishing nets. Lines of black posts, fastened together with a top rail, look like upturned railway tracks. There are thick beams leaning into each other, elderly lovers bound by a metal headband.

The sky is so wide that you can see different weather conditions in one glance: bruised clouds, stretched white ones, clear blue sky. As the sun sets, a glitter line dances across the water towards the boat.

I remember the moment I knew, with a rare flash of intuition, that I was going to write a book about this river. I was standing on a bridge in one of my favourite cities, Torino. Underneath

my feet oarsmen and women were slicing through the clear
water. Living in Parma, I had, until then, thought of the Po as
a slow, ugly river. Hemmed in by Italy's industrial heartlands
in the Veneto, Emilia-Romagna, Lombardia and Piemonte, I
had usually seen it only from bridges and the windows of cars
and trains: sluggish and dirty, it was often overshadowed by
the tubular tangles of power plants which used its waters to
cool off. The river's sheer vastness – one of its many ancient
names was "Bondincus", meaning "bottomless" – I simply
found off-putting.

But then, in Torino, I suddenly saw it differently. The river
wasn't quite dainty, but it was slim and clear. It still had force
– you could hear it dancing down the city's weir – but it was
downsized for participation. There was an elegance to it, and
I began to think of all the other great cities it cut through, or
was linked to via tributaries and man-made canals: Ferrara,
Mantova, Parma, Cremona, Piacenza and Pavia. I considered
the appeal of writing about a river: you don't choose where it
takes you, so you end up in unexpected places, not just neglected
cities but towns and villages you would never otherwise visit.
It was as if I didn't even have to decide where to go – the river
would do that for me. With my feet planted on the Umberto I
bridge, I had never made a decision so quickly.

Compared to many of the planet's longest rivers, the Po is
relatively short. Its 652 kilometres seem almost insignificant
compared to the 6,640 kilometres of the Nile, the 6,400
kilometres of the Amazon or even the 2,888 kilometres of the
Danube. But its shortness means the Po belongs entirely to just
one country. Even its watershed (c. 74,000 square kilometres) is
almost all in Italy (the exception being 3,000 square kilometres
in parts of Switzerland). The river stretches from one end of Italy
(high up in the Alps, only a few hundred metres from the French
border) to the other (the Adriatic Sea just south of Venezia). And

although comparatively short, there is something majestic about the Po. Virgil called it *fluviorum rex*, "the king of rivers". The poet Guido Ceronetti once wrote that "you need to understand the Po to understand Italy" and I began to hope that the river might offer a vein from which I could take samples of the blood of my adopted country.

When viewed from an Italian perspective, the Po actually seems fairly mighty: the river has 141 tributaries (ninety-five to the left as the river flows, and forty-six to the right). Its (Italian) drainage basin of 71,057 square kilometres represents around a quarter of all Italian territory, around twenty million of its inhabitants, 3,500 municipalities and roughly 40 per cent of the country's GDP. The south side of the river (the right bank) is often troubled by water scarcity, with smaller tributaries having very variable flows from the Apennines. But the north side of the Po is fed by major rivers (from west to east: Ticino, Adda, Oglio and Mincio) which descend from four lakes accounting for 70 per cent of the water volume of surface freshwater in Italy (Lakes Maggiore, Como, Iseo and Garda).

The river's importance, historically, has been that of a vital highway and an unreliable moat. It was, for millennia, an aquatic thoroughfare, by far the easiest way to transport goods from the Mediterranean all the way to the hinterlands of Emilia, Lombardia and Piemonte. Every duchy or principality fought for access to the river in order to levy charges on trade and so, all along its banks, there are ancient castles and customs houses. But the river was also like a moat which, for centuries, delineated territories and stalled invaders from the north. From Hannibal and his elephants to Holy Roman Emperors and the *Landsknechte*, armies and navies have always met on these often impassable plains.

I'm aware that a waterway can be an erratic historical guide. As Olivia Laing wrote in her book on the River Ouse, "the earth hoards its treasures and what is buried there remains until it's disinterred by spade or plough, but a river is more shifty, relinquishing its possessions haphazardly and without regard to the landlocked chronology historians hold so dear. A history compiled by way of water is by its nature quick and fluid..." Haphazard was, I came to realise, a fair description of my journey. I travelled by all conceivable means of transport: boat, foot, bicycle, bus, train and car. I swung between the left and right banks according to what interested me. The river has changed course so often that I decided it was legitimate to follow not only the river's present course but also, sometimes, its ancient ones.

For centuries the Po's edges were very smudged. Its bed was really an immense marsh which was partly comparable to the Somerset Levels. In this "Padanian plain" ("Padus" is one of the river's many names, of which "Po" was a later contraction) there was a class of riverbank dweller who was ingenious and resourceful: milling wheat and cultivating unexpected cash crops like clams, eels, sturgeon caviar and, in the ever-flooding fields, hemp, silk and rice. I discovered that if the river was often the site of battles between the different seignory powers of northern Italy and beyond, the river's boggy floodplains were also a shelter for the excluded and the dispossessed. The Po travels through such horizontal land that it floods frequently, and most territories close to it were, until the twentieth century, dangerous and unprofitable. It was there that the very poorest of the Pianura Padana had their crop shares and shacks. Since the waterway was always, until Italian unification, the boundary between one territorial power and another, Po-side settlements attracted smugglers, outlaws and itinerants who needed to jump from one jurisdiction to another. The degree to which the forests of the Po's floodplains gave cover to petty criminals is evident from odd place names: there's a peninsula near Parma called "the island of the interned" and, near Piacenza, a village called Rea, which might come from a word which means, more or less, "the guilty".

"It's as if there's an anarchic and libertarian spirit which attracts particular individuals to the Po," the musician Adriano Scillitani wrote recently; "people who have decided to live in their own way and thus have a vision of the world different to ours". It's something which has been noted for centuries, with all sorts of explanations: the Po just draws "personalities who are a bit strange", says Riccardo Varini, the Reggio photographer. "It's a land of contraband where you breathe an air of almost gypsy-ish liberty."

That counterculture along the river's edges was perhaps inevitable because the land there was precarious. It wasn't only the delta that flooded. Both left and right banks as far inland as Monferrato, almost at Torino, were also frequently breached. Even near the source, in the Cottian Alps, land was under snow for months on end. There was an impermanence to land and, perhaps because of that, there are many examples of communities offering each other an insurance by deciding to hold land in common. I'm always drawn to communitarian spaces which defy mainstream privatisation, and along the Po there were many examples: musical ensembles that formed socialist squats to alleviate agricultural poverty, lot-drawing woodlands that gave villagers permanent access to land, tax-free enclaves where the people distributed their own resources.

Those pockets of ordered or anarchic resistance to private ownership intrigued me. Their frequency along the river's banks suggested that personal and social eccentricity was an integral part of the Po's story. But I was also drawn to those commonholds because, with their constitutions or articles of association precluding sell-offs and thus an inevitable transformation into industrialised farms, they maintained a much closer fidelity to the native ecology of this river. As you would expect, the Po has been poisoned by the by-products of factories and farms: until serious clear-up efforts began in the 1990s, when "defence from the waters" became accompanied by "defence of the waters", the river had been used as a drain for pollutants. The size of that drainage basin, and the fact that the Pianura Padana is so heavily industrialised, means that the river suffered from effluents throughout the twentieth century. It has also been dammed and deviated. Its beds were raided for sands and gravels during the boom years of Italy's "economic miracle". Invasive species have strangled and starved the natives. A lot of the journey, I knew, would be ugly and depressing, so I looked out for those resilient spaces where shared ownership had preserved an ecological inheritance. The rare hornbeam trees were as much a part of the history I hoped to trace as were the nobles and their repetitive wars.

So I set off with lots of leads and ideas and the expectation that I would, at least, usually know where to go. But I've only just started and I'm already lost. There are five rivers now: the Po Grande, the Po Maistra, the Po Piccolo, the Po di Gnocca and the Po delle Tolle. Even those five endings in the delta, forming a leopard-skin of ponds, islands, inlets and sandbanks, have other names and tributaries: the Po Grande is also called the Po di Venezia and, later, the Po di Pila. The Po di Gnocca is also known as "della Donzella", the Po Piccolo is often referred to as "Po di Goro". There's a sixth branch to the south, the Po di Volano, and another to the north (the Tartaro-collettore padano-polesine, which is the original route of the river before – you hear a lot about this – the famous "break of Ficarolo" in 1152).

Before I even get to those many branches, there are various *buse*, slim twigs which shoot off them. The Po di Pila becomes the *busa di scirocco* (south), the *busa dritta* (straight on) and *busa di tramontana* (north). It almost seems deliberately confusing: as the verbose futurist Corrado Govoni once wrote, the delta is "an absurd and disordered overlap and intersection of currents in the blind search for any opening into the Adriatic... an intricacy of arteries and thin veins". No wonder the Romans called the vast salt marshes of this delta the *septem maria*, the "seven seas".

There's much impermanence in this delta: the river floods and soaks, then the land is salvaged and defended. The sea rises and is then nudged another way. That advance and retreat between land and water has been going on for centuries. The small town of Mesola was "media isola" – middle island. Polesine meant "marshy lands". Often the names arose simply because there were many more animals than humans. Oca Marina was a place of wild geese. The town of Scardovari was named after the rudd (*scardolle*) they fished and the next-door village is called Bonelli ("islands" in dialect).

In one of his madrigals about this soaked landscape, Torquato Tasso spoke of "*secchi ed ondosi calli*", of "dry and wave-filled streets". His archaic Italian – *quinci* and *lece* – sounds deliberately squelchy. As I squint at my phone in the sunset, trying to understand where I am, there are more waterways than roads: not just the many iterations of the river, but hundreds of different irrigation tracks given names like *scolo* (drain), *fossone* (big ditch), *collettore* (collector) or just *canale* (canal or channel).

This sullen flatness disperses all enthusiasm and orientation. It's as if there's no purpose other than the water's sad obedience to gravity. The only way to fit in is to go horizontal: to lie low, rent a boat and drift. From here, human endeavour seems not only futile, but also ugly: the only verticals that dare puncture that 180 degrees of sky are man-made: the red and white chimneys of an abandoned power station, the grim pylons, the cranes repairing the fat, white lighthouse at Gorino. As well as restful, the delta is a melancholy place, historically associated with dissipation and death. This is where Dante fell ill and died and his description of the river here is funereal: "the Po descends / to be at peace with his followers" ("dove 'l Po discende / per aver pace co' seguaci sui"). The river is always masculine, "il Po".

In one of my favourite novels, Renata Viganò's *L'Agnese va a morire,* a sturdy female partisan criss-crosses this delta at the brutal end of the Second World War. Viganò describes the grim realities of this no-man's land: "you smelt the dead stench of swamps, the whiff of rotten walls, of damp rags, of mould, like in the houses of the poor..." The delta, she wrote, was "a sad, grey place with a disconsolate horizon". The water, in her pages, is never romanticised: a "green canal" is "slimy as a snail..." The destitution of the delta dwellers was apparent well into the twentieth century. Federico Fellini collaborated with Roberto Rossellini on the episodic film *Paisà* (1946), the sixth and final part of which is set near the mouth of the Po. He said that this delta had a primitiveness unlike anything he had seen in the rest of the peninsula: "we had been in Sicilia and in Napoli, amidst a spectacular, Spanish sort of poverty," he said. "In the Po delta, however, the poverty had something wild, something silent. When we came across people, they displayed an Eskimo strangeness. It was as if we were on the polar ice-caps. And yet they were Italians." It was, he said, "a landscape of low, desolate hovels".

When you watch documentaries about the delta from the 1940s and 1950s, the conditions are stark: reed huts on the mudflats, children in ill-fitting clothes, newspapers used as wallpaper on the wattle, white flags raised on long sticks as the only way to call a doctor or a priest. Malaria and malnourishment were common, and many families only had water when, as they said, "the Po was sweet" (freshwater is called *acqua dolce*). Sweetness is a distant hope out here. The waters smell of rich rot, of scum

11

and disintegration through damp: now, at low tide, the posts and reeds reveal all their sludgy, black fur.

These shallows have always been inaccessible to great armies or naval fleets, and so have often been a refuge for misfits and fugitives. Heretics gathered by this lagoon to escape the wrath of papal theocrats. It was here that Giuseppe Garibaldi fled after the fall of the Roman Republic in July 1849, hoping to reach Venezia which was still holding out against the Austrians. His pregnant wife, Anita, died during the escape, expiring on a mattress laid in a boat somewhere between Ravenna and Comacchio (there's now a nearby village named after her). Another of Garibaldi's entourage, fleeing north, was betrayed at Porto Tolle: Angelo Brunetti, nicknamed "Ciceruacchio" ("Chubby") because of his bulk, was shot along with his two sons.

This delta still feels like a frontier for people on the fringes of civilisation. As I twist the handle of the outboard motor to get closer to the dunes I can see isolated caravans. The coast of the Sacca degli Scardovari (*sacca* means "pouch" or "pocket", but in this delta implies a large lagoon) has rows of fishing cabins on stilts. Their platforms are hung with greying nets, sharpened poles and plastic jerrycans. They look like detached houses on an unusual estate, each with a white van parked on the bank behind the water. The gold rush in the delta is for clams: the industry is, officially, worth close to €100 million per annum, but unofficially it's estimated to be double that. So as you get closer to the coast, you see vans and refrigerated trucks speeding along the narrow, raised roads on their way to supermarkets and restaurants.

I pull the boat up and go ashore. I pay the man I hired it from and we chat. He tells me about the brutes from Chioggia who arrived fifty years ago when the clam business started to boom. There was a lot of money to be made, and pistols occasionally came out, he says.

Chioggia is the northern point of the Po delta. I like to think that it was one of the "gilded horns" (*le corna dorate*) to which Virgil alluded. The Po was often compared to a bull (as it could be both placid and useful, then suddenly enraged and uncontainable) and those horns at the head of the river, pointing into the Adriatic, might allude to Chioggia at the far north and Comacchio in the far south. They were the satellite settlements of their controlling cities, Venezia and Ferrara respectively. They even resemble their cities: Chioggia, at the far northern tip, is a miniature Venezia (albeit with cars): white marble, long steps on dainty bridges, ornate workshops. The streets are even called, as in Venezia, *calli*, and it seems to sit unnaturally on the sea itself (the name, Chioggia, is derived from "constructed artificially"). Two surnames – Tiozzo and Boscolo – are so common (with over 10,000 in the last census, in a city of under 50,000), that official documents contain nicknames, a bit like "Jones-the-bread" in Wales.

Comacchio – the other "horn" – is only separated from Chioggia by about 60 kilometres, but they seem almost complete opposites. Comacchio was repeatedly besieged and sacked by the Venetian Republic, before coming under the protection of the Estensi nobles from Ferrara, a city which it slowly came to resemble thanks to its rust-coloured bricks. For centuries it was the poor sibling of its august northern rival. Here they traded salt, shot duck and attempted to survive malaria. The main cottage industry was the capturing, smoking and pickling of eels. This work was the unlikely backdrop to one of Sophia Loren's earliest films, *La Donna del Fiume* ("the woman of the river"). Almost all the necessary tools were made from the pollarded willows which grew fast in these wetlands: the *lavoriero* (a series of woven funnels which became one-way valves to trap the eels which had travelled all the way from, it was thought, the Sargasso Sea) and the *bolaga* (a woven bulb, into which the eels were placed and kept in the water to maintain their freshness). The men and women working the lakes were sometimes night-time poachers using wooden harpoons. Their lamps, covered so as not to be seen, burned dry hay or, later, acetylene, and they used a flat-bottomed boat called a *vulipicio* that was so light it could be dragged across banks and marshes if they needed to evade either the authorities or, during the war, the German occupiers. As always, this was a place of insurgents and brigands: Loren's lover in the film is a smuggler.

Comacchio was described by Ludovico Ariosto as something of a redneck frontier town where the people were so rough, and weary of the mudflats, that they yearned for choppy waters:

e la città ch'in mezzo alle piscose	And that fair town, [...] which fishy marshes round enclose,
paludi, del Po teme ambe le foci,	And Po's two currents threat with double breach;
dove abitan le genti disiose	Whose townsmen loath the lazy calm's repose,
che 'l mar si turbi e sieno i venti atroci.	And pray that stormy waves may lash the beach.

(Trans. William Stewart Rose)

Given its precarious position a few feet above the waters, Comacchio was symbolised by Trepponti, an irregular, pentagonal bridge straddling the Pallotta canal as it divides into four different offshoots. The bridge, in pink brick topped with white Istrian stone, has five arches over five bodies of water and five staircases. As you look through its arches, all turning in different directions, the water creates superimposed circles. It's a town which deliberately draws the sea into itself, like the one-way funnels the Comacchiesi perfected to trap the eels: "with a way-in open and a way-out closed", as Tasso said. At the far end of the town, the 143 arches of a yellow loggia (built in gratitude for being spared by flooding in the early seventeenth century) conduct you to the Santuario di Santa Maria, the very point of the funnel.

Given centuries of rivalries between those two horns, you can see why someone on the southern end of the delta might have a grudge against the clam raiders from the north. But the real battle for supremacy on this delta was between Venezia and Ferrara and, just over 400 years ago, one city state decisively defeated the other.

It's only clear when you come ashore how completely nature has been nudged, contained and dislocated through human intervention. The river is what's called "perched", significantly higher than the surrounding land. The *argini* (banks) are topped by a narrow road and from up here the Po di Goro is clearly a few metres higher than the ploughed clods of the surrounding fields. All the engineering here is geared towards managing water levels: there are locks and sluice gates beside the road and the fields. Pump houses straddle canals with parallel tubes, the size of water-park slides, emerging from their grand façades.

Coypus are everywhere, both alive and dead. These beaver-like rats, called *nutrie* in Italian, plop in and out of the water and, frequently, waddle across the roads and get killed. They were introduced from South America to satisfy the demand for fur, but that demand has declined, if not disappeared, and now the coypu multiply in the wild with no predators except cars and, occasionally, wolves. They munch through the crops and erode the precious banks. As I cycle along the narrow road – on the map it looks like a paperclip on a pond – I see the hairy lump of a dead coypu every hundred metres or so.

From this raised road, the narrow lines of land in the delta look like tussocks of grass sprouting between glassy tiles. The ponds and lakes are called *valli*. The pace of water is so slow it seems immobile. There's almost no horizon, no obstruction to the natural light. But the more closely you look, the more you see how busy it is. Pygmy cormorants – black wings outstretched to dry out after a dive – seem to be bigging themselves up for a fight. Much further away I can see maybe two hundred birds. Through the binoculars the egg-shaped bodies of the flamingos seem incongruous on those matchstick legs. I don't know why they're so charming: maybe their sheer size – both individually and as a flock – or their insouciance to the nearby road. But they offer exoticism and colour like cherries on a mud pie. As I cycle closer, one flaps its great wings and I see the flash of red and black on the plumage and that dipped-in-ink beak.

Meanwhile humans are extracting what they can from the water. Some canals have lines of boats with what's called the *bilancia,* a net held by its four corners which catches fish like a prospector seeking gold, raising and sifting the water. In the distance are the *saline* with their piles of glinting salt.

The history of this river is, largely, about man's attempt to contain it. Tens of thousands of years ago the whole Pianura Padana – that low-lying plain between this delta and, more or less, Torino – was just swamps and mudflats.

Land formation was partly a natural process of sedimentation. Even today, the river deposits so much silt in this delta that about 60 hectares of land are added to Italian soil every year. On time-lapse videos, you can see how, over the decades and centuries, the delta of the Po has expanded like a car jack towards Istria on the eastern side of the Gulf of Venezia in Croatia. The town of Adria is a sign of just how far the land is moving outwards. Originally called Atria, which was the Etruscan for "east" or "light" (like atrium), this former port gave its name to the whole sea into which this mighty river disgorges itself – the Adriatic. But now it finds itself a dozen kilometres from the coast. There are fossilised dunes 20 kilometres from the tip of the delta: now they're just rippling, grassy knolls in nature reserves.

But over the millennia there has also been assiduous human intervention, what in Italian are called *bonifiche*, land reclamations. The Romans conducted a "centuriation" all around Adria, creating square plots surrounded by drains which were given to war veterans. The land was fertile, and mud and clay were used to make bricks and tiles. Access to the river was always profitable because the Po was an aquatic turnpike, the means of delivering salt, amber, bronze, garum (the Romans' fish paste) and much else upstream. The Romans built a coastal road – the Via Popilia, connecting Rimini to Ravenna and Adria – although now it's many miles inland.

Back then, the main branch of the Po was the "Ferrara Po", also known as Eridanus. Although there were many offshoots, originally the main body of water flowed from Bondeno to Voghenza and from there into the Adriatic by the lost Etruscan city of Spina (west of Comacchio). The minimal differentials in altitude meant that the course of the river was surprisingly unsettled. Because of heavy rainfall throughout the sixth century, the Po's main course became the Copparo–Ariano branch to the north and Spina, and later Comacchio, became brackish lagoons.

As happened on the Somerset Levels in England, those marshes were later drained by monks, or at least by serfs working on the orders of the monastery. Comacchio was donated by the Lombard monarchs to the monastery of the Irish missionary St Colombanus. Settling on "Pomposa Island" in the sixth to seventh centuries, those monks were in charge of both the profitable salt trade and the sale of emergent lands. The monastery's moment of greatest splendour was at the turn of the millennium, when their abbot, Guido, invented the annotation of the musical scale.

"Solfeggio" – or "do-re-mi" – came from the first, Latin syllables of the hymn of St John the Baptist. By then the monastery was under the control of the Benedictine order and, in 1062, a stunning square tower was built, with additional and widening windows added on each storey to reduce weight and give visual, and spiritual, uplift.

When you go there now, to admire that iconic tower and the preserved, tinselled tibia of St Guido, it's hard to imagine it as an island surrounded by sea and rivers. Now it's all farmland. But everywhere you look there's evidence that this used to be the centre of the delta: the soil is a sandy-grey. The local wine is called *vino delle sabbie* ("the wine of the sands", with its mildly salty taste). There's a pink brick, three-arched bridge over a grassy ditch in the grounds of the monastery, an elegant monument to the waters' retreat.

By the Middle Ages, two great powers were competing for control of the River Po's shipping lane: the Venetian Republic and the Estensi dukes based in Ferrara. Theirs was a conflict which would simmer for centuries. The Venetian doges had become wary of Ferrara's growing financial and territorial power, based in part on the drifts of glinting salt crystals at Cervia. During the "Salt War" (also known as the "War of Ferrara" in 1482–4) the Venetian Republic was allied with the papal forces and the Genovan Republic, and conquered much of the Estensi lands – from Rovigo to Ficarolo. It even besieged Ferrara itself. The result was that the Estensi lost all their territories north of the river (today the left bank of this eastern end of the Po is still in Veneto, and the right in Emilia-Romagna).

The relics of that ongoing friction between Venezia and Ferrara are evident all over the delta. Amid the fields, you come across what were called the *delizie* (the "delights") of the Estensi empire.

"Delight" is a strange word for what were really defensive structures: it sounds more like a description of aesthetic stupefaction than of functional fortification. But the "delights" were the fifty-plus buildings erected on Estensi territories throughout the sixteenth century to defend against both the Venetians and the water. The pink-brick Torre Abate (1568-9) was supposed, initially, to be instrumental in Duke Alfonso II's land reclamation, which added about 30,000 hectares of land to his duchy. But later it became an integral part of his military expansion into the delta with a watchtower added to the diminuendo of brick arches which straddle the water. It seems so incongruous now, a monumental building surrounded by stagnant water, reeds and vast fields with their cartoon-size pumpkins.

The Estensi defences were stepped up a few years later with the construction of Mesola castle (1578-85). When you go to Mesola and see that "delight" it is undeniably charming and you can understand why these defences were considered delightful: the castle has square turrets turned diagonally against the main body of the building, and it looks angular amid the curving colonnades of the surrounding oval of modern shops and bars. Sandwiched between the bends of the Po di Goro and of the Canale Bianco, it has a kind of grandeur, but also a delicacy and poise. But the size of the castle seems at odds with this tiny town, its presence incomprehensible unless one understands the strategic importance of the mouth of the river.

In 1597, Alfonso II died without heirs and his lands reverted to the Papal States. It meant that Ferrara, and its southern side of the delta, was suddenly ruled by absentee landlords who had been, until then, allies of the Venetian Republic: the Venetian navy had played an instrumental role in the Holy League's victory in the Battle of Lepanto in 1571, coming to the rescue of Catholic allies under the leadership of Pope Pio V. But that alliance meant little years later when Venezia finally had the opportunity to enact its long-term strategy of protecting its own lagoon by silting up Ferrara's side of the estuary. The problem facing Venezia had been eloquently described years before, in November 1569, by Luigi Groto, a playwright and orator known as the "blind man of Adria". In a speech to the Senate of the Venetian Republic, Groto had complained of the effect of the floodwaters from the Po. The waters, he said:

> turn fields into lakes and houses into cisterns, where you can neither sow nor plant and even if you do plant and sow, in these soaking holdings the buried seeds neither germinate nor rise, and grown trees languish and die...

During floods, he said, "in just one hour the crops and vegetables, the vines and willows, the flocks and herds, the houses and their owners, the churches and the altars, the mothers with their children at their breasts, the wives with beside them their husbands, can be swept away..."

The flooding, he claimed, was caused by a regular silting up of the riverbed, meaning that the river didn't flow into the sea easily but often backed up and broke its banks. His logic was convincing:

> If, when this river becomes murky, we take a carafe of his waters and allow it the time to clear and deposit his dirt on the bottom, we will find that one third part is mud. Now imagine how many carafes of this water descend every day, just in the Po, and clearly all the turbidity stays on the river-bed or is scattered on the mouths of the ports, and as the river-bed rises so do the waters...

The problem of sedimentation was exacerbated by the fact that two other major rivers – the Adige and Brenta – also discharged into the sea just south of the Venetian lagoon.

On 17 December 1598, the year immediately after Alfonso II's death, the Venetian senate finally approved the new *taglio* (cut) by eighty-six votes to sixteen. Work began in 1600 and it took 257,823 Venetian ducats, and over four years, to complete the excavations. The digging was frequently stymied by strikes and sabotage, often – it was alleged – conducted by papal forces whose waterways were directly affected and who now found themselves at odds with their erstwhile allies. About a million and a half cubic metres of soil were dug, and the eventual cut – turning sharply south immediately after Contarina – was 6,864 metres long.

At 7 p.m. on 16 September 1604 the new river course was created. More than fifty apertures were made in the last bank of soil between the Po and its new route. The water flooded in, speeding along its new course south and flooding, in time, over 20,000 hectares of papal land. The Sacca di Goro was silted up. That watercourse – previously known as the Po di Corbola – inevitably took the name Po di Venezia.

That river diversion came to be known as the Porto Viro Cut. The efficacy of that confrontational intervention can be seen from the subsequent maps of the delta over ensuing centuries: the land slowly encroaches into the Adriatic, billowing out south-south-east, while the Venetian lagoon remains unaffected. The radically altered topography meant that the boundaries between the Venetian Republic and the papal lands were unclear: it wasn't until a century and a half later, in 1749, that an accord was signed and boundary stones erected. One still survives – a leaning brick obelisk you can see through the fence of a large farm complex. That boundary, rather than heading east on the 45th parallel, now descended much further south, gifting the Venetian Republic fertile farmland.

New estates were built which were, finally, protected from flooding. Venetian nobles began to use their new territories of the delta to build summer retreats and grand hunting lodges, their surnames (Donà and Contarini) becoming the names, too, of the villages that grew up to serve their estates (Donada and Contarina). As you saunter around this delta, the names of Venetian aristocrats – Venier, Vendramin, Morosini, Tiepolo and Mocenigo – are remembered in the lakes, bights and manors. You sometimes see those grandiose buildings from the river: Ca' Zen is now a hotel with immaculate lawns, groves and gravel. But the building's flaking turquoise shutters and symmetrical brick façade, with long wings to the east and west, show its age. It was built in the early seventeenth century and, like many churches along the Po, the entrance of Ca' Zen's chapel faces the river, almost as if the water were something to be watched and acknowledged, even in church. This, they say, is where Byron visited his lover, the married Countess Teresa Gamba.

That sense of a frontier slowly populated by pioneers is apparent in the names of other hamlets and villages. Everything here is new: Santa Giulia was named after a landowner's sister, Giulia (replacing the more poetic "Polesine dei Sospiri", the "marshland of sighs"). The island of Donzella was named after another's daughter. "The island of seagulls" became – either to attract tourists, or because of their activities – "the island of love". Gorino Sullam was named after Giuseppe Sullam who, in 1837, bought wetlands from the Austrian Empire and slowly reclaimed them, turning them into farmland.

Even centuries after that land reclamation and slow colonisation, this delta still appears new and lacking in historical depth. Apart from those solid and stern Estensi "delights", each settlement is very modern: one-street towns which look entirely built in the last sixty years or so. Often the houses are garishly coloured: bright oranges, cerises, magentas and limes, as if making up for the dull farmland all around. As with the birds out in the mud, there's a contrast of monochrome and sudden colour. Between each town are straight canals, curving branches of the Po and *mortizze*, the "dead" sections of the river – like ox-bow lakes – which have now become stagnant ponds.

I become used to the loud plop of another coypu as it belly-flops into the thick green froth of water. Eutrophication is a major environmental problem here: it's the over-enrichment of the water from the run-off of synthetic fertilisers used throughout the Pianura Padana, giving rise to algal blooms which deplete the oxygen and darken the waters. As you stop, map in hand, to understand which stretch of water you're now crossing, it barely looks aquatic: the surface is more like a bowling green. One recent study suggests that the dissolved inorganic nitrogen load, brought by the river to the sea each year, oscillates between 50,000 and 200,000 tonnes. The river accounts for 65 per cent of all freshwater nitrogen and phosphorus loads into the Adriatic. It doesn't take long to understand why. Almost every field here is straddled by a spraying boom as long as a crane's horizontal arm. The farming here is heavily industrialised: the serene stillness of the delta is punctured by the syncopated bangs and revving of farm machinery and one woman I talk to about this year's crops nonchalantly refers to a farm as an *impianto*, a "system" or "installation". The farmsteads themselves are often hidden amid cypress groves and copses of maritime pines, the only blip of foliage on the slim horizon.

When you think of a delta – and this one extends for 380 square kilometres – you imagine a vast expanse of water with isolated slivers of land. Here, inland from that very watery tip, it's the opposite. The river has been channelled, boxed in as tight as possible. The land reclamation sped up in the late nineteenth and early twentieth centuries as steam-powered pump houses could do the job much faster using what they called "Cardiff coal". Near Comacchio, 8,806 hectares of land were reclaimed between 1919 and 1933, leading to the loss of the Trebbia, Ponti and Isola lagoons. In the same area, another 2,256 hectares of land were created between 1951 and 1964, causing the disappearance of the Pega, Rillo and Zavalea lagoons. Between 1957 and 1975, the 18,000 hectares of the Mezzano lagoon disappeared, turned into farmland. Through the twentieth century, the number of *valli* were reduced from fifty to just twenty-four.

That frantic land reclamation lifted thousands of subsistence fishermen and their families out of poverty. They became farmers and, often, dealers in the Etruscan treasures the land gave up as it was drained. But there were unintended consequences of what was called the "colonisation" of the waters. As water was extracted from the loam and peat, the land itself subsided, making it only more vulnerable to incursions from the sea and the river. This subsidence was exacerbated by the discovery of liquefied methane in the mid-twentieth century: by the 1940s there were 400 wells across the delta, extracting methane and thus, unexpectedly, lowering the land still further, often by two or three metres. The more land reclamation took place, the greater the height differential between the Po and the land: the river thus became even more perched, its banks raised and reinforced.

As lakes turned into farms, one of the great industries of this area almost disappeared. Eels were replaced by more lucrative clams. There's still a niche production of pickled eels, and you can visit the grand fireplaces where they used to be grilled, but it's really only part of the heritage trail now. Eels are relished by adventurous foodies but are no longer a popular dish for mainstream palates. I often hear people complain that the eels don't even come to Comacchio anymore because there aren't the vast lagoons and inlets.

When you read, or watch documentaries, about lives on the delta in the first half of the twentieth century, the water seems uncontained, sloshing where it wanted to create a landscape of mud, reeds and willows. The delta's inhabitants were impoverished, malnourished and often diseased, but there was a rugged simplicity to their soggy landscape. Perhaps that's why so many great films were set here, like Luchino Visconti's *Ossessione* (*Obsession*), a Po river version of James M. Cain's *The Postman Always Rings Twice*, or Michelangelo Antonioni's *Il Grido* (*The Cry*). In both films, the protagonist is an itinerant, shifting locations like the vagrant river. There seems little solidity or foundation, only the topographical emptiness of the delta that seems to match an existential one.

The river was the setting for many of the iconic neo-realist films not only because so many of the great directors (Michelangelo Antonioni, Florestano Vancini and Cesare Zavattini) grew up next to the Po, but because its world was so simple, so pared down that it was almost like a theatre set with those slim tracks as the stage. The backdrop was the sky, and there was little – apart from the odd bicycle or lonely building – to distract from the action. Even the willows were pollarded to bulbous stumps. The river provided dramatic tension – a place of suicide, murder, infidelity, and, as ever, a threatening source of floods – but most of all it added to the simplicity and menace of the films. As one of the characters says in Bernardo Bertolucci's *Prima della Rivoluzione* (*Before the Revolution*), the river "is down there, always hidden, never showing itself, but always overshadowing you…". And that water reflected everything, creating a dimpled mirror which disconcerted the viewer.

As Italy modernised beyond recognition in the post-war years, the incursions on rural lands of industrial and housing estates, of pylons and power stations, reduced the wilderness of the Pianura Padana. But that only made the river, if anything, even more attractive to filmmakers. Adapting Renata Viganò's novel, *L'Agnese va a morire* in 1976, Giuliano Montaldo deliberately chose the Romagna lowlands because, he said, they offered "a greater possibility of reconstructing in a faithful way the Italy of 1943–45". Those lowlands still had that dangerous openness which gave the book its tension: the landscape is so bare that the characters can't really hide, only deceive their enemies and each other in full view. That risk of exposure was only softened by the Po's theatrical prop: its notoriously thick fogs.

That physical barrenness is what repeatedly called another director, Ermanno Olmi, back to the river. It was along the Po that Olmi found "a simplicity, a sincerity of which there is little in the world of the so-called elect". "I believe", he once said, "that a dignified poverty is a school for life for western civilisation which lives within abundance. Simplicity is the ability to distinguish every day what is essential from what is superficial. We have the necessity to go to a school of poverty, not to invoke a return to the past, but to curb the disasters which richness produces."

From Taglio di Po – the town named after the famous Venetian cut of 1604 – the main branch of the river heads west. There's another offshoot of the river to the south, the Po di Goro, so technically I'm now cycling along the fringe of an island, the Isola d'Ariano. After a couple of kilometres, the river almost bends back on itself completely, heading south-east before turning west again. In the middle of, and mirroring, that crescent is another island, called the Isola di Balutin. It's exactly on the 45th parallel and joined to the left bank by a peninsula of dice-shaped boulders now so overgrown with thistles and willows that you would need a machete to pass through them.

This island was, for ten years, the site of a half-serious, half-satirical utopian experiment. Like so many idealistic attempts to re-found human society, it started in the aftermath of war, in 1945. Its founder was a professor of Slavic languages from Milano, Luigi Salvini, who had married a woman from the poetically named village of Bellombra ("beautiful shade"). Salvini had seen for himself the hatred of war – he apparently survived an attempted poisoning in Zagreb in 1942 when a meatball was laced with arsenic – and his so-called "free, independent, periodical, transitory and illiterate" community was an attempt not so much to change the world as to retreat from it for three summer months every year. Radios and newspapers were banned in the "Tamisiana Repubblica di Bosgattia", as were honorific titles.

The name was a deliberate mouthful. A *bosgato* (with one t) is the local dialect word for a pig – a "wood-cat" perhaps. But it was the "Tamisiana" in name of the community, Salvini explained, which was all important: it didn't refer to the dialect term for a flour sieve (*tamisa*) but the pan with which prospectors on the riverbanks hunted for the *storione*, the sturgeon, and its precious load of caviar. Salvini's mid-river state had its own stamps and currency (the *çievaloro*, or golden grey mullet). Passports were offered by the satirically bombastic "very serene council of elders of the cofraternity of..." To become a citizen you had to be able to catch and unhook a catfish. Temporary visitors (and every community tires of the stream of curious onlookers) were housed in a big tent called the "*Casa dello Sbafatore di Turno*" ("the house of the latest gate-crasher"). Female citizens were called *ginepotami* (women of the river). The Bosgattians invented recipes based on eels, mullets, *bruscandoli* (wild hops), catfish and – when life was really good – the sturgeon.

Being a linguist (he had become a professor in Rome), Salvini was inevitably good with words, and he mixed up the local dialect to such an extent that no one was ever certain whether he knew more about the locals' ancient diction than them or whether the "professor from Rome" was just having a laugh and making it up. But they all liked him. If his islanders had come ashore to stock up on wine or beef, paying with the *çievaloro* currency,

Salvini would go round the shops a few days later and settle up with lire (the fixed exchange rate was one *çievaloro* for five lire). Now, sixty-five years since the community moved off (Salvini died in 1957, in his mid-forties) there's nothing left except the memories and the elusive stamps with naive drawings of tents, fish and *ginepotami* collected by communitarians and historians.

So I, too, move on. I want to get to Santa Maria in Punta. I can see a couple of lakes, houses and woods on the map and am intrigued to trudge to the far end of this pointed oval of land between the converging sides of the Po. At the end of that rotund peninsula is the point, at last, where the Po becomes a single river (bar a few distant offshoots upstream). It's where the Po di Goro joins the river from the south.

I don't get far because there's a creeping weed which covers the ground and trees, its light-green tendrils corkscrewing around the lower branches. It's clear that something's awry. Alder and willow are bent over by the pull of its tangle. I had been warned about this. Linda, a photographer friend from Parma, had shown me her silhouettes of these vines in winter: they cover everything as if a fishing net had been thrown over the forest and pulled it downwards. It's *Sicyos angulatus*, the so-called *zucca pazza*, the "mad pumpkin" or, in English, star-cucumber because of its picturesque seed pod. Because the plant has such large leaves and grows so fast, it was originally introduced to provide shade for Italian orchards and, perhaps, as a rootstock for cucumbers. But as with the coypu and catfish, the invasive species took over, spreading much further than expected. A single plant can produce up to 80,000 seeds and it thrives on the wet floodplains of the Po.

Only a few miles into the journey, I'm losing count of the invasions: here, Canadian poplars, grown for biomass, fibres and matchsticks, have replaced the leaning, water-laden black alders. The poplars are planted with rigid geometry: every plantation is identical, attractive in its ordered lines, but dull, too. The sturgeon used to be the prized beauty of the Po, but even in the 1940s and 1950s there was an awareness that this symbol of the river's generosity was in decline. As sturgeon populations dwindled, so the river's finest delicacy – sturgeon caviar – became ever rarer. The sturgeon is almost forgotten now, replaced as the big beast of the river by the huge, ugly bottom feeder, the *siluro*, or wels catfish. In fishing lodges, you can see endless photographs of men holding up a fish much longer than the tallest of them, as big as a small dolphin. Estimates suggest that the catfish now accounts for an astonishing 27 per cent of the biomass of the Po. In 2015, just outside San Benedetto Po where the river meets the Secchia tributary, a catfish was caught which set a new record: it was two metres sixty-seven long, nearly nine feet, and weighed in at 127 kilograms. The invaders keep getting fat.

Hacking my way through the bright green vines, I come to the first of the two lakes on this odd peninsula. There are whole families of coypu, their nostrils just out of the water, and long tails wagging slowly like a slim rudder. There's a stylish merganser duck, with her ginger mohican. On a bare branch sticking out of the water, a heron guards the lake.

Further on, an abandoned brick shed has appreciative slogans spray-painted on its walls amongst the weeds: *cullati nel silenzio* – "cradle yourself in the silence".

I had almost given up on reaching the point of Santa Maria. It's far further than the feather-shaped peninsula on the map might suggest. But I trudge on, past a dozen abandoned houses: brick and timber cottages with roofs that now only consist of thick foliage. The graffiti, as usual, is good: skulls and slogans. I like it here, the solitude and roughness. So I walk on across the damp ground. A dozen metres from the water I almost give up. But I scramble through the undergrowth and find myself on a sandy beach in the middle of the Po surrounded by thistles, bonfire circles and beer cans.

To the north, a bulldozer is lumping blocks of white boulders to shore up the *argine maestro*, the "magisterial bank". The distant clanking barely disturbs me, but the image itself does. It's obvious that the surrounding land needs protection from this river, but there's something illogical or arrogant about raising and reinforcing the banks so that the river becomes ever more perched. The laws of gravity make me assume that payback is surely coming, and the sound of burning diesel reminds me why we have freak rainfalls of unprecedented intensity in the first place. It's only one bulldozer, but it unexpectedly needles me: a symbol of our desperation to avoid consequences, like constantly borrowing more money to pay off debt. Here human intervention has lowered the surrounding land and narrowed and thereby raised the river. Now that the river is above, rather than below, the land, the process can't be reversed. The banks have to be constantly raised and reinforced.

I go and sit in one of the two green plastic chairs that face the water. Looking upstream, you can see the speed of flow by watching all the shredded bags and shoe soles going past. To the left is the Po di Goro, heading towards the clams and that lighthouse. To the right is the main body, the Po-proper. But in front of me the river is, at last, a single being. The many threads of the delta have become one.

TWO

Polesine

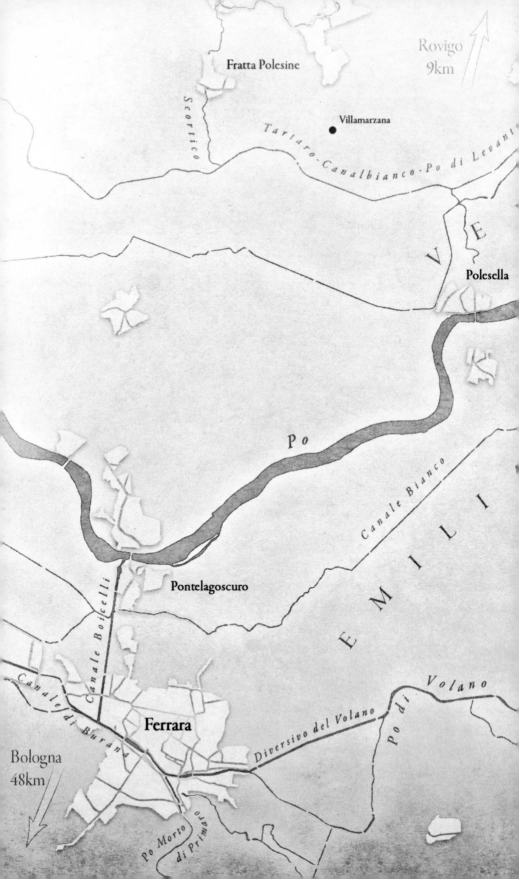

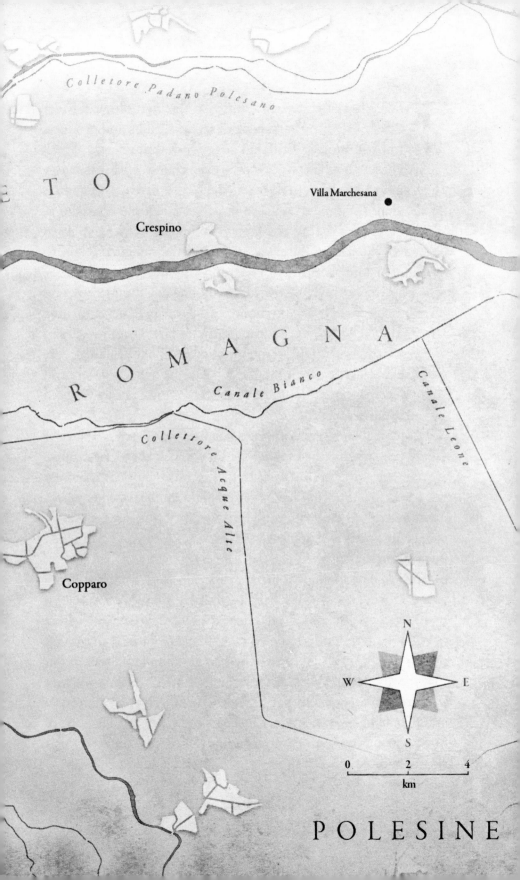

The Po has often been identified as the mythological River Eridanos. Many bars, pizzerias, parks, clubs and products (most famously Eridania sugar) use that ancient Greek name. The small village of Crespino even claims, with admirable chutzpah, to be the actual site of the Greek myth of Phaethon and Eridanos, calling its wide square Piazza Fetonte (Phaethon).

The story goes that Phaethon was taunted about his paternity. To prove who he was, he asked his father, the sun god Helios, to lend him his sun chariot. But Phaethon lost control of the horses, scorching the earth. Zeus struck Phaethon with a thunderbolt and he fell to his death in the mythological river. There his mourning sisters, the Heliades, were turned into poplars weeping tears of amber. "To this very day", wrote Apollonius about Eridanos, "the marsh exhales a heavy vapour which rises from his [Phaethon's] smouldering wound; no bird can stretch out its fragile wings to fly over that water…"

It's a tale which seems appropriate for this stretch of the river where poplars line the banks. The Po was central to the Bronze Age amber trade in northern Italy. From the Baltic, that shiny resin was brought by boat into the Padanian heartlands where artisans crafted it into jewellery. The story of scorched earth, too, is apt for this shadeless land which is burned and cracked during summer droughts.

The Po, back then, was utterly different from how it appears today. During the Bronze Age, it's thought that there were two main branches which divided near present-day Guastalla (just north of Reggio Emilia): the Po di Spina flowed to the south and the Po di Adria to the north. The surrounding land was so flat that the divergent river often found other beds, overflowing into the large area between that fork. It gave the river a reputation as a menacing tyrant: "madly he bears them down, that Lord of floods, Eridanos," wrote Virgil in his *Georgics*, "until through all the plain are swept beasts and their stalls together."

But now the single river is channelled by these great banks. I still find it strange that you don't walk down to the river, but up to it. The *argini* are so monumental that they are stepped into three plateaus wide enough for tractors to cut the hay and roll it into hairy cotton reels. There's a thin road on top with oblique lines every few hundred metres on which you can slide down to each village a few metres beneath the level of the water.

The *argine maestro*, the main bank, is often eulogised almost as much as the river. It's the outer boundary of the floodplains and so is rarely – except in floods – in contact with the water. According to Ermanno Rea, that main bank allowed the river to express its "vitality and mobility" as it spills over the *sponda* (the primary bank) and laps against the "magisterial bank". That *argine maestro* is where people go for strolls or bike rides. It's a place to catch occasional glimpses of the water, which comes into view and then disappears again. And because that main bank is tall and tiered, when you descend on the river side, you're suddenly alone in the wilderness. There's usually a large crescent of land between the banks: the designated *golena*, the "floodplain". These spaces are often home to simple clubs: there are picnic tables, basic bars, pontoons and pétanque pits. There are occasional houses, but most are empty. Sometimes the river is a few fields away, and it's a wet walk before you can enjoy the glassy water fringed by autumnal foliage.

Here the river is still wide and, after the torrential rain of the last few days, decidedly dark and lively. There are gurgling noises on the outside of the bend as the water churns against low foliage. Driftwood, used as free rafts by the gulls, speeds by every few seconds. Grey plastic bags and bottles float on islands of grey foam.

The name for this area on the left bank of the river, south of Rovigo, is Polesine. It's the Venetian version of the Latin *policinum*, meaning "marshland" (or, more rarely, an island emerging from the river's waters). Many villages near here are called something-Polesine, and it recurs upriver, too, near Parma. For much more than half of this river, almost all the way to Torino, the place names mean "bog", "swamp" or "soaked". There are also many towns called Argine (bank) or Fossa (ditch). Just as frequently, the place names refer to the land that emerges from the water: Mezzani means "half-island" and the many Motte (Mottegiana, Le Motte) are – like motte and bailey castles – mounds of mud.

The Po's habitual flooding in this area has reduced the land to an eerie architectural cemetery. I walk to the "Isola di Mezzano", just south of Papozze, because I've seen photographs of a grand, abandoned villa where, they say, the Counter-Reformation saint Carlo Borromeo once stayed. But the herring-bone indentations in the mud of the villa's former drive suggest this is now only a tractor route. I walk along it for half a mile and eventually come to a building hidden by mature white poplars. The pink bricks have lost most of their sandy rendering and the balcony railing is rusted. Rows of broken beams look like the teeth of a broken comb. It's like an accidental nature reserve – full of herons, bulrushes and frogs – squeezed between agricultural land on all sides.

This area – with its ample supply of clay and wood – used to be one of the major brick-producing districts in northern Italy. At Villanova Marchesana, slim red-brick chimneys, half covered in ivy, rise high above the willows and poplars of the floodplain. One is attached to a five-storey building, the Fornace Toti, now missing its roof and windows. Nearby is another abandoned furnace, Fornace Etna. Concrete and steel have long since made them redundant, and now the cycle is being completed: their bricks and timbers are slowly being absorbed back into the ground from which they came.

But even back on the farmland outside the floodplains, it's the same story. In almost every other field there's a ruin: grand but abandoned, its roof tiles long gone. They are covered with graffiti inside and out, declarations of love for football teams, girls and, sometimes, for philosophical positions. Fig trees grow like weeds next to cracked walls. Shutters, ripped off for firewood or to make chicken coops decades ago, leave bare windows out of which ivy pours. Thick beams, weathered grey, sag like washing lines. When you talk to the locals, they give the same reason for all the ruins here – the empty houses and the abandoned barns. "Fifty-one" is all they say if you ask why a grand villa is sinking back into the soil.

Polesine had always suffered floods. When, in 589, the River Adige burst its banks (in the "Rotta della Cucca" near present-day Veronella) it completely changed the hydrological panorama of the Veneto region. And the "Boje" peasant rebellion of the mid-1880s is thought to have begun when the Adige, again, burst its banks near Ceregnano in 1882, washing away subsistence farmers' fields and shacks. But it's 1951 that lingers in living memory.

In early to mid-November 1951 it had been raining heavily across northern Italy for days. With 141 tributaries, the Po is obviously the recipient of vast volumes of water. It's very rare that the flood waves of those distant tributaries all flow into the mother river at the same time. Usually the distribution of rainfall is such that the *onde di piena* – the "waves of fullness" – are staggered. In 1951, however, they all hit the Po contemporaneously. In the past, overflows from the river had often been absorbed by the floodplains; but by 1930 the surface area of the Po-side floodplains had been reduced 50 per cent compared to 1878 (and there would be a further 20–30 per cent decrease between 1930 and 1980). Deforestation in the Apennine mountains meant that water retention was reduced to the south of the river and rainfall duly careered into the valley.

There was also, on 13–14 November, a scirocco, a southerly wind which raised the sea level near Venezia by 151 centimetres, with a deleterious effect on the speed at which the river could flow into the Adriatic. That scirocco also raised the level of the river's waters by 20–30 centimetres on the left (north) bank, precisely the bank that was a metre or so short of the planned flood defences due to lack of funding.

Emergency defensive work in the preceding days had protected the upstream villages around Mantova. Despite a shortage of heavy machinery, meaning that most defences were built up by hand, the citizens of Bergantino, Castelmassa and Canto managed to protect their villages. Slightly further downstream the river narrows, funnelling the water higher. Where a river narrows humans build bridges and those two bridges at Occhiobello and Santa Maria Maddalena had voluminous supports which displaced the water, raising it still higher.

Various sociological studies have attempted to understand why the citizens of Occhiobello and Canaro didn't show the same diligence as had been demonstrated further upstream. Some have suggested that in these areas – where *latifundismo* was still normal, with huge estates on which the peasants had no land or even property of their own – the residents had less incentive to protect their dwellings. That poverty also meant that radios and telephones were luxurious rarities, and that raising the alarm and coordinating actions were far harder. Instead, false rumours spread, suggesting the river had already broken its banks and that it was better to flee than to take a stand.

It had just got dark on the evening of 14 November when the first breach occurred in Paviole at 19.45. Within half an hour there were two further breaches in Occhiobello. Estimates of the flow of water onto the surrounding land put the figure at between 6,000 and 9,500 thousand cubic metres (roughly three Olympic swimming pools of water) per second. It was as if the river had effectively altered course, pouring out to its left into Polesine. As soon as the banks were breached, they were eroded, too, so that by the end of the crisis, over a month later, the three breaches in the banks measured 220, 204 and 312 metres respectively. It was only on 20 December that the river stopped flowing through them: in that time, eight billion cubic metres of water had crashed into farmlands the wrong side of the river's banks.

Photographs from the early days after the initial flooding show waters that look like the high seas: vicious, foaming waves, almost nothing breaking the surface of the water other than the odd bell tower or stable roof. The figures were stark: eighty-eight people died – many in a bus that got stranded in the middle of the night. Four thousand five hundred cows and 7,800 pigs were killed. In the months after the flood, 80,000 people emigrated away from Polesine. Many families never went back: the majority of entire villages moved to Lombardia and Piemonte where there was work in factories and where the flats, in modern apartment blocks, were high above ground.

In many ways these villages never recovered. When you wander around everything seems deserted: churches, crumbling castles and little museums are all closed. Mature willows have taken up residence in the abandoned houses. These are mostly silent places. What noise there is only reminds me of the elderly or the lonely: old men play cards in steamed-up bars, shouting at each other and the Chinese barmaid. Fields are now ploughed by single tractors, the driver sitting alone all day. This is all that's left: sparsely populated villages full of reminiscence and regret. That sense of being in a time capsule increases when you see road signs, almost a century old: small, metal fingers on the corners of buildings in the main square.

The Po's river defences were fortified in the late 1950s, a few years after that flood. But although they now hold the river at bay, they also physically separate the river from the villages which had previously been integrated with it. When you see images of these settlements from before the 1950s, they huddled by the river: it's where the laundry was done, where reeds were cut and firewood sourced. The banks were little more than bare mounds and the river so imposing that these settlements were described as coastal (*rivierasco*). The Po was, according to many writers, like a maternal breast, offering constant comfort and sustenance. Now, though, the river is shut off, and the villages are living with their backs to it.

I walk towards Polesella along the raised bank. To one side, on my left, is the river: bending away from me so that it looks like a vast lake fringed by gingering leaves. On my right are distant church steeples in the treeless landscape. A kestrel glares down from its wire watchtower. When it takes flight, the small birds on the freshly ploughed field take to the air noisily. Herons bend their knees, ready for take-off, as I pass.

As I get closer to Polesella, the footpath, now squeezed between the river and its bank, is one long mural, full of spray paintings of birds, nudes, fat faces, fish, cherry blossoms, indecipherable letters and tributes to the local gang, the "Golena Boys" ("lads of the floodplain"). The mural goes on for a hundred metres or more, until you reach the bridge of this once-famous village.

There are quite a few German- or Austrian-run fishing resorts here. In each one, I see the same photographs: two or three burly anglers struggling to smile as they hold a swollen catfish horizontal on their forearms. In one, an unusual Austrian guy, drinking beer by himself in his dark house, lets me pitch my tent in his garden right next to the river. I ask him what I can give him for my pitch and he smiles. "Beer."

I sit in the dark and read about the legends of the river by torchlight. I like the one about Slengher. He was a poor boy who worked as a boatman, transporting merchants from one side of the river to the other. One day he saw a young girl holding a flower and fell in love. But he was struck dumb by Clepie, the spirit of the river to whom the girl belonged. Learning of the curse, the young girl decided to challenge Clepie to a contest: whoever could talk the longest, without interruption, would be declared the winner. If the girl won, Slengher would have his voice restored, but if Clepie won, the girl would forever belong to the river spirit. The girl started talking. She yakked away without pause for two days until the river spirit could take no more and gave the young boatman his voice back. I don't know why that story seems apt for this river, but there's something about its insistence on silence that I like: the spirit takes away the boy's voice and can't abide the chatter of the girl's. It's as if prolixity is out of place besides the Po.

The river legends are often love stories. There's a large ox-bow lake further north (in Trecenta, near the mostly man-made channel which combines the old Po di Levanto and the Tartaro rivers). It's called the Gorgo della Sposa ("the whirlpool of the bride"). The story goes that a young woman was in love with a poor local boy, but that her family insisted she marry a rich noble. She tried to persuade them that it was useless, that she only loved the poor boy, but her family was determined to clinch the wealthier option. So the young woman fled to her lover's house only to find him murdered. Later, in the carriage going to Ferrara for the fateful wedding to the richer man, she paused to admire the river. She got out and looked at the water and suddenly saw the face of her dead lover. She dived in to be with him and was pulled under and never seen again. Inevitably, they say that on moonlit nights you can still see, in the water, the white lace of her wedding veil.

Tonight there's no moon. The rain is hammering down on the tent now like hundreds of nails tapping a desk. When it stops I can hear the river lapping at the mud below. Francesca, my wife, phones to tell me the Po is on the news. They're talking about rising levels and showing footage of serious flooding upstream. "After writing all your stuff about the mafia and murderers and criminals," she laughs, "if you get killed by a river you're properly stupid."

The next morning I'm up early. The river's much closer, perhaps only ten metres from the tent, but not a danger. I watch it for a while. It's muddy and fast, and the half-dozen cables and ropes securing the floating pontoon to the willows are squeaking against the bark.

This stretch of the river by Polesella was the site of a famous battle in 1509. Just like grassy battlefields that contain few clues to the carnage from centuries past, nothing of the battle survives here except its protagonist, the river. It was rain that gave the Estensi their advantage back then. During the "Salt War" of 1482–4, the Estensi had lost almost all their lands to the left of the river – the area now called Polesine – and Polesella became Venezia's foothold on the river. Venezia was now considered, by various European superpowers, as too powerful: it held many cities across northern Italy as well as important ports in the south. The League of Cambrai was formed in December 1508 to contain Venetian expansionism into Bologna and beyond. The alliance was, originally, between the Papal States, the French monarchy, the Holy Roman Empire, and the Lords of Ferrara, Urbino and Mantova.

In skirmishes around this village, some of Ferrara's noblest allies were killed. Ludovico Pico – a *condottiero* from nearby Mirandola – was killed by a Venetian culverin (a basic musket), and another Ferrara soldier, Ercole Cantelmo (son of Duke Sigismondo of Sora), was captured when his horse charged the enemy and became stuck in the muddy swamps. He was immediately beheaded. That his own father was watching added emotive appeal to the story, and Ariosto addressed the grieving father in his commemoration of the murder:

Che cor, duca di Sora, che consiglio	What counsel, Sora's duke, was thine, what heart,
Fra mille spade al generoso figlio	When thy bold son thou saw'st, of helm bereft,
A menar preso al nave e sopra un schelmo	Amid a thousand swords, when – dragged apart –
Troncargli il capo?	Thou saw'st his young head from his shoulders cleft?

(Trans. William Stewart Rose)

Guicciardini in his *Storia d'Italia* echoed the indignation (*"inaudito esempio di barbara crudeltà"*) as did Mario Equicola, another early sixteenth-century humanist, who blamed the wicked hand for not only killing Ercole but also "the glory of our age".

Revenge came in December 1509, just before Christmas. What I like about the descriptions of the Battle of Polesella – written, naturally, by the victors – was that the river played an integral role. It had been raining heavily and Duke Alfonso I had most of his fleet far upstream, beyond Bondeno. The waters were rising and the flow accelerating. Alfonso sent a message to his brother, Ippolito, telling him that the Venetian galleys would soon rise above the dykes and be exposed to the Estensi's weaponry. Ippolito bored holes in various dykes, placing hidden arquebuses and culverins in the openings. For over a kilometre along the river's right bank, the Estensi troops were dug in, hidden, and their weapons loaded.

At dawn on 23 December, the Estensi attacked. As Ippolito's cannon smashed hulls and his snipers picked off Venetian sailors, Alfonso came down the angry river with all his cannon aimed at the half-asleep Venetian fleet. The Estensi troops sunk five galleys, captured a dozen more, and killed, it was estimated, around two thousand men. They chased the Venetians all the way to the delta, retaking Comacchio.

The victory was famously commemorated in Ariosto's *Orlando Furioso* (Canto XL):

Ebbe lungo spettacolo il fedele

Your faithful people gazed on a long show,

Vostro popul la notte e 'l dì che stette,

That night and day, wherein they crowded stood,

come in teatro, l'inimiche vele

As in a theatre, and hemmed on Po

mirando in Po tra ferro e fuoco astrette.

Twixt fire and sword, the hostile navies viewed.

Che gridi udir si possano e querele,

What outcries may be heard, what sounds of woe,

Ch'onde veder di sangue umano infette,

How rivers may run red with human blood,

per quanti modi in tal pugna si muora

In suchlike combat, in how many a mode

vedeste, e a molti il dimostraste allora.

Men die, you saw, and you to many showed.

(Trans. William Stewart Rose)

Ercole's father acquired his son's remains and had his head stitched back onto his body. He was embalmed and buried at the Church of San Francesco.

The river has changed its course so often over the centuries that sometimes you're drawn to places a dozen miles or more from the current river. I head north from Polesella, over a series of short bridges straddling thin streams and straight canals. The Tartaro-Canalbianco-Po di Levante is a bit of both, a combination of the Tartaro river and man-made canals which eventually join up with the ancient, most northerly branch of the Po itself. I turn left over the waterway and onto Via 43 Martiri (43 Martyrs).

Half a mile later I'm in the small village of Villamarzana, a crossroads town famous for the massacre that took place here in 1944. Two fascist officials had been killed in September 1944, and when, weeks later, four fascist spies were sent to Villamarzana and the surrounding countryside to infiltrate the partisan resistance, they disappeared. Investigations into the killings were unsuccessful and so, on the night of 13 October, thirty-eight men and five children were rounded up and tortured in Rovigo. On the 15th, they were shot. Only one man survived, though he, too, died a year later.

Next to the canal is a memorial chapel and, outside, a long line of the names of the victims. There are wreaths and Italian flags. On the patchy rendering of the chapel, metal lettering spells out the warning from history: "they fell for freedom from every internal and foreign tyranny. From their blood should emerge a warning for future generations to perpetuate a fair, free, democratic country." There's another plaque commemorating the massacre on the walls of the town hall and, next to that, a plaque to a former mayor placed there on the fiftieth anniversary of his murder in 1924: it lauds him as a "socialist mayor of this council in the dark years of poverty, oppression and pre-Fascist, agrarian slavery".

Of all the martyrs of fascism, that mayor, Giacomo Matteotti, is perhaps the most well known. There are 3,292 streets named after him in Italy. He was born in the next-door village of Fratta Polesine in 1887. He was vociferously against Italy's entry into the First World War and was interned in Sicily for much of that war. He became a deputy in the Italian parliament for the Socialist Party and after Mussolini seized power in October 1922 frequently denounced fascist violence, corruption and electoral fraud. His last speech to the Camera was on 30 May 1924, in which he decried the intimidation and tricks in the previous month's election. He knew he would be killed: "I've made my speech," he said at the end. "Now you prepare the funeral elegy for me." On 10 June he disappeared, bundled into a car in the centre of Rome and stabbed to death. His body was found on 16 August in a wood in Riano, to the north of the capital.

Fratta, Matteotti's birthplace, stands close to the site of an ancient settlement called Frattesina. It was on the old Po di Adria, a branch of the river which slowly disappeared in, it's thought, the first century BC. The settlement was only discovered in 1967, and archaeological digs continued for the next twenty years, revealing a sophisticated culture in which amber was a vital commodity.

After the Venetians had conquered much of the Polesine in the sixteenth and seventeenth centuries, Fratta became, like the delta, a summer resort for wealthy Venetians. It's just a small village now, with a deep, slim canal (the *Scortico*) and small bridges. But on the far side of that canal are incongruously palatial villas such as the Villa Badoer, designed by Andrea Palladio in 1554–5: the immaculate symmetry of the pronaos (the portico of a classical temple), and the soft whiteness of the long staircases leading up to it (it was built on the site of the old castle and is raised above the surrounding land), give it a deliberate sense of calm, neoclassical superiority. But it's oddly welcoming, too, its curving, lateral colonnades (disguising agricultural outbuildings) reaching out like arms for a hug.

It's hard to imagine this rather grandiose village as a centre of insurgents and, later, defiant socialists, but in both the nineteenth and twentieth centuries Fratta Polesine became nationally famous for its patriotic martyrs. After the final defeat of Napoleon Bonaparte, and the restoration of the Austro-Hungarian Empire in northern Italy at the Congress of Vienna in 1815, many Italian patriots formed secret societies to continue their battle for a united Italy. The Carbonari were the most famous, but there were also the Federati and the Guelfia, a secret society which Costantino Munari, a Jacobin from a hamlet on the left bank of the Po, hoped to fuse with the Carbonari.

On 11 November 1819, the perceived patron of the subversives, Giuseppa Cecilia Monti, invited various Carbonari to a banquet. Monti was married to a Bonapartist general, Jean-Baptiste d'Arnaud, and was part of a network of Polesine conspirators. It's unknown whether the sound of patriotic shouts was heard by the Austrian police, or if the meeting at Villa Grimani Morin (another grand residence deliberately designed to echo the next-door Villa Badoer) was revealed by a spy, but the house was raided and a dozen Carbonari were arrested. One confessed that he had entrusted compromising documents to a local man called Antonio.

Two months later, Antonio Fortunato Oroboni, the illegitimate son of a Ferrara nobleman, was also arrested at his house in Fratta. Munari's *Costituzione Latina* – a sort of insurgents' manifesto – was found hidden in the chapel of Oroboni's house. After three years in prison, he was sentenced to death with his co-conspirators, a sentence later commuted to fifteen years in

Spielberg prison in Brno in what is now the Czech Republic.

Oroboni is one of those figures from history who has been mythologised by a single source, and the other documentation is so thin it's hard to unpick the stories about his pious patriotism. The mythologisation comes from the memoir of the Italian patriot Silvio Pellico: *My Prisons*. Pellico was incarcerated at Spielberg, and although he only briefly met Oroboni in person, they would converse from their prison windows. Pellico drew a portrait of a man who, rather than a revolutionary against the good order of the Austrian Restoration, appeared more like a Christian martyr: "Many had harmed him," wrote Pellico. "He was wounded, but he forgave everyone and if he could narrate some praiseworthy aspect of one of his enemies, he did so gladly." Pellico's description of Oroboni's patriotism even as he was dying of tuberculosis turned him into one of the earliest Risorgimento martyrs: "So many times Oroboni told me as he looked out of the window at the cemetery: 'I should get accustomed to the idea of rotting down there: and yet I confess that the idea disgusts me. It doesn't seem to me that one could be as well buried in these countries as in our dear peninsula'." Pellico recalls the patriot's last words as "I forgive in my heart all my enemies".

I walk from one villa to another. Fratta Polesine seems top-heavy with mansions belonging to the landed gentry. They're part of the Carbonari heritage trail now. You can walk from Villa Oroboni to Villa Carnoldi, where another Carbonaro, Antonio Villa, was arrested. He, too, was sent to, and died in, Spielberg prison. But the village stops abruptly, becoming flat fields with no birds, trees or humans.

In the cemetery, the Matteotti family chapel is easy to find. There, draped with an Italian tricolour, surrounded by fuchsia cyclamen and permanent wreaths, is his charcoal-grey tomb. Below a photograph of Matteotti is one of his most famous utterances: "kill me, but you will never kill the idea I have in me." A month before my visit, someone had placed a handwritten letter addressed to Matteotti next to the photograph: "last year I told you about how Italy, politically and socially, has taken an ugly turn. After a year, the situation hasn't improved. We struggle every day, as we can, against the injustices which surround us, carrying forward your values for a fairer, freer world."

On the way to Ferrara, just south of the right bank, I go via Copparo. I want to see another of the Estensi "delights", the *turiòn*. It's a testament to the skill of the Estensi architects that this square, brick-built, almost windowless tower is so arresting. Perhaps it's just the contrast: it's like a medieval watchtower in a modern shopping mall, a sole reminder of authoritarian town planning. There's contrast to the *turiòn* itself, too: although imposing, its bricks are slim. The tower is a bare square, but crowned by overhanging crenellations. It was supposed to become part of a castle – you can still see the sockets in the brickwork where walls came off at right angles – but it now serves as the town's library.

Bricks define Ferrara. The city is encamped within monumental city walls that splay down into parkland. Almost all the grand architecture in the city – its angular bastions, the moated Estense castle, the Casa Pisani with its Ghibelline merlons (swallow-tailed crenellations), the remains of the Castello dei Curtensi, even the birthplace of one of the city's most famous sons, the Dominican friar Girolamo Savonarola – are built of brick.

The city's defensive buildings (including the now-destroyed Castel Tedaldo and the papal Fortezza) were on the river front, overseeing, protecting and taxing the river traffic. But the city's waterways today are completely altered: the old canal which used to lead straight to the castle moat has been built over, and ever since 1152 – when the Po burst its left bank in that famous "break of Ficarolo" and it found a new, more northerly, bed – Ferrara has slowly been deprived of its aquatic thoroughfare. It was this shift in the river's course, as much as all those battles between Venezia and Ferrara for ownership of the river, that really nudged the balance of power away from this city. The water – so dreaded in times of flood – was now flowing further away, straight from Ficarolo to Occhiobello and Francolino. In theory the Po still flows through this city: there's the "Po Morto di Primaro", and the "Po di Volano". But the first, a "dead Po", is almost static, petering out south of the city, while the Volano isn't the Po proper, just a thin offshoot which heads east of the city, reaching the Adriatic below Pomposa Abbey and the Mesola woodland. Ferrara's red-brick grandeur grew in future centuries, but it was no longer able to command the river in quite the same way.

In the fifteenth and sixteenth centuries, Ferrara's real power was cultural rather than military. The city claimed to be, as much as Florence or Urbino, the centre of the Italian Renaissance. The painter Dosso Dossi (1489?–1542) was a court artist who is considered the equal of Bellini, Michelangelo and Titian. He used walnut oil instead of tempera, meaning that even Giorgio Vasari (usually scornful of his works) was forced to admire the effect: "the oil in itself softens and sweetens the colours and renders them more delicate and more easily blended... in short, by this method the artists impart wonderful grace and vivacity and vigour to their figures." Dossi used orpiment generously: it was a yellow derived from arsenic whose impurities created an orange that was ideal for flaming sunshine or candles. In Dossi's *Melissa* the golden fringe of the enchantress's rug cascades over her toes. The flames she is poking have both a vigour and a fragility. The armour gleams and the foliage on the trees goes from a feathery corn-yellow to almost black. The Italian art critic

Roberto Longhi once placed Dossi on the fault line between northern and southern Europe: his art, wrote Longhi, mixed the "violet ashes" of late Giorgione with the "damp fog of the Po valley" and the "lucid rays" of the south.

Dossi was a narrative painter, basing his Melissa on his friend Ludovico Ariosto's character in *Orlando Furioso*. The imagery is so dense in the painting that it's surprisingly similar to reading Ariosto: you're speedily side-tracked. (Comparing the two, another art critic, Mauro Lucco, writes of how both Ariosto and Dossi enjoyed "narrating, imagining, rambling..."). Both artist and writer were sometimes scorned for providing superficial "parerga" – parergies, or the pleasurable embellishments – rather than religious pieties. But Dossi was ahead of his time, often being called impressionistic by daring to do more with less: in his *Scenes from a Legend*, the white town in the background shimmers and disappears like, in Longhi's words, "butterfly wings".

Ferrara was also the location of one of the most memorable conspiracies of the sixteenth century. The Duke of Ferrara, Ercole I, died in 1505, leaving Alfonso I (the future victor of the river battle at Polesella) to inherit the duchy. Alfonso's younger brother, Ippolito, was a cardinal and – among their other siblings – there was a "natural son", Giulio, who had also been brought up in court. Ippolito had fallen in love with a young woman who rejected him in favour of his illegitimate half-brother: "Giulio's eyes alone," she allegedly said, "are worth more than all of you." The furious cardinal and his retinue followed Giulio one day as he rode out into the woods. They surrounded him and beat him so badly he lost his sight. Some reports say his eyeballs were deliberately skewered out.

When Alfonso refused to discipline Ippolito, the blind Giulio and another brother, Ferrante, began to plot. The only way to have justice now was to kill the duke. When the plot was discovered – or maybe invented – by Ippolito, Giulio fled to

Mantova only for his protector, Francesco Gonzaga, to hand him over to the Ferrara authorities.

Giulio spent fifty-three years in prison, incarcerated alone in the Torre dei Leoni. In those fifty-three years, the woman who had expressed love for his eyes married a nobleman from Sassuolo and Giulio's brothers and sisters – even their children – died. Alfonso I's grandson, Alfonso II, came to power in 1559 and one of his first acts was to pardon his grandfather's half-brother. By then the blinded, half-blood Giulio d'Este was eighty-one. His age alone would have made him notorious, but this victim of fraternal jealousy was, it's said, still wearing the clothes he had worn in 1505. He died just over a year later.

The story was made into a touching film by Florestano Vancini, *E Ridendo l'Uccise*. Vancini cleverly elided the tale with another of the city's memorable events, the death of Gonella. Gonella (c.1391–1440) was the Estensi's jester and like most jokers he didn't always know when to stop. He pushed it further than was wise, and the more people laughed, the more he – short and gingerish – recited silly rhymes. His destiny was linked to the Po: Duke Niccolò III and Gonella were very close, but one day the duke was ill with fever and Gonella believed that a shock would cure him. So when they were out walking together, Gonella pushed him into the river and, fearful of the duke's fury, ran off to Padova. The duke did get better, but he ordered his jester back to the city. Gonella arrived standing on a barrow full of Padova soil in the hope that if things didn't go his way, he could claim he was still on foreign land. But Gonella was taken to the gallows as punishment for his impudence. As the joker's neck was placed on the axe block, a bucket of cold water was thrown on his head. That was the duke's scary joke – an eye for an eye, or water for water. But the cold and the fear gave Gonella such a shock that his heart gave out and he died.

Water was always a central preoccupation of the Estensi dukes. Alfonso I attempted to irrigate the fields south-east of the city, and create a canal as a transport hub between Ferrara and Bologna, but that connection between the Po and Reno rivers silted up and the land seemed constantly flooded. The city became notorious as an island in a swamp: despite all those land reclamations by Alfonso II between 1564 and 1580, Ferrara was still described (in a papal *Compendiosa Descrittione dello Stato*) as a "squalid little city surrounded by marshes". Even centuries later, in 1907, the Ferrara parliamentarian Pietro Niccolini, in his analysis of agrarian destitution, moaned that "the lagunas spread their dead waters" over 100,000 hectares: "It's a burdensome setting, motionlessness... and the fogs almost always wrap the horizon making it seem uncertain and boundless."

The Ferraresi make a virtue of this flatness, relishing being called the "Italian Holland", and boasting that about a quarter of a million hectares of land would be under water were it not for centuries of *bonifiche* and canal creation. And it's interesting how the river seeps into the city's literature. After Ariosto, Torquato Tasso became – between controversies and imprisonments – the Estensi's court poet. Because they were near-contemporaries, and both connected to Ferrara, comparing and contrasting Ariosto and Tasso has been a game of literary salons ever since the sixteenth century: Galileo far preferred Ariosto, calling him "magnificent, rich and admirable" compared to Tasso's "narrow, poor and miserable" verse. But Tasso is sometimes more complex and rooted. He seems less servile towards the regime and he wrote far more about the Po. One of his earliest pastorals, *Aminta*, was set on an island of the river, and while the then-fashionable invocations of nymphs and satyrs leave me pretty cold, his deferential address to that regal river, lauding its power and imploring its assistance, captures the place that the Po had for him and his courtly contemporaries:

Re de gli altri superbo, altero fiume,	King of all others, proud, haughty river
che qualor esci del tuo regno e vaghi	Whenever you leave your kingdom and roam
atterri ciò ch'opporsi a te presume,	on land that opposes you, deliver
e l'ime valli e l'alte piagge allaghi...	To the low valleys and the high beauties your foam...

(Sonnet 83)

That opening line is an exact replica of the ninth line of Petrarch's sonnet on the river in which he permits the Po to carry away his *"scorza"*, his "rind" or physical remains. Tasso, too, felt such an affinity for the river that he imagined his remains would be received by it. But mostly the image of the Po in his poetry (and the river features heavily in *Gerusalemme Liberata*) is that of a power that can't be contained. The imagery is always of imperial omnipotence:

... Così de gli altri fiumi il re tal volta,	... So when his banks the prince of rivers, Po,
quando superbo oltra misura ingrossa	Doth overswell, he breaks with hideous fall
sovra le sponde ruinoso scorre	The mossy rocks and trees o'ergrown with age,
né cosa è mai che gli s'ardisca opporre.	Nor aught withstands his fury and his rage.

(Canto I, LXXV) (Trans. Edward Fairfax, 1600)

Centuries later, the city's acclaimed writers, painters and filmmakers were using the river, and its delta, as a metaphor for humanity's inner turmoils. Giorgio Bassani (famous in the English-speaking world for *The Garden of the Finzi-Continis*) imagined the central Corso Giovecca (built on top of the old canal) as "a great cart track, fraught with cobbles and uneven like the bed of a stream...". Even when admiring the city's architecture – "the contorted and decrepit alleys of the medieval heart..." – Bassani saw the earthy reds and pinks of the river's bricks (*"rosea"*, *"rossastro"*, *"rosseggiare"*). He wrote an elegiac book called *L'Airone* (*The Heron*), in which he describes the "barren lands of the reclamation", with their "long, flat sandbanks, covered with a thick, dwarf vegetation the colour of tobacco, similar to the hair of an old nag". That novel was largely set in the delta, but it starts and finishes in Ferrara, and that sense of pointlessness and waste is what brings the story to its climax.

Ferrara at this time of year – mid-autumn – is subtle. It's wrapped in fog and closed to the world as soon as the unseen sun goes down. Through the faint lights you see solitary cyclists. By nine it seems deserted. You can hear cutlery being shuffled and laughter from third-floor windows. It has a great buskers' festival in early autumn and its blue-tubed football stadium is almost in the city centre itself, so it's not an unlively town. But normally, in this fog, people are invisible. Sounds are muffled. D'Annunzio wrote about the "deserted beauty" of Ferrara, inevitably eroticising it with his usual creamy clichés: "...the dream of voluptuousness which is buried beneath the bare stones..."

Many writers have noticed a certain lassitude to the place. My favourite building is Palazzo Schifanoia, the "avoid boredom" building. There's even a village nearby, whose name has the same meaning, called Schifanoglia. One of the people interviewed by Ermanno Rea in his *Il Po si racconta* refers to a "laziness which is essentially sensuality. Ferrara's laziness comes from far away, from history's obscurity, and has a flavour of courtly life, a Ducal laziness..." Bassani, too, writes about one young woman's stride as exhibiting "*maestosa languidezza*", a "lofty languor", and commenting on "the boredom and idleness of the province".

There's a wistfulness in Bassani's writing, not just because the decadent city's glories were long in the past but because, for him, as a Jewish anti-fascist, the Shoah made even the recent past remote and unreachable. So post-war Ferrara becomes a city of ghosts, like the character of Geo Josz who comes back from the dead just as a plaque is being put up to commemorate him. He shows his hands and wounds to the unconvinced and uninterested. It is, writes Bassani, a city of "luminous dust".

It's hard not to be aware of the past. Outside the castle, on a corner column, is a *padimetro*, a historical account of the heights of the Po ("Padus") through the ages: various years, from 1705 onwards, are marked with an arrow on the stone showing how high the waters were at the nearby town of Pontelagoscuro. Nineteen fifty-one tops the chart, at four metres thirty, almost the level of the flats and shops above the colonnade. Next to it is an overbearing statue of Savonarola, his arms outstretched. And then, a little further on, is the small rectangle on the castle wall marking the site of the massacre on 13 November 1943, when eleven people were executed in revenge for the unsolved murder of the local fascist dignitary, Igino Ghisellini, two days before.

Critical of his city's shrugging collusion with anti-Semitism and fascism, Bassani turned that killing into a short story, "Una notte del '43". That slaughter by the castle is the backdrop to the marriage of an ailing man and his beautiful wife. Reduced to staring out of his window overlooking the castle, the man sees everything but, because he also sees his unfaithful wife, decides to see nothing. He pretends to be asleep so as not to admit to himself his own cuckolding. If anything, the film adaptation by

Florestano Vancini is even better than the short story, portraying a bare, black and white Ferrara inevitably enveloped in fog. Like the short story, it's a tale of deliberate blindness and treachery: the victims of the killings, described by the fascist authorities as "traitors" on the moat wall, were actually betrayed, and the cuckolded husband is betrayed not only by his wife but also by himself. Like indifferent citizens, he sees everything but is deliberately sightless.

Michelangelo Antonioni was another film director from Ferrara. Working in those post-war decades when Italy suddenly changed from being a predominantly agrarian to an industrial society, Antonioni's early landscapes are dotted with symbols of modernity: petrol stations, refineries and factories. One of his very first short films was called *People of the Po*, and although the music is annoyingly emotive and the narration dull, the images are unforgettable: the reed huts (*tuguri*), the abandoned, floating flour mills, the smoky barges. The Po is the lead character, but rather than rhapsodise this elemental setting, Antonioni offers a surprising simile for the Po, calling it "as flat as asphalt". The river is no more romantic than another road.

Normally, when writing a travel book, there's a rough resemblance between your research and the reality. They might not align precisely, but what you read before setting off is usually at least comparable to what you see when you get there. With this river, though, the discrepancies are vast. I've been reading books about how this tract of water was, for over two millennia, the most important thoroughfare in northern Italy. It linked Venezia and the Adriatic to august cities like Ferrara, Mantova, Parma, Pavia and Torino. Controlling the river was like controlling a flight path, or an airport. It wasn't just a source of taxes and power, but a fundamental element in every aspect of people's lives: it was where – far from the sea – they enjoyed sandy beaches and milled their flour.

But now the river is irrelevant, an area left behind by modernity. Littering the riverside are more ruins, not just abandoned farmhouses but metal skeletons, factories rusting brown and surrounded by barbed wire and "danger of collapse" signs. There used to be sugar refineries here, using the beet grown on these fertile fields, but they have been demolished or bombed. During the Second World War they produced alcohol as an alternative to scarce diesel fuel, and were thus subject to Allied air raids.

T. S. Eliot's description of his "sullen" river, the Mississippi, is so appropriate for the Po: "… the brown god is almost forgotten / By the dwellers in cities… Unhonoured, unpropitiated / By worshippers of the machine, but waiting, watching and waiting." The only business along the river now is perpendicular to it, on the many bridges that cross it.

It's bleak, but that, in a strange way, is what attracts people to this landscape. These villages are insulated by fog. It gives them a moody anonymity. And when you go into one of the hostelries the atmosphere is equally liquid – windows steamed up, pensioners drinking mid-morning white wine while playing *briscola* – but, unlike the atmosphere outside, it's loud and warm. If you ask them about the river, you can understand why it's so often been portrayed as a god because it is deeply loved and feared, giving and taking and, now, disappearing from sight, seemingly redundant and ignored.

The elderly are the last living witnesses of a way of life that has vanished. When they describe their parents' and grandparents' jobs the indolence of modern life really strikes home: many were *scarriolanti*, the "wheel-barrowers" who toiled in the claggy mud all day to build these irrigation channels. When work was slack in irrigation, the strong men would work as *sabbiatori* (or *sabbiaroli*), shovelling sand and silt onto boats: "… shuddering the spade underwater" as Cesare Pavese wrote in his poem "Crepuscolo di Sabbiatori" ("twilight of sand-shifters").

Life was a battle against the water, the mud, the current and the hunger, and these men in the bar remember the stark poverty like a warning they long to pass on. One tells me about the *trognaio*, a ragged itinerant who snuffled along the banks, digging up the potato-bean tuber. Scavengers were called *spigolatrici*, picking loose corn from the fields. Other roles were almost animalistic: the *cavallanti* (the "horsers") were men linked, like oxen, to one thick rope who pulled big boats upstream (boats could do around 100 kilometres a day or more with the current, but only 10–20 against it). Sometimes ponies – called *bidetti* – were used (that's where the word bidet comes from, I learn, since you straddle it like a horse). The farmhands were called *terzaroli* because they had to give a third of their produce to the landowner. By 11 November, the day of San Martino, everything had been harvested and winter crops planted, and so that date was traditionally the end of the agricultural contracts. "To do the San Martino" meant to pack up all your belongings and find somewhere to bed down until the winter passed and spring broke through.

Above that underclass were other jobs, linked to the shifting, silty bed of the river. The *meatore* was the man who gauged the depths for the ships: "the river's always new", one man says to me, explaining that the sandy bed shifts constantly. Dredgers ploughed the mud, occasionally turning up treasures like the Montefortino helmet (a pre-Roman bronze helmet, used by the Celts and Etruscans, discovered in the riverbed near Revere). There were hunters – usually two men using a long, flat boat called a *sandolina*. The men would use a wooden duck to attract real birds (those primitive objects, now cracked with age, are still seen in houses and bars). One man, at the back, paddled silently while another lay on his stomach with a three-metre cannon called a *spingarda*. That cannon fired so much shot – up to a kilogram at a time – that often they could kill dozens of ducks in one firing. The recoil was so great that it would force the boat backwards a dozen metres or more.

Under the water there was an abundance of food: freshwater prawns, pike, perch and, above all, the mighty sturgeon which could often grow to over two metres and feed an entire village. Now the prawns have been replaced by invasive versions from Alabama. Gone, too, are the floating double-hulled mills which used the current to mill flour. It's estimated there were once as many as three hundred of these mills along the river, between Cremona and the sea, in the early nineteenth century. In an area with no steep rivers and seldom much wind, only the Po had the force to drive a millstone round here. But because you couldn't have fixed mills due to the varying heights of the river, and because the best current was out in the middle, these catamarans drifted in and out, channelling the water between their two hulls which turned a *superiore* or *soprano* (the upper stone) on the *dormiente* (the sleeper below).

The millers were notoriously rough diamonds, living alone on their wooden boats: given the presence of flour and wood, the danger of fire or explosions was such that they lived in the cold, cooking often only flour gnocchi with a lard and cheese sauce. It was such dusty work that, over decades, they inevitably suffered respiratory problems; and the constant noise of grinding stones rendered many of them deaf or, at best, hard of hearing. But they never went hungry. They controlled the flour of the Bassa (the lowlands around the river) and they had sidelines. The mooring charges and the flour taxes were so high that often these floating mills became magnets for contraband and people who wanted to hide, allowing night boats to moor, unload and scavenge for driftwood and gossip. Legislation against those mills meant that they were never allowed permanent moorings as they would get in the way of those human horses dragging tugs upstream. Throughout the early twentieth century they were all replaced by onshore steam- or diesel-powered mills. Of those three hundred or so mills, only one remained after 1945. But it was a profession immortalised by one of the most famous trilogies about the river, *The Mill on the Po* by Riccardo Bacchelli.

The old men in this bar remember their youth, in the 1940s, when the river was so clean that every day in the summer they would go to the river's beach. A lifeguard was employed by the town council for three months every year.

"He would hit you on the head with his oar if you went out too far," one man smiles. "My mother used to give him a few extra notes to keep a special eye on me."

Everyone has a vivid story of a drowning, as if the river were a god which demanded its victims, its annual human sacrifices. As they say here, in dialect: "*Al Po al dà e al tös*" – the Po gives and it takes away. But I've also been told that these sandy, sometimes wooded banks were where couples went to – they often use a more colourful phrase than this – *amoreggiare*, to frolic. When I ask the elderly men in the bar about this, they laugh, as if I had asked them where children come from: "we were all conceived there!" one guffaws in dialect.

Maybe it wasn't only the seclusion or the softness of the ground that made the riverside a place to undress together. Like hugging a tree, there's a gentle but insistent energy beside this river. That's part of its attraction. You're drawn to its power (people sometimes called it *sua maestà*, "his majesty"). The film director Franco Barilli once said, "the Bassa is pure sex, it's erotic energy, it's a primitive, vital pulse". Maybe it's that proximity to nature – its strength, its demands – that encourages natural acts. And it's hidden, somehow, from the conventional world of urbane civilisation. Ermanno Olmi once said: "going beyond the banks of the river, I had the impression I had entered another world, a sort of truce of humanity, in which all tension was deleted and in which every relationship with the rest of the world was broken. It seemed to me like the penetration of a frank space…" It all sounds voluptuously carnal: there's the truce, the erasure of tension, the world on hold and held at bay. Perhaps that sense of relief and release, of flowing through banks, means that its drownings are balanced by its conceptions.

But now the river is ignored and irrelevant. It has no purpose for the majority of people here – it's just an obstacle to be overcome. Once in a while, as I walk along the sodden banks, I see a lone angler or someone caulking an upturned boat by a clearing… but there's no life here. It's mostly unpeopled. It offers solitude and quiet, but it makes me anxious. I sometimes wonder about that ancient warning that *induà a nas pénsa, lacqua la rump* – "who doesn't think about it, will be broken by the water".

THREE

Il Mantovano

IL MANTOVANO

Verona
15km

Mincio

Lago
Superiore

Lago di
Mezzo

Lago
Inferiore

Mantova

Governolo

Ostiglia

San Benedetto Po

Canale

Suzzara

M

B

A

R

D

Cavo Lama

Secchia

**Reggio
-Emilia
27km**

E

M

I

L

I

A

R

Panaro

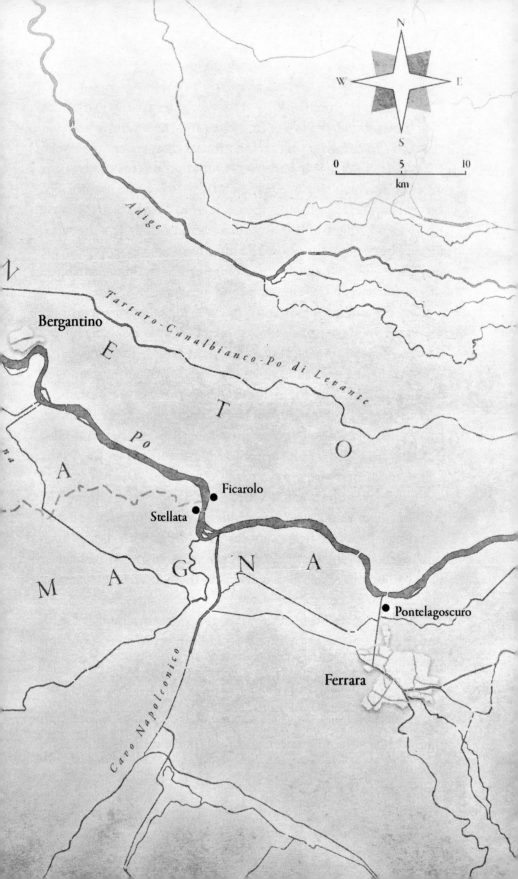

The beery river, frothy and brown, glugs past. It's still high, tugging at the lower branches and their yellow leaves.

Pontelagoscuro is an unattractive town: once renowned for its *via coperta* – it had over a hundred metres of riverside arcades in which to store merchandise – it became a notorious target for aerial bombing in the Second World War because of its two bridges and many sugar refineries. It was bombed almost horizontal and now the muddy riverbank is one of the few places which has remained more or less the same: a ribbon of green between the chimneys and antennae.

I keep trudging upstream, under bridges, past gravel pits, walking round fly-tipped tiles, sofas and mattresses. The purple flowers of meadow sage peek through the long grass. It's so damp here. Many buildings look like neglected bathrooms, smudged grey by mould. The fog makes it seem as if you're looking at everything through gauze. As the Po bends away in the distance, there's no separation between the white river and the white sky.

Every now and again the footpath along the river leaves the water and brings you via the banks to a grand *idrovora*, arched buildings straddling water with slim chimneys on either side. And between them are more industrial ruins: grey aluminium claddings, concrete frames, hollow buildings with more "keep out" signs hanging on the gate. There are runs of rusting barbed wire topping breeze-block walls. And then, after a mile or two, you're back by the water.

The *golene* are flooded now: stretches of woodland are sunk under many metres of water. Fat, oblique trunks emerge from its shiny surface. The star-cucumber's huge leaves sag and their hairy stems have thinned to a soggy brown. Diseased trees stand bare and skeletal. Everything is sodden. It looks like the water has recently been at least a metre higher: a perfectly horizontal line bleaches the lower foliage of the false indigos and alders that have been immersed in the flood.

Every few miles are brown signs to another floodplain, brown being the colour for something "natural". At Porporano, among the puddles and ponds, tall oaks and ashes are strung with ivy and bindweed bunting. Coots – charcoal-black with white beaks – waddle across the cycle path. In this bleached landscape, almost the only bright colours are the smooth circles of orange persimmons hanging from the trees.

As usual, all the place names near here remind you that this whole area used to be marshland: the town of Moglia comes from *molia* or *moja*, meaning a place invaded by waters. Other hamlets – Bagnolo and Bugno – recall the effects of floods. The Po basin has around 50,000 kilometres of canals and here there are more waterways than roads, so many canals and drainage channels that it's hard to keep up: the Canale Boicelli, Canale Bianco, Canale delle Pilastresi, Canale di Fossalta, Cavo Napoleonico, Canale di Burana, Canale Diversivo di Burana, Canale della Bonifica Reggiana-Mantovana. There are the Secchia and Panaro rivers, the Canale della Bonifica Parmigiana Moglia, the Canale Sabbioncello. The straight lines of those canals, and the many perpendicular plantations of poplars standing in the lustred mud, give the landscape an oddly deliberate, lineal appearance.

This is one of the narrower parts of the river where two forts used to face each other and control the river traffic. Someone tells me there used to be a chain which was pulled taut between the strongholds to impede ships which hadn't paid their passage. The fort on one side is Ficarolo, with its wonky tower. This side is the Rocca Possente, a pink fort whose star shape gave this town its name, Stellata. The castle is now cracked and closed to the public following a recent earthquake.

This area of the Po – between its two right-bank tributaries of the Secchia and Panaro rivers – was where hundreds of Germans drowned in the Second World War, trapped by water on all sides. They had chosen this area as a strategic place where they could isolate themselves from attack by destroying the bridges over those tributaries. And from here it was supposed to be a direct route north, through the Germans' stronghold of Verona and the Brennero Pass. But it turned into a trap. In July 1944, Operation Mallory Major had destroyed twenty-two of the twenty-four bridges on the entire length of the River Po, cutting the Germans' supply lines. Pontoon crossings were frequently recreated by Germans at night using boats and floats, but they had to be dismantled during the day to avoid more Allied bombings.

It's thought that the Germans lost 70,000 men (half of whom were captured) in the Allied offensive of April 1945. Many of their greatest losses were here on this stretch of the Po: they left behind, on the right bank of the river, 15,000 horses and hundreds of vehicles. When you look at photographs from 23–24 April that year, you can see, all along the banks, mile upon mile of burned-out cars, trucks and tanks. With no bridges to cross, and with all the boats already having left, thousands of retreating Germans tried to swim across the river using any floats they could find: empty fuel tanks, house shutters and random logs. For weeks afterwards, the bodies of drowned Germans were found downstream.

One of the officers and later a noted military historian, General Fridolin von Senger und Etterlin, believed that "the Allied bombings of the Po River crossings finished the Germans in Italy". Abandoning almost all their equipment, and losing much of their personnel, the war was finished. "North of the Po," General von Senger said, "we were no longer an army."

In the years after the war, that bounty left by advancing, and retreating, armies was a mine for resourceful locals. Given the quantity of that abandoned equipment – sometimes on the banks, but often scattered in fields and woodlands nearby – a new profession was born along the river: the *recuperatore* or reclaimer. If you stop and talk to any of the farmers round here they love describing the resourcefulness of those years: the silk from the Allied parachutes was used for first communions and weddings well into the 1950s. German helmets were so common they were deployed as hoppers for chicken feed, cooking pans or to clean out long drops. For years farmers fixed tyres with the plastic patches the Allies had brought to repair punctures on their inflatable bridge supports. The ribbed, cylindrical gas-mask containers were turned into mini water tanks on knife-sharpening wheels. The Allies' foldable Goatley boat had waxed cloth sides and was used by cobblers for years after the war for making boots. During the floods of 1951, rescuers even launched the old Allied Duck boats that had been left behind.

But perhaps my favourite story about that resourcefulness is from the left bank, in Bergantino. One of the people I talk to tells me it's always been a bit of an outlaw town: "It's called Bergantino because it was a place of brigands," she says. "It was notorious for banditry and piracy. The town was excommunicated three times in the eighteenth century for not paying its taxes." It certainly feels like a border town – right on the edge of the regions of Lombardia, Veneto and Emilia-Romagna – and is, as my new friend says, "marginalised but free", in the simple sense that it's remote or forgotten.

Bergantino became famous in the early twentieth century as a town which produced artisanal fairground rides. Between the wars, two inventors from the town had made carousels with wooden cars but Albino Protti wanted to go one better and make a children's ride with aeroplanes. He had designed a prototype using chains to lift the kids, but it was tame and when the war broke out he was conscripted and sent to North Africa. Captured and deported to the United States to work on the cotton plantations, he saw, for the first time, a hydraulic truck. He studied it and thought about it for his fairground ride. After the war, he patented his design, and created a ride using the discarded barrels from German and Allied tanks as strong arms to lift the little toy planes. The mini fuselages were made from the torpedo-shaped fuel tanks which the Allied bombers discarded all over the Pianura Padana after their bridge-bombing raids.

Protti's success was imitated by dozens of others and Bergantino slowly became the centre of the Italian fairground industry. I hear different figures about how many people were involved: 150 families in the 1970s, or 105 families in the 1960s. But in a town of only, then, around 3,000, the percentage of people creating rides and games was clearly high. The town has a tiny but charming museum which tells the story of popular entertainments and fairgrounds through the ages. There are still a few hundred people here involved in the industry, but the rides today seem tackier than those old inventions. As I move on, walking upstream, one of the fields looks like a carousel cemetery from a horror film: crooked big wheels, cracked elastic belts and empty bulb sockets.

The name of the small town Sermide derives from the Sarmatian warriors from Scythia (the steppes of eastern Ukraine and southern Russia) who were hired to defend the river from barbarians during the collapse of the Roman Empire. It once had a grand castle but only its red-brick tower with its swallow-tailed crenellations survives. As you walk under its one arch, the relief brickwork announces the "Amministrazione Communale Fascista". Although the third word has been flattened, it's still legible.

Being almost equidistant from Ferrara and Mantova, Sermide was constantly contested by those city rulers, the Estensi and the

Gonzagas. So many wars devastated this town that its history becomes very confusing: in 1630, during the Second War of Monferrato (when the main branch of the Gonzaga line died out) the town was sacked; in the first Italian War of Independence (1848–9), Sermide earned the moniker of the "Lioness of the Po", holding out against Austrian troops until Field Marshal Radetzky stormed it and burned it down. It was his bloody suppression of Italian patriots that led Johann Strauss to celebrate him in his jaunty waltz. In the Second World War, a sugar refinery and nearby bridge made it yet another target for Allied bombings.

When you wander around now it seems as if there's no one here. There's a peeling poster announcing the union meeting house is up for sale. A register of flood heights on the church shows a mark, from 1872, twice my height or more. The population has halved in the last two decades and, given the now affordable housing, the few who move in are immigrants. There's an Islamic funeral director between the grand church and the tower.

Italian writers who have done this same river journey in the other direction mourn this emptiness. "We're on the edges of the provinces, where they live like the forgotten people of a civilisation that always arrived late and slow," Guido Conti wrote wistfully when he got here. "The sense of marginalisation mixed with decadence and abandonment could be confused with an air of constant holidaying… we feel like tourists arriving the day after the destruction of humanity." Gianni Celati, one of the best writers about the Bassa, once said the main square in Pomponesco "was almost always empty, but that emptiness was recognisable as a kind of welcome". As always, when you do find someone to talk to it's hard to stop them because they're either lonely or else so keen to share the treasures of this muddy, wet town and its neighbouring villages. They don't just talk about the war, and the history, but most of all about "the river". The word they all use is *tramandare*: they long to "hand down" what they know before it's lost forever.

I phone a retired local historian called Pietro and he tells me to meet him in the bar. When he arrives it takes him ten minutes to get to me past all the card players. We settle in with mid-afternoon glasses of Fortana, the local red wine, and he tells me about the floating bridges. Like so many of the elderly people I talk to about the river and its culture, he's melancholic about that lost world. He has the fastidiousness of someone eager for everything to be recorded and remembered correctly. He talks me through the different types of boats – dozens and dozens of names which he reels off with evangelic zeal: the *magana*, the *sandolo*, the *battana*, the *burchiello*, the *battello*, the *zattera*... But it's the floating bridges that most enthuse him. They were feats of human engineering, he says. The head position of *pontiere* (the "bridgeman") was a serious role. Romano Prodi's father was a "bridgeman", I'm told – it's said as an endorsement of the former Italian prime minister's solidity and seriousness.

Making the bridge was the easy bit, says Pietro. You lashed the barges (flat-bottomed, rectangular boats called *chiatte*) side by side. But they constantly had to be undone, too, to let vessels pass. The centre of the bridge was unloosed, and the current pulled it apart; but then the ends had to be pulled back by many hands against the current.

"It can be a treacherous river," Pietro says happily, "especially at night or when the water is high. Those bridgemen were constantly on high alert. You had lumps of ice, or tree trunks, which could smash a barge or two if you didn't see them coming. You've got impatient navigators in their boats who will honk for you to open up the bridge, uncouple the *chiatte*, and let them through. You've got farmers and traders who want to go the other way, and for you to lash it back together again. You've got a till full of all the takings on the toll which some passing bandit might fancy sticking a pistol in your face for."

The size of the bridge operations from a century or more ago is surprising. The Boretto-Viadana bridge, slightly upstream the other side of Mantova, had 120 boats creating a floating bridge across hundreds of metres of water. It employed eighteen people. But the tolls are where you get a true insight into another era. Pietro shows me the old tariffs for the barge bridge in San Benedetto Po: in 1874, it cost four-hundredths of a lire for a pedestrian to cross (the cost was the same for a calf, pig or donkey, unless the donkey was loaded, in which case it was six cents). Sheep or goats cost only two cents. It cost three lire to take across a threshing machine, or one lire fifty for a horse- or mule-drawn coffin (half if the coffin was empty). The sheet of tolls is so long there are thirty-six different prices: for carriages, for steam engines, for different numbers of livestock. By 1893, there were only twenty-two different tolls, but inflation had increased the cost for a pedestrian to five cents, the donkey or calf to fifteen cents, and a coffin to two lire forty. In the small print at the foot of both tariff sheets it says costs will be doubled if the river is *in piena*, literally "full".

I wander on towards Revere. Like so many of these towns, it has only a single tower as a reminder of the twelfth-century castle which used to overlook the river. It stands like a folly now, opposite the Gonzagas' Ducal Palace. On the other side of the water, the red and white hooped chimneys of Ostiglia power station are flanked by pylons looking like metallic A-line dresses. I cross the river to the ugly left bank to get a closer look: more pylons leer over the landscape, more red and white chimneys and fat tubes run from the power station to the river. I had naively expected a mildly bucolic town. Pliny, in his *Naturalis Historia*, talks of people in Ostiglia putting beehives on boats so that the bees could find new nectar. But it's a town of architectural chaos:

the red-brick ruins of ancient buildings are squeezed between grey concrete. The twelfth-century castle was dismantled in the eighteenth century to provide fortifications for Mantova and now whiteish, high-rise flats dwarf the ruins. Vegetation is taking over empty villas, with ivy crawling inside the upper windows of one of them. And everything is in the shadow of those barber-shop chimneys.

Painted on the side of some concrete next to the water is a quotation: "men are like rivers: the water is the same in each, and alike in all; but every river is narrow here, is more rapid there, here slower, there broader, now clear, now cold, now dull, now warm." The attribution consists of just two painted letters – LT (Leo Tolstoy).

I walk back to the river for respite. It bends into a horseshoe here, with Ostiglia at the apex. It's slightly narrower – you could almost land a stone the other side. Sprays of trees line the banks, and there are rectangular houseboats and fishing sheds floating on the belching water. The sky is purpling, and – if only by contrast to the post-industrial mess beyond – it's almost restful.

By the time I get to Governolo, about a dozen miles south-east of Mantova, the river has risen even further. I can see serpents of froth in the middle of the current like shaving foam. It doesn't sound quite normal either: it's growling softly. You can see here why rivers are often thought to be cleansing, purging or purifying: this body of water is visibly carrying plastic rectangles of food packaging, streaks of red I don't like the look of, dead fish. I wonder what's in its depths, invisible to the eye. The houses in the floodplains – once white but now blotched black by mould – are one-third underwater.

On slightly higher ground, I watch various people scrambling to save their stuff. An old man in a check shirt is at the first-floor window of a stable, pulling chairs up by a rope and urging his stout wife to tie the knots faster. Another chap is trying to stop his garden furniture floating away. I offer a hand but he shrugs and says "*ormai*", a way of declaring "what's done is done". He gives up and decides to sit in a deck chair in his waders enjoying a fag.

The poplar plantations seem rooted on water. In the reflection, their upper halves are now their bottom halves and there's no ground, only sky. The entire trunks of the alders and willows are gone, and you can only see their canopies nudging above the surface. An old signora walks past me and pauses to watch the scene.

"Not as bad as 2000, right?"

I nod as if I knew.

"I could wash my hands from the balcony back then!"

A herd of sixty or so goats are being moved and they scurry here and there, tumbling down the bank until the goatherd, an Albanian, shouts directions. He and I stare at the water together as the goats nibble our trousers.

"As long as the sea is pulling, that's the thing," he says, repeating – as we immigrants do – what we've been told: "*finché il mare tira*."

This is Governolo, on the elbow where the rivers Mincio and Po meet. The contrast between the frenetic salvage operation one side of the bank and the sedate luxury the other could hardly be more marked. Within thirty seconds you're in a small green which is clearly, from its concave form, an old riverbed. A line of rusting cogs, two metres tall, used to raise and lower this "Conca del Bertalazzo" (the "Bertalazzo lock") to control the flow of the River Mincio into the Po. I wander over to the remains of the castle – a red-brick tower now adjoined to a creamy white house. A plaque commemorates the fallen patriots, many Piemontese, who died here in the 1848–9 uprisings against the Austrians.

Governolo is famous because this is where, it's said, Attila the Hun was turned back by Pope Leo X. There's supposed to be a marker somewhere on the exact spot where the pope bribed or threatened the invader, who duly decided not to cross the water. I pedal up and down the banks for a merry hour looking for the plaque. I cross bridges over the Mincio and over dozens of drainage channels and canals. Then I turn round and come back to the Po. I watch a man with a walking stick trying to catch lettuces which are floating away from his veg bed.

Eventually, there's a modern looking cube of a farmhouse set in gravel and I knock.

A woman comes to the top window. "*Allora?*" ("So?")

"Are you from here?" I ask stupidly.

"Why should I tell you where I'm from?"

"I'm looking for the plaque, where Attila..." Before I finish, she points to her left and pulls the shutters closed.

Round to the side, on the wall, is a large white rectangle of marble. The incised letters are the same white, so you have to shift left and right to read it:

Hic est locus celebris ille ube in padum / olim mintii. Influentibus undis, Leo Primus Pont Max / Anno DiNi CCCCLIIII Athilan Flagellum Dei...

The marble was erected by Francesco Gonzaga in 1616 on the side of the village oratorio which has long since disappeared. The attempted English translation beneath is rather charming:

This is the famous place where once ago flow into the river Po the waves of Mincio, the great pontiff Leone the first, our Lord's year 454, armed with threatening presence of the apostles Peter and Paul, with his admirable eloquence dissuaded Attila, the scourge of god, from devastating the town of Rome and the whole of Italy...

At dusk, I decide to look for the farm where I'm giving myself the comfort of a bed. I walk down the diagonal slip road from the bank and the place has a self-assured solidity: a terracotta courtyard, a smell of manure in the air, a noisy cockerel perching on an upside-down wheelbarrow. Inside, that farmyard welcome increases: there's a large room with a vaulted brick ceiling. By the fire, there's a spread of their own cheeses and chutneys, and a flask of red wine. The hospitality in these lowlands is always both solicitous and informal – it feels more like you're sitting at the family table which, often, you are. An old signora pulls up a chair alongside me. I had told her I was writing about the river, and she wants to share the family photo album.

"*Ecco*," she says, "the Germans." They were stationed in this farmhouse in the war. She fingers a picture of herself, little more than a toddler. She turns the page and it's Americans. "They all ate here," she says, pointing at the floor.

That night I watch *Il Mestiere delle Armi* (*The Profession of Arms*) in bed. The room is chilly, but the blankets warm – perfect for an Olmi film set in the Governolo winter of 1526. It's a war film without much action: it's about a slow death here in Governolo. The papal forces were attempting to halt the descent of the German *Lanzichenecchi* who were aiming to reach Rome through the bottleneck of the Gonzaga and Estensi territories. The Estensi provided a few *falconetti* – little cannons – to the *Lanzichenecchi,* and the leading *condottiero* of his generation – Giovanni of the Black Bands – was shot in the leg. Taken to the Gonzaga palace, he died there aged only twenty-six. That's about all there is to the plot of the film, but its recreation of a wintry war along the river is moving, with the elderly von Frundsberg from Mindelheim pitted against the young Italian noble, the son of Giovanni de' Medici and Caterina Sforza.

This river has almost always been the point of contact between the invaders from the north and defenders from the south. The Huns, the Holy Roman Emperors, Charles V, the Duke du Villeroi in the War of Spanish Succession... every century, it seems, envious armies were attempting to take control of the Pianura Padana. These flat fields were ideal for battles, but troops were invariably held apart for weeks or months by the swollen condition of the Po. There were only a few obvious places to cross. Surprise was almost impossible, so armies camped either side, sometimes trying to cut a deal.

Mantova floats like a wedge on the water. It was once protected by four lakes, but one of them, the Paiolo, has long since been drained. The three remaining basins are really bulges in the Mincio river a few miles before it flows into the Po. Legend goes that the city was created by the tears of Manto, the wife of Tireseus, whose son Ocnus founded the city and named it after her. Plenty of other legends surround the city. It's said that Longino, the Roman centurion who pierced Jesus' flank on the cross, was himself martyred here. The church built on the place of his burial contains, they say, the sponge with which Jesus was given vinegar and a vial of his blood.

Those famous lakes were a deliberate defensive strategy designed and created in the final decade of the twelfth century to give Mantova a very wide moat. Dante – putting words in the mouth of Virgil, born in Mantova – wasn't very complimentary about those stagnant waters. In talking about the course of the Mincio river he wrote:

Non molto ha corso, ch'el trova una lama,	Before that confluence, it finds a level
ne la qual si distende e la 'mpaluda;	Where it broadens to a stagnant fen,

e suol di state talor esser grama.   Which reeks in summer like the
very devil

(Trans. Ciaran Carson)

Dante goes on to say that locals realised that *lo pantan* – the quagmire or bog – could be a stronghold ("the fen as impassable as any rampart"), and so the city became – like Chioggia and Venezia – a city defended by its aquatic isolation. One of the resulting bridges was the mill bridge where the farmers came to mill their wheat and sell it to the rich citizens.

It's a layered city: as you enjoy the eleventh-century brick rotunda, the saw-like crenellations and double lancet windows of the Palazzo del Capitano, the square turrets of the brick castle, the grassy courtyards and secret gardens of the Ducal Palace, you can briefly forget that this city is insulated by water. It seems like any other landlocked polis, until you come to its edges and you see those great lakes. In the summer, they're cross-hatched with mosquitoes and iced with lotus flowers, introduced by friars in the early twentieth century who hoped to alleviate hunger by using the roots as cornflour. The foodstuff never caught on, but the flowers did. Elsewhere on the water, horned water caltrops (or chestnuts) emerge from their pale-green rosettes.

Throughout the Middle Ages, Mantova was a strategic city. Placed in the middle of the Pianura Padana and of the Milano–Venezia–Bologna triangle, Mantova had to be negotiated by any troops heading south to Rome. So it became like a pawn bossing the centre of the chessboard: a small piece which just happened to be in the right place. To survive, the Gonzaga family, which ruled the city from 1328 to 1707, was constantly forced to make alliances and marriages with one side or the other. The marriages were often stymied by a hereditary curvature of the spine (or "hunchback") which made the daughters unattractive consorts for European princes. The Gonzaga gained a reputation for being ruthless precisely because they were so vulnerable.

The family had come to power in a coup in which Luigi Corradi da Gonzaga had killed the previous captain of the city, Passerino Bonacolsi, and his son. For the next four centuries, that pattern of taking power through assassination continued: Luigi's grandson, Ugolino, was killed by his brothers in 1362, probably at the prompting of the Venetian Republic which resented his allegiance with the Milanese Visconti. In 1368, when the other brother, Francesco, died or was murdered, Ludovico took power. His son was equally violent: he accused his wife, Agnese Visconti, of infidelity and she was beheaded in 1391. Much later, Vespasiano Gonzaga – who tried to create an ideal city from scratch in Sabbioneta (on the "sands" by the Po) – beheaded his first wife, Diana di Cardona, and (probably accidentally) killed his son.

Despite that bloodletting, the city was also a centre of cultural magnificence. From 1422 until his death in 1446, Vittorino da Feltre ran his famous humanist school at Ca' Zoiosa, educating the sons of nobles but also of poorer traders and farmers. Andrea Mantegna, the brother-in-law of Giovanni Bellini, was resident in Mantova for most of the second half of that century. He painted the Camera degli Sposi in the Ducal Palace, and his compositional innovations began to fill the city. But it was in his private work, like the *Lamentation of Christ*, that his viewpoint proved truly radical. In that painting he revealed an almost shocking humanisation of Jesus and his death: the blotchy pink marble has more colour than the paling body. The angle is deliberately jarring: swollen feet first, a focus on his crotch, nipples and throat.

There were many others who made the city renowned. Baldassare Castiglione, author of the famous *Book of the Courtier*, which extolled the elegance, grace, learning and nonchalance of the courtier, was born just outside the city, and he became an ambassador for the Gonzaga family. From 1524 to 1546, Raffaello's pupil, Giulio Romano (named by Shakespeare in *A Winter's Tale*: "that rare Italian master") lived in the city, designing the august loggia and exedra of the Palazzo Te, sited on an old lime tree (*tiglio*) forest that gave the palazzo its odd name. Inside, Romano painted his Room of Giants during the 1530s: like Dosso Dossi's Sala delle Cariatidi in Pesaro from a few years earlier, every inch of wall and ceiling is painted: columns and arches crash onto giants as Zeus flings down his meteorological rage from the cupola. The fury of the deity, and the extravagant size of the palazzo and its paintings, seem almost calculated to belittle the burghers of Mantova and remind them of their place in the world.

Often the strategic ruthlessness and artistic magnificence were intertwined. When Francesco Gonzaga led the Italic League to victory against the invading French monarch, Charles VIII, in Fornovo in 1495, a painting was commissioned in which his military triumph was depicted as the result of the Madonna's blessing. A Jewish banker, Daniele da Norsa, who had dared to paint over a different Madonna in his own house, was forced to pay for Mantegna's lush symbolism and had his house torn down. Much of that artwork is no longer in the city, though. As the Gonzaga dynasty fell on hard times, its lavish art collection was sold to the Stuart monarch, Charles I. Mantegna's *Madonna della Vittoria* was filched by Napoleon's troops in 1798.

One of the reasons the *Lanzichenecchi* had swept into Padania in 1630 was because the Mantova duchy had fallen into the hands of the French: the direct line of the Gonzaga family ended with Vincenzo in 1627, and the city was now ruled by the Parisian Charles I Gonzaga-Nevers. Within three years, the *Lanzichenecchi* had sacked the city. Carlo Botta, the historian who liked his anecdotes perhaps more than accuracy, says that the Germanic troops "became madmen, they killed the Mantovani for fun and the limbs of those killed were roasted and eaten in the public piazzas".

The narrative of the cruel Austrians always finds an echo here. Just to the west of the city centre is the monument to the Martyrs of Belfiore, Italian patriots who were accused of plotting against the Austro-Hungarian Empire in the early 1850s. Some of the arrested patriots – there were 110 of them – were priests and their code used the Latin version of the Lord's Prayer. Despite the appeals of the city's bishop, eleven were executed and denied burial. Their bodies were only discovered during the Second War of Independence against the Austrians, in 1866, when two Italian foremen – dredging for sand for the city's defences – came across the cadavers. The foremen pretended to their Austrian commanders that they had to work through the night and used the darkness to remove the bodies for burial a few weeks later when the Austrians were driven out.

For weeks I've been looking forward to arriving at San Benedetto Po, the other side of the river to Governolo. It grew from humble beginnings: in the tenth century there was a simply a small chapel on an island between the Po and Lirone rivers (the Lirone has vanished, but the monastery, founded in 1007 by Tedaldo of Canossa, is still called "Polirone"). Eventually affiliated to the Benedictines of Cluny in France, it received so many endowments that it was soon one of the richest monasteries in Europe, with lands reaching from Tuscany to Lake Garda. An entire town grew up in the curtilage of the church, cloisters, library, refectory and barns. As in Pomposa, in the delta, the monks were adept at reclaiming land from the marshes: in 1336, the River Secchia was diverted (shifted eastwards towards Mirasole) and the Po was gradually banked up.

Matilde was the granddaughter of the monastery's founder. A bulwark of papal authority in this buffer zone against invasions from the Holy Roman Emperors, she actually had relatives on both sides. Canossa is in the hills south of Reggio Emilia, but the "Canossian Lands" extended from modern-day Lazio to Lombardy, and Matilde – having seen both her father and first husband murdered – was notoriously tough. According to legend, when in 1077 her first cousin, Henry IV (Duke of Bavaria and future Holy Roman Emperor) came to Canossa to beg the forgiveness of Pope Gregory VII (at the Synod of Worms the year previously, Henry had refused to recognise him as the legitimate pope), she made him kneel in the snow outside her castle for three days and nights before he was allowed to prostrate himself in penitence before the pope. That frosty exclusion became known as "the humiliation of Canossa". Matilde was buried in this monastery (until she was taken to Rome in 1644 and interred in St Peter's) and everywhere you can see images and carvings of the pomegranate, her voluptuous and fertile symbol.

As well as designing the Palazzo Te, Giulio Romano redesigned this monastery and looking at it I remember how far his taste is from mine. The naves are such an exuberant confusion of cherubs, lions and garlands, of recesses and framings, that it's a relief to get to the cloisters with their pencil-slim columns and calm geometry. The grand monastery was suppressed by Napoleon in 1797 and now the town is a sort of ecclesiastical theme park: tourists admire the wide square with its oversize church, look at the sculptures and artwork and the museum. But it's slightly unlived in, as if the devout buildings sit like an undigested meal on the stomach of this town.

When Italian historians talk of those marauding soldiers from the north, it's usually with regret for the diseases they brought with them. This monastery had 120 monks when the *Lanzichenecchi* arrived and sacked Mantova in 1630. Shortly afterwards, thanks to the plague, there were only fourteen. I'm possibly intrigued by those northern invaders because I see Italy through a northerner's eyes, or else because my wife's surname – Lenzi – is conceivably derived from the *Lanzichenecchi*. But the usual killer was simply the river. In 1609 the Po flooded badly, and a marble plaque calls the river, evocatively, that "tyrant guest". The river is still high right now, and much of the talk in the bars isn't about the water sloshing over the banks, but coming in under them through all the aquifers. Someone tells me about something called *bodri* a few miles upstream: riverside lakes which are fed by floods and underwater channels to the Po. It's as if, despite the never-ending attempts to bank the river, water will always seep out somewhere.

FOUR

La Bassa Reggiana

LA BASSA REGGIANA

Sabbioneta

L   O

P o

Brescello

Boretto

Canale Rondele

Collettore Impero

Enza

Collettore Vittoria

Parma
15km

E   M   I   L   I

Fossa

uzzara is just over the border between Lombardy and Emilia-Romagna, at the very north of the Bassa Reggiana, the "Reggio lowlands". It used to be an island of mud, hence its name (*lutum* in Latin, which then merged with the name of a nearby river, the Zara). The Po now snakes a one-minute walk to the north of it.

Luzzara is famous less because of the Battle of Luzzara (on 15 August 1702, during the War of the Spanish Succession between Franco-Spanish and imperial forces) than the fact that it was home to Cesare Zavattini. Often working with Vittorio De Sica, Zavattini was one of the central reasons for the brilliance of post-war Italian cinema. He wrote the screenplays for *Ladri di biciclette* (*Bicycle Thieves*), *La Ciociara* (*Two Women*) and dozens of others. His novels and fantasies were often portraits of people down on their luck, like the figure of Totò il Buono, and Zavattini constantly celebrated the creativity and resilience of the people of the floodplains. He did so not only through a daunting output of films, books and journalism, but also through a recognition that his fellow villagers' art – music, paintings and photographs – was as worthy as his own. An unusual combination of genuine humility and international connections allowed Zavattini to champion Luzzara's many eccentrics as authentic artists. He invited the American photographer Paul Strand to the town, a collaboration which produced one of the most moving photographic sequences of the twentieth century, *Un Paese*. Showing the rugged faces of a village which appeared outside of time itself, *Un Paese* meant that Luzzara became globally renowned as a remote, foggy village suckling on the river. Zavattini was aware that he was hitching his career wholeheartedly to this homeland, mythologising it and himself: "I'll be reprimanded once again", Zavattini once wrote, "that I have personally given Luzzara an almost mythical importance, that I have privileged my place of birth over other parts of the world." He wrote that he would be "mad with joy to be able to say that I have taught the Luzzaresi what Luzzara is."

Now I've finally reached Luzzara (unpoetically by car) it doesn't disappoint. The Gonzagas' brick Palazzo della Macina suggests both agricultural abundance and manorial power. There's a colourful theatre, the Teatro di Corte, with its balcony and stucco festoons, squeezed between the unpainted buildings of the square. Of the old Gonzaga fortifications, only the red tower still stands and there's no trace of the old Augustine convent. But it's a village which has a decisive character. Many of the central streets are named after the partisan martyrs of 1945: Fausto Melli, Adolfo Tedeschi and all the others who fell in action or reprisals during that dreadful spring.

I've often heard people say that the Bassa is the Mexico of Italy. It's a line which conjures up images of deserted squares in the midday sun. It makes one think of agricultural poverty, swaggering music and political struggles, maybe the odd gunfight among the barns. But it's very different at this time of year of fog and frost. The only similarity is the silence. Never short of words, Zavattini wrote about Luzzara's silence often: "It's unique and it's not the usual absence of noise, but instead a synthesis of noises, of human voices, ancient and contemporary, which become silence through accumulation, equal to the white which is mysteriously generated from a vortex of so many colours. It wouldn't be wrong to define it a historical silence..." It sounds slightly pretentious, but it makes perfect sense to me here with all these deserted streets, "for sale" signs and plaques to battles and fallen anti-fascists. It's a rowdy silence and not only, I think, because of that history of martyrdom, but because of that vast, silent stalker a stone's throw to the north – the Po. It makes (almost) no noise, but glides past like a bully, always ready to rise up. And it's that sense of brooding quiet which gives Luzzara, and so many similar villages, its chilled but also edgy atmosphere.

Zavattini once said that "one wears the Po like a suit", and there's often a sense that it's on your back even when you don't see it. Perhaps that's why I like seeing the effect of the river as much as the thing itself, trying to glimpse the ways in which that ominous body of water alters the way people live. It's not something it's easy to enunciate, but the closer you get to the river, the more you sense that reality is loosened somehow. It's as if the solid certainties of terra firma give way when they come into contact with the shifting sands, muds and floods of the Po.

In those floodplains between the two banks, there's a sense that things could go two ways: land could become lake, or vice versa. I've gone to parts of the river that are scorched fields on one visit and, a month later, static water. Nothing stays quite the same and that precariousness has always attracted those who either weren't of sound mind or who wanted to escape the rigidity of straight society. In his book, *Viaggio al principio del giorno*, Alberto Bevilacqua wrote of how the riverbanks were the "banks of the mad": "down there, they've always lived in defiance of logic: witty and wild-eyed, or in an underworld... ruled by whimsy and mistiness... a bit was invented and a bit not."

As I walk along the river, I often see huts and campervans: sometimes they look jolly, with hubcaps painted bright colours and tended verandas with buckets of empty bottles. Sometimes these huts are nothing more than Sunday salons where friends gather for weekly meals and afternoon flops in foldable fishing chairs. But many of these shacks are decidedly down-at-heel: hand-carved weathervanes which don't twist because they're rusted or because there's never any wind. One has a noil of smoke from the flue, but when I knock no one opens up.

Eccentrics and the socially excluded exist everywhere, of course, but it does seem as if the wilderness of these floodplains – where one could hide, howl and forage for wood – attracted more than the national average. The most famous, in this Bassa Reggiana, was called Toni al Mat, "Mad Tony". Born Antonio Costa in 1899, he was the son of an Italian prostitute living in Switzerland. He never knew his father. He became Antonio Leccabue when a man from Gualtieri, a few miles upstream of Luzzara, married his mother. But by then Antonio was living with an adoptive family. He suffered from rickets and goitre and was frequently expelled from school for his eccentric behaviour. When his mother, and three siblings, died of food poisoning in 1913, he believed his stepfather had deliberately poisoned them, causing Toni to change his name to from Leccabue to Ligabue, the name by which he is now known.

Ligabue was confined to a mental asylum and eventually expelled from Switzerland and sent to Gualtieri. There, he worked as a day labourer on the banks of the Po, but increasingly became an itinerant among the wooded floodplains. He would amaze the locals by doing odd things like washing his rabbits with soap. Many households had one of his pet rabbits, and occasionally, suffering food shortages, they ate them and Ligabue would get furious. He paid grocers with his paintings and slept in hay barns, often digging a hole in the hay so that he could sleep sitting upright because of his respiratory problems.

One of his favourite haunts was the Isola degli Internati (the "island of the interned"). I want to see it, but the tracks leading to it are all underwater now: they descend into stagnant water held by the sickle-shaped banks. Even the hoops for the pumpkin polytunnels are buried in this cold water, their curved apexes only just poking above the water like regimented metal monsters. The water has subsided from last week but you can still see how high it rose: the grass of the bank is bleached white to within a metre of its top. Alders and willows have tangles of river detritus caught in their canopies. From here you can just make out a chemical factory on the other side of the river like a cartoon confusion of chimneys and tubes pumping out smoke and steam.

Ligabue spent much of his adult life in Gualtieri and its floodplains. There's a miniaturised augustness to this place: the arcaded main square, Piazza Bentivoglio, is exactly 100 metres each side, with a theatre, church, ice-creameries, bars and shops among the arcades. The imposing Palazzo Bentivoglio is another of those red-brick residences for the local dignitaries, its walls widening at the base as if it were wearing flares. It's picturesque – there are multicoloured, terraced houses on cobbled streets and perfectly pollarded willows – but, as usual, you see almost no one. And, like a lot of these small towns, it's enduringly agricultural, with small fields and open barns in the middle of the housing.

When he wasn't here, Ligabue was frequently confined in asylums – once, during the Second World War, for breaking a bottle over a soldier's head. When you watch footage of him (from documentaries made late in his life), it's unsettling. He carried a mirror around his neck, partly because he often painted self-portraits, but also because he was always punishing himself by staring at his reflection and wailing. During the painting of one self-portrait he gathers up his skirts (he was a cross-dresser), crouches and goes through his exorcisms. He turns his back on the self-portrait, looking over his shoulder at the image he has drawn of himself, and whines as if it frightens him.

He was almost shamanic with animals, communicating with them through his squawks and barks on the riverbanks. All his pictures had animals in them: spiders and insects worry the canvases, and his famous cheetahs and leopards are often circled by snakes. Standing in front of the Sistine Chapel, he once said that "the painter who doesn't put animals in his pictures isn't a painter".

He became famous later in life, partly thanks to two renowned sculptors who recognised the importance of his naif portraits of locals with garish colours, the slightly Swiss backdrops and bright African animals. Zavattini championed him. He started to make money: there were exhibitions in Rome and his paintings were used in Bertolucci's films. Ligabue got a car and a chauffeur, but he remained, to locals, "Mad Tony".

Although he wasn't originally from the Bassa, it was here that his art flourished, where he was received, recognised and cherished. Two of Italy's other great naif painters of the twentieth century also came from here: Bruno Rovesti, a painter of bright, dreamy riverscapes, was based – like Ligabue – in Gualtieri and Pietro Ghizzardi, famous for his wobbly nudes in sombre charcoals, was based in Boretto. In all three, the deliberate avoidance of perspective, and the startling colours and jamboree of animals and bodies, make the canvases seem intense, busy and oneiric.

I keep hearing stories about puppeteers. When I look up the next village I'm staying at, there are often references to someone who became a local celebrity through their ability to put a cloth over their fist and make people laugh. Chignolo Po, a small village upstream, had such distinguished puppeteers they ended up in Paris (they say Chignolo was the reason the Parisian Theatre Guignol got its name). Often someone in a bar will ask me "have you heard about Sarzi?", and everyone starts telling stories.

There's a major difference between a string puppet (*marionetta*) and a glove one (*burattino*). The great Parma puppeteer Italo Ferrari once said that between the two there was a different understanding of humanity: "the string-puppeteer believes man is perfect and has made an artist in his image. The glove puppeteer is persuaded of human imperfection, and that's why the misshapen, grotesque, legless puppet emerges, possibly to give him a bigger head."

The puppets were often called *teste di legno* (meaning knucklehead or blockhead). It reflected not only the wood from which they were carved, but also the fact that they represented stubbornness and stupidity. The other material from which they were often made was simply the cloth used to sieve flour (*buratinus* in Latin), hence *burattino*. That extraordinary simplicity of the art form, creating life from offcuts of wood and cloth, meant that puppeteering was easy access and deliberately coarse. Italo Sarzi – born by the river in Casalfoschino, near Sissa – once said, "the puppet has to be rustic, his body a rag. It's a deformed thing that only begins to move when you insert a hand."

In many ways, the puppet shows were a poor person's version of the *commedia dell'arte* which satirised the counts, squires, capitalists and upper classes. In those comedies, the hapless Capitano Spaventa, the greedy Venetian merchant Pantalone and the verbosity and infidelity of Il Dottore were given an enjoyable comeuppance by the scheming servants – the cunning Harlequin or the trickster Brighella. Tristano Martinelli (the creator of Harlequin mask) was from Marcaria, just the other side of the river from where I am now, in Gualtieri. The puppeteers drew on those comedic traditions (there was, after all, a character in the *commedia dell'arte* called "Burattino"), but the puppeteers were much more anarchic: literally hidden from view and thus, perhaps, able to be even more caustic. The comic actor Ettore Petrolini once said that "in the shack of the puppets the soul of the people sings". And the humble puppets took that *commedia dell'arte* even further: even the underclass was now parodied and held up for ridicule. Bargnocla, the poor cobbler created by Ferrari, is little more than his name suggests – a lump or bump.

As with the naif art, it's hard to pinpoint quite why this irreverent art form thrived along the banks of the river, but it's something proudly noticed by those who are from Emilia. They will tell you about the Ferrari family from Parma, the Maletti and Campogalliani families from Modena, the Monticelli from Reggio. Zavattini once said that "for us, the puppets are a traditional heritage... in the puppets I almost saw the personalities from my own town, I saw there the faces of my people." Fulvio De Negris (who wrote a slim biography of Sarzi) said that "within the Emilian territory there's a precise propensity for the theatre of the wooden heads. Schools were formed, dynasties created. Personalities were invented that became masks of the city itself." To an outsider, it seems part of that same resourcefulness which turned Bergantino, that borderline town on the floodplains, into a centre of artisan carousels: the ability of itinerant entertainers to make people laugh and gasp so much that they were prepared to pay for it, not least because – in these tiny villages – a puppet show was often the only semi-professional entertainment there was.

Bargnocla debuted in a stable in the winter of 1892 and repeatedly you hear that the context for these shows was the *teatro dell'aia*, the "theatre of the farmyard". The Italian genius for jollification and subversive silliness has often been noted (our word "zany" comes from *zanni*, the Venetian nickname for the acrobats and slapstick artists from Bergamo who performed many of the *commedie*). But in Emilia there's both an earthiness and a precariousness which makes a rag doll, amid the manure and sawdust, seem one of us: poorly dressed, they're ugly, legless, needing money and love but are soon, we know, to be put in a box. And the puppet literally speaks the language of the public: the reason I often struggle to follow the shows (they're sometimes called, humbly, *siparietti*, literally "little curtains") is that they're more than half in dialect.

It's easy to overemphasise the agricultural quality of puppeteering. The puppeteers' repertoire drew not just on barnyard humour, but also on classical comedies. Underneath the lack of pretension, there was much learning and study. What strikes you most, tramping through these seemingly deserted hamlets, is that every other one has a theatre. Tiny, it's true: usually a single door under the porticos of the matchbox main square – but still going, with bright posters for the next event, and able to create a tiny bit of grandeur through a red rope and worn, velveteen seats. Puppeteers were performers and spectators there, too, and their art was a discipline in which the paterfamilias was often as autocratic as the high society he parodied, bossing his wife and children relentlessly since they were all part of the wandering ensemble.

Those family dynasties inevitably had strained father/son relationships. Italo Sarzi considered himself more an underground anti-fascist than a puppeteer: implicated in various anti-Mussolini satires, he was forced to flee to Switzerland in 1936 and during the Spanish Civil War he was a courier in the Pyrenees for the Republicans. Thinking it safe to return to Italy, he was arrested, imprisoned and internally exiled in Calabria, in Sant'Agata di Esaro near Cosenza, for three years. During the Second World War, he used his puppeteering props as a front for moving messages and victuals among the partisans and his performances were sometimes a front for clandestine meetings.

The Sarzi story overlaps with one of the most miserable events of the war. He often stored the equipment in a farm belonging to a family with seven sons. The Cervi family shared his politics and since they lived not far from Via Emilia, their farm was a good place to pick up and drop off his equipment. But all seven brothers were murdered in a sweep of partisans in the Bassa conducted by Fascists in December 1943. Many streets in Italy are named after the *sette fratelli Cervi*. Their mother died of a heart attack within a year (during another raid on the family farm) but the brothers' father, Alcide, lived until 1970, keeping alive the memory of his sons and the fight against the reignition of the fascist flame. Every summer in Gattatico the

Cervi farm has a big "anti-fascist" feast. The Sarzi story is a sub-plot to that tragedy. Much of his family's equipment – the stage, puppets, costumes and lights – was burned when the brothers were arrested, a fate which befell Sarzi again in Rome in 1958, when he lost 600 puppets after an act of arson by, probably, members of the Movimento Sociale Italiano.

Those acts of murder and vandalism confirmed both Sarzi's calling and his commitment to political activism. His productions were never blatantly political, but at the centre of his acts was always a sense that he was in a shadow knife fight. In his explanatory notes for his post-war "experimental puppet theatre", he reminded his readers of the long-standing radicalism of puppeteering: "the traditional repertoire of wooden heads has always been based on a critique of habits, a satire on the hypocrisies and the current conformisms." Reversing his surname, Sarzi for a long time toured with an act called "I Pupi [the dolls] di Izras". It sounded Hispanic, perhaps, almost Arabic.

My favourite story about Sarzi comes from when he was working in Novara in 1951. He wasn't sure he wanted to continue the family's puppeteering tradition: it was partly modesty, because he didn't feel he had his father's talent for voices and dialects, but also because of a desire to find his own vocation. But in November that year, as winter was coming on, he saw two bus-loads of cold, scared children who had been evacuated following the Polesine floods. Sarzi ran home to get his puppets, picking up those characters who spoke the children's Veneto dialects: Brighella, Fracanapa and Pantalone. He realised then, making those suddenly homeless children laugh, that he couldn't escape his calling. "To see people gripped by a puppet which manages to transmit emotions is something which makes the public, as well as the puppets, come alive."

The village of Santa Vittoria is just a few miles south of Gualtieri. It's a sleepy place – mostly modern houses with crazy paving and a tree or two in their thin patches of lawn. This place was originally a marshy wasteland called Gambararia because it was where the poor gathered to fish, trap frogs and find prawns (*gamberi*). But when the local stream, the Crostolo, was banked and ditches dug in the fifteenth and sixteenth centuries, land was suddenly plentiful and foraging anglers became, over the next centuries, sharecroppers. The land was so rich that when they dropped flat seeds in the cracks, thick stems and wide leaves emerged, the flowers fruiting into rotund watermelons and pumpkins. Irrigation meant that thirsty crops, like melons and rice, replaced fish and frogs as the staples and soon that productive soil attracted city investors: from the 1770s onwards, the Greppi family, from Milano, started buying up land and gradually created an estate, experimenting with new crops like silk and tobacco. They built an imposing villa, the Palazzo Greppi.

The Bassa was increasingly attracting outsiders: after the independence uprisings and revolts of 1848–9, the Austrian military presence was intrusive and there were barracks even in remote places like Gualtieri. They brought bands and waltzes (what the locals called "jumpy dances"). Itinerant labourers were involved in the land reclamations: *birocciai* (carters), *facchini* (porters) and *ghiaiaioli* (gravellers) did the grunt work after the serious floods of the 1850s. The railway line between Parma, Guastalla and Suzzara was laid in the 1870s and 1880s, and new faces were arriving in the villages and hamlets outside the towns. In 1865, forty people had asked for a passport from the Guastalla authorities. Five years later, it was 140.

Wandering salesmen brought their wares to sell: cooking pots, jewellery, books and religious trinkets. Some arrived with new gadgetry like bicycle-powered sharpening wheels. Among the newcomers there were always a few deserters and fugitives. In his book about Santa Vittoria, Carmelo Lanzafame wrote that these "marshy and low-lying places, divided by subtle and changing dynastic borders, linked by few streets and dotted with little centres on the edge of the main banks of the Po, were obviously ideal for anyone smuggling or for whoever couldn't or wouldn't reside elsewhere". Loners, outlaws, chancers, seekers, fortune tellers and musicians drifted from one riverside village to the next, often earning enough small change to eat pumpkin tortelli in local taverns, where they pulled out their fiddles and entertained the patrons to pay for their drinks. Their songs were often rounds – *zirudelle* – so everyone could pick them up and repeat them once they had gone.

By the late nineteenth century, every source of peasant income was dwindling. Silk cultivation had been a sociable activity for much of the century and the countryside was still lined by mulberry boulevards which provided the nutrition for silkworms. The women called the worm (it sounds gleefully disdainful in dialect) the *bèg*: once wrapped in their silk, the worms were killed in boiling water so they couldn't eat their way out through the precious fibre. Those mulberries also provided firewood for humans and leaves for the livestock. But a new disease, called pebrine, meant that the larvae were suddenly dotted brown and unable to wind themselves in precious silk. Many orchards were felled and replaced by regimental plantations of poplars.

Other traditional fibres were being replaced: about 15 per cent of all arable land in the provinces of Bologna and Ferrara was dedicated to hemp cultivation in 1870, but demand dropped starkly as cotton began dominating the international fibre market. Hemp had also been an important product for the boat builders and repairers along the Po because it was used to caulk the hulls. That usage, too, was being slowly replaced by bitumen or pitch.

Rice cultivation was hammered by the opening of the Suez

Canal in 1869, which made it easier for Asian imports to undercut the Italian market. In the 1860s, Italy had only imported a few hundred tonnes of rice. By 1880, it was importing 53,000 tonnes and four years later 94,414 tonnes. The number of people working in the Padanian paddy fields (the *risaie*) dropped from almost a quarter of a million in 1870 to 145,000 in 1910. A plant disease (the *brusòn*) was also damaging many of the rice plantations. As local producers had to trim costs it was the labourers who took the hit: in 1888, the average wage for a day's work in the paddy fields was only one lira.

A tax on flour in the late 1860s, an epochal first error of the government of the newly united Italy, made staples like bread and pasta more expensive. Because polenta was often the only slops available, pellagra became a common disease: the dark, peeling skin caused by niacin deficiency was often most visible around the neck and thus looked like a noose. Misery was so widespread that it was the name given to tradescantia, those purplish plants which grew easily and fast. When I watch one documentary about Santa Vittoria the narrator says rhetorically: "there was a funeral every day".

Those harsh agricultural conditions led to a sustained revolt (from 1882 to 1885) known as "la Boje". The reason for the odd name is much debated (it might come from dialect for "bubble" caused by boiling rage): it began when the Adige river broke its banks, and the strikes spread quickly to farms in the Mantovano and Cremonese areas where sharecroppers began to adopt the key demands of their Veneto counterparts: that their 12 per cent share of the harvest should be doubled. The political and military energies which had contributed to the Risorgimento were now, often, being directed to the causes of unionism, socialism and anarchism, and the Bassa Reggiana was recognised as an important centre of those nascent ideologies. One of the country's most important socialist politicians, Camillo

Prampolini, was from Reggio Emilia, and in 1897, ten of the fifteen socialist deputies elected to parliament were from rural constituencies in Padania. A few years later, in the 1900 national elections, socialists received 26 per cent of the vote in Emilia, double the national percentage for the party.

Santa Vittoria was – in the words of one historian "an extreme case of this tendency towards popular associationism". In February 1890, the villagers had created their own labourers' cooperative. Three years later it had almost two hundred members, and by 1896, twenty-three affiliated cooperatives. In 1902, of the 2,309 inhabitants of the village, 1,513 were adherents of one cooperative or another. Meetings were often held in the Osteria Vioni, which doubled as a grocer and liquor store and thus served as an outlet for the cooperatives' produce. In 1900 an agricultural cooperative was founded in Santa Vittoria which began renting local farms: by 1907, it was farming 171 hectares in five different estates. Workers on those farms were now receiving 20–30 cents per hour.

There were two aspects of Santa Vittoria which made it remarkable. First, its labourers united to buy the enormous Greppi estate and its grand villa in the centre of the village: a new Cooperativa Agricola was constituted in November 1911, with shares costing one hundred lire each. That month the 350-hectare estate was purchased for 715,000 lire. The building eventually became informal social housing, offering grand rooms to labourers more used to shacks and slums. It became the storehouse for other mutual aid organisations, many of which extended credit and allowed payment in kind. Inevitably, the village attracted other radicals: one of Italy's iconic anarchists, Giovanna Caleffi from Gualtieri, became a schoolteacher in the village.

But apart from this political radicalism, what distinguished Santa Vittoria was its violins. Musical groups had often been hitched to political movements: in 1911, Gualtieri's town band had – in the time-honoured tradition of left-wing division – splintered into two. There was, nationally, already a divergence between the moderate and radical socialists, and the division of Gualtieri's band reflected that split in miniature: half of the band refused to serenade the newly elected councillors. They were ordered to return their instruments, but on appeal were allowed to continue using them. So suddenly Gualtieri found itself with two bands: the Corpo Filarmonico Operaio (the Workers' Philharmonic Corps) and the Banda Operaia Indipendente (the Independent Workers' Band). The town council financed the band and not the corps, and so a rivalry was born, fired by the need to outdo the other in terms of recruits, skill and popularity. That led, inevitably, to displays of ardent musical virtuosity.

By 1905, the musicians and luthiers of Santa Vittoria had formed their own cooperative, the "Lega Violinista". The Santa Vittoria labourers also created their own group, la Fanfara Avanti (the Onwards Fanfare). The name reflected a belief in assured progress. In admiring prose, many historians recount how the peasants followed a joyous path from impoverished labouring to musical education, political enlightenment, prosperity and partying. It seems true that an inexplicable number of villagers became musicians (Santa Vittoria is sometimes puffed as "the village of a hundred violins"). At one point, thirteen families – many with numbers of children in double figures – were supporting themselves, in part, through music. In an era of ever-diminishing agricultural returns, joining an ensemble became a source of quick cash. Groups were invited to festivals, weddings and funerals and became known themselves, slightly oddly, as "concerts": the Bagnoli Concert, the Cantarelli Concert and so on.

The symbolic expression of music as liberation was the fact that often the bands would play on the Ponte delle Portine, the same bridge where the labourers used to sit to be picked up by gangmasters for agricultural work. They played on the bridge because it was on the divide between two different jurisdictions, and if the authorities came from one end to arrest them for playing in public without permission, they could shuffle to the other without, it was said, even stopping the music.

My kids' piano teacher says she has the Bassa in her blood. It was she who first told me about the Fojonco. Surviving only by raiding red wine from locals, the three-legged, lazy bird of prey is one of the many legendary animals of the Bassa. It endures because it reflects aspects of the mindset and landscape from which it emerged: a relish for fizzy, watery red wine and a lassitude which is laziness and humour rolled into the ridiculous. There are now shopping centres and fun-loving drinking clubs named after the Fojonco. One of the tribute acts to the violinists of Santa Vittoria has a song called the "Tango of the Fojonco".

The animal gave rise to two of Italy's most charming short stories. Giuseppe Pederiali was from Finale Emilia (the name says it all, sort of "the end of Emilia"), and he showed a wry fondness for the idealists who are scorned by society. His scholarly loner, Aldro, listens to the legends of old and dedicates his life to proving the existence of the Fojonco. The conceit is taking the ridiculous very seriously: when Aldro is appalling his university colleagues in the zoology department by lecturing on the animal, one admiring student asks an earnest question. Every word of it – the provinciality, the pseudo-academic seriousness, the reclining silliness – makes me smile: "my mother, who is from Fanano, has told me about the Foionco [variant spellings only add allure and seriousness to the search: there are even schisms within the nomenclature of the creature]. She says that it is so lazy as to wait for an earthquake's turbulence in order to couple with its female. Can you confirm this particular?"

There's often a link to erotica in the encounter with the Fojonco, as if the unceasing search for the bird is a metaphor for the improbability of the young scholar ever getting laid. It's when Aldro sources another mythological creature – the Bosma – that he is visited by the horny hostess of the B&B where he is staying and celebrates his success with her in a nocturnal romp, with terrible consequences. In another short story, "The Lambrusco Bird", Betonica first sees the Fojonco when lying in the hills with his girlfriend, Maripia: they had begun to enjoy each other's company more than the wine when the Fojonco swept down: "a dark stain moving in front of the bottle and the glasses." Years later, his wife leaves Betonica partly because he "had got to the point of evoking [the Fojonco] while they were making love".

Those mythological animals served a purpose beyond the comedic. Every house and field here is surrounded by ditches and their stagnant, precious water. Those ditches often have steep banks and, though the water's not deep, they're dangerous to children. So perhaps it was to dissuade kids from playing near them that, over the centuries, legends arose about these fearsome creatures. The Bosma was a dragon which lived in putrid waters and wells. The Anzlìn was a nocturnal serpent much talked about in the hostelries, though its purpose was possibly to dissuade thieves from roaming around in the dark. But Pederiali's succinct stories go deeper. They're parodies about the misguided who might just, through the tenderness with which they search for animals, enchant the landscape again. The aim of Aldro or Betonica was not to kill, stuff or eat, but to hold up these creatures to disbelievers as the final proof that humans don't always know everything and that, if we could go slowly and carefully, we might see new wonders.

~

I head to Boretto, where the Po is straight (*Po retto*). Being the last outpost of Venetian influence on the Po, Boretto makes much of its connection to that august lagoon: its church, as in Venezia, is called St Mark's, and a lion – a gift from the Venetian Republic – stands outside it. The port is more a lido now, with picnic areas and couples strolling along the promenade. At one end, outside the small museum, is a rusting ship once used to dredge the river: it has a wide suction pipe emerging from its prow which sucked up and sprayed the sandy mud left and right to clear the channel, firing the sludge via hoses onto the barges on either side.

It's only a short walk to Brescello, a town rendered famous as the location for the hugely successful Don Camillo films of the 1950s and 1960s (adapted from Giovannino Guareschi's short stories). Bronzes of the two main characters stand in the piazza now, the cassocked priest and the portly politician squaring off at a distance. Like so many of these riverside towns, Brescello is both sturdy and deserted: wide, cobbled streets and a piazza with porticos which make your footsteps echo through the damp air. Everything ancient has been erased. There used to be a Pasquino statue here (a "talking statue", known as a pasquinade, was plastered with a community's invectives and satires) but, like the pentagonal walls of the fortress which used to defend the town, it's long gone.

Brescello is famous as the place where Marcus Salvius Otho, briefly Roman emperor, took his own life by stabbing himself in the heart. From 58 to 68 CE, Otho had been exiled to the Iberian peninsula by Nero. There Otho plotted his revenge, forging an alliance with Servius Galba and, in 68, he began an uprising. After Nero's suicide, Galba was pronounced emperor only for Otho to arrange for him to be murdered and become emperor himself. Aulus Vitellius, commanding Roman troops to the north of the Alps, refused to recognise the accession and launched an attack, descending on the Italian peninsula. The rival troops from north and south met, as usual, on the flat fields surrounding the Po. Having lost a decisive battle at Bedriacum (near Cremona), and allegedly to avoid more bloodshed, Otho made the decision to leave the battlefield and his life.

Brescello was considered an important port by the Romans and they attempted to solve the problem of frequent flooding and the rising water tables by placing amphoras (those terracotta containers for wine or oil) under buildings and roads as foundations: holes were made in the amphoras' pointed bases and they were laid end to end on a slight incline so that water would flow away inside them. Used vertically, too, they acted as natural bladders, absorbing the water which came up from below.

Recently, though, the real threat to Brescello hasn't been water, but organised crime. What happened was, in some ways, a textbook study in how organised crime inveigles itself into an unsuspecting society. It started with a strategic error by the Italian state: the policy of *soggiorno obbligato* – "compulsory residency" – was an attempt to remove *mafiosi* from their strongholds in the south and place them in the allegedly more law-abiding north. Rather than reform the criminals, however, it often gave them an opportunity to build criminal empires in the naïve, or unsuspecting, societies in which they were placed.

In 1982, a mafia boss from the small Calabrian town of Cutro, called Antonino Dragone, was forced to reside in Quattro Castella, near Reggio Emilia. Dragone connected with other mobsters who were under "compulsory residency" orders in Emilia and who were already active in drug dealing and extortion. Dozens of other families from Cutro moved north: many were part of organised crime, but others were simply looking for work in the Calabrians' construction firms in the boom years of the 1980s.

"Whoever imagines the mafias as only violent or murderous

organisations," Enzo Ciconte, one of the best writers on the 'Ndrangheta, once wrote, "is unable to understand how these people who behave in such a 'normal' way can be considered mafiosi." Through their politeness and occasional largesse, these newcomers were often hailed as upright citizens. The ties between Brescello and Calabria were cemented by symbolism. In 1990, the town of Isola Capo Rizzuto, near Cutro, offered Brescello a painting of the Madonna Greca. It was put up in Brescello's church. In 2008, after an indulgent trip south by a delegation from Brescello, there was a formal twinning between Brescello and Isola Capo Rizzuto. This infusion of Calabrian influences was just as strong in Reggio Emilia, where a new slip road was named, bizarrely, after Cutro.

It seemed, on the surface, nothing more than a friendship between two remote parts of Italy. But those firms received many contracts because they undercut their rivals by using gangmasters to keep costs low and offered cash incentives to crooked politicians to enable them to win contracts. The benefit of those contracts wasn't simply financial, but social: the Cutresi were beginning to forge local friendships and allegiances. Their construction firms were soon handling such large contracts that they were able to launder the voluminous cash that the clans had gleaned from narcotics sales. Able to invest in heavy machinery, these Calabrian construction firms were issued lucrative permits to extract gravel and sand from the Po and were awarded contracts for flood-defence work on the riverbanks. Soon there were so many Calabrians from Cutro living within one area of Brescello that it was nicknamed "Cutrello". One investigation estimated that the Calabrian contingent now made up 9 per cent of the Brescello population (of around 5,000), meaning that politically they were influential, able to bring votes to any politician who, in return, promised them public contracts. One informant later said that between the late 1980s and early 1990s, Dragone's control of Reggio Emilia and its province was "absolute".

There were, as usual, feuds. In 1992, one resident was shot five times while answering his door in the middle of the night. His murderers were using a fake Carabiniere car. By then a new Calabrian clan, the Grande Aracri family, was attempting to take over control of the territory from the original bosses. Two members of the Dragone clan were murdered (in 1999 and 2004) and Francesco Grande Aracri became the boss. He lived in Brescello and owned two construction companies, shares in a third, six houses, nine commercial properties and had at least sixteen bank accounts. Often his generosity earned him the gratitude of the locals: in 2002, the flooding of the Enza and Po rivers threatened hundreds of houses and Francesco Grande Aracri provided eighty-one trucks of sand as protection.

Anyone who complained was silenced. The owners of the central bar in Brescello refused to pay protection money and put a notice in their windows denouncing "mafia threats". The town's mayor immediately sent traffic wardens to take down the sign and denounced the libellous comments. Traffic wardens were also instructed not to put fines on certain luxury cars. But even after the infiltration became public, in 2015–16, most Brescellesi were oblivious to the problem. The mayor (the son of Grande Aracri's lawyer, himself a former mayor) said of the main mafioso: "he's very kind, very calm, very composed and polite."

In early 2016, the town council was *commissionariato*, meaning that external administrators were appointed. Brescello became the first council in Emilia-Romagna to be dissolved for mafia infiltration.

FIVE

La Bassa Parmense

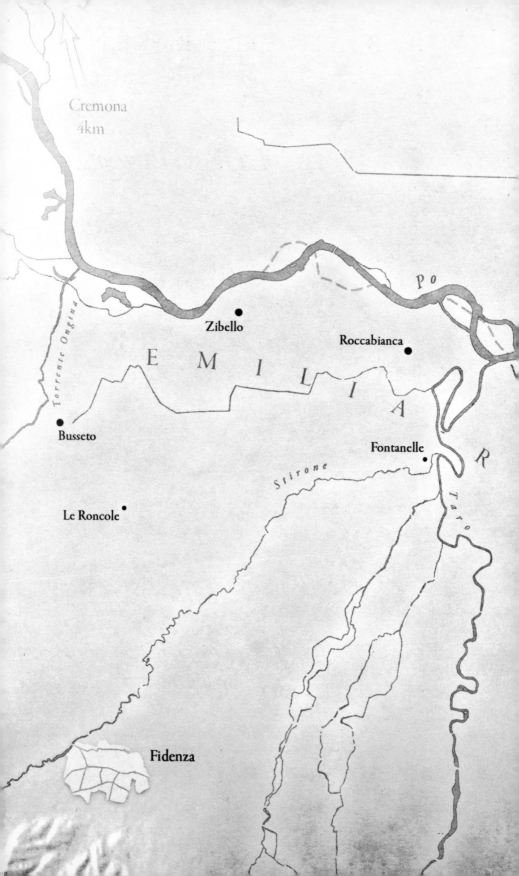

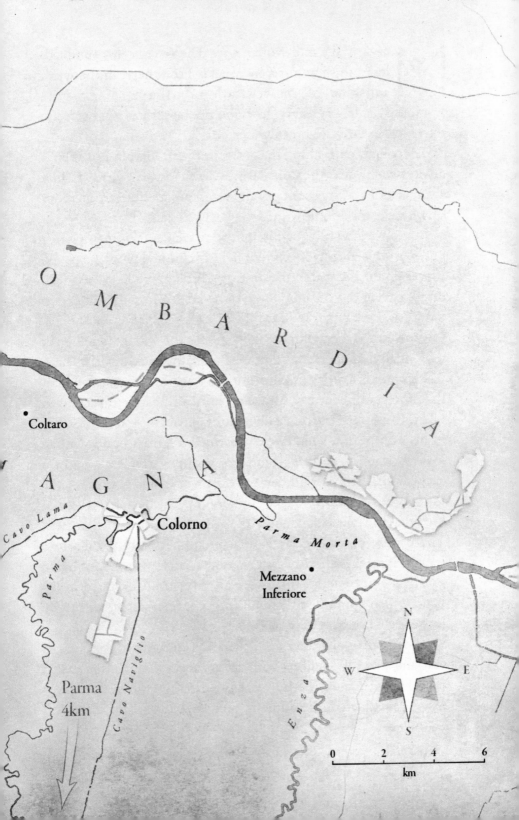

LA BASSA PARMENSE

Coltaro

Colorno

Mezzano
Inferiore

Parma Morta

Cavo Lama

Parma

Cavo Naviglio

Enza

Parma
4km

O M B A R D I A

A G N A

N
W E
S

0   2   4   6
km

Mezzani. It's mid-winter now. The river seems subdued, less full than in recent weeks. From here, in the weak sunshine, all the vegetation on the left bank – the Lombardy side – is sandy-grey and the bare trees are perfectly mirrored in the jade-green water.

There's no path along the river, so I turn inland. But there's always water near the Po. "Parma Morta" is the "dead" Parma river, a series of stagnant ponds which are an aquatic memory of where it used to flow into the River Enza.

I sit and the stillness dissipates anxieties. You can hear a bustling which is no longer yours: the occasional plop of a coypu slipping into the water, the dive of a little grebe, its rusty neck disappearing out of sight. Everything here seems abandoned to nature and better for it. It's a "dead" river which has come alive. I watch a moorhen glide serenely across the water, its red beak looking like someone has thumbed oil paint halfway up its face.

Mezzani is a village that produced one of the finest bands of the nineteenth century. Although born in nearby Brescello in 1841, Giuseppe Cantoni, a flugelhorn player, moved to Mezzani in his youth and, aged twenty, formed his own band. Unlike lots of other, slightly agricultural groups, Cantoni's had no accordions, drums or fiddles, but only woodwind and brass: the rasp of the *bombardino* (the euphonium), the deep heartbeat of the tuba, the cheerful squawk of the *quartino* (a mini clarinet). There were clarinets, flugelhorns, trumpets and trombones, representing the whole tonal range of an orchestra. Cantoni had fourteen children and they were all, over time, enrolled in his band which continued through four generations of the family (his great-grandson only died in 2012).

There's an exuberance and gaiety to Cantoni's music – it's so fast and playful – and as with the puppets it was often called music of the *aia*, of the farmyard or threshing floor. But it was also sophisticated, introducing polkas, waltzes and mazurkas to the masses. Cantoni's son Riccardo studied at the Parma conservatoire and Arturo Toscanini, the famous conductor, was an admirer. In its heyday, in the late nineteenth and early twentieth centuries, the Concerto Cantoni was in great demand: every gathering in the Bassa – whether a *sagra* (a sort of village festival), wedding, or harvest festival – wanted their full, energetic sound. A few hours before the party started, the clarinettist would find the tallest vantage point – either a bell tower, balcony, treetop or barn roof – and trill the *invito*: the tune would carry across the fields and everyone would be reminded that there was a party that evening.

In 1933, the band performed 187 concerts, more than three a week, and – as at Santa Vittoria – music became a means to escape agricultural poverty. One musician said that, in five concerts, he paid off debts that his family had had for two years. Bertolucci repeatedly used the band, as he had Ligabue's paintings, in his films (in *Novecento*, *La Strategia del Ragno* and *La Tragedia d'un Uomo Ridicolo*). The group was so influential that it had many imitators – at least two dozen comparable acts emerged across these lowlands – so that its speedy, brassy sophistication became a new sort of folk music.

"They were the gods of the Bassa," says Eugenio, the affable leader of the band today. They still play the same repertoire at parties and, often, funerals. Eugenio enthuses about how, just as Verdi was composing his operas only a few miles from here in the mid-nineteenth century, the Bassa was full of musical currents: "with the Austrians stationed here, there was so much from Vienna and Mitteleuropa, the waltzes and so on, but there were also French influences from Colorno, and then also something almost jazz-like in their live performances, with one soloist after another showing their virtuosity." Some parts of the Cantoni repertoire are so demanding that even classically trained musicians have sometimes sent back the sheet music saying they're unable to master the many pages of hemi-demi-semi-quavers. According to Eugenio, the popularity of European dances influenced Verdi just as much as the Cantoni: "'Va Pensiero' is all a waltz," he says. "You can tell it's an Emilian waltz because we put the emphasis on the third beat, not the first... 'La Donna è Mobile' is a mazurka."

But the thrill of the Cantoni music is how much it somehow captures the natural world: the *quartino* trills are bird-like (their most famous song is called "The Nightingale"), the euphonium and tuba sound so much like lowing cattle you can almost smell the manure. The relentless pace of music reminds me of a scurrying mouse, dashing one way then the next, catching its breath against the wall before its next dart. As with the naïf art and the puppeteers, it has a hypnotic combination of red-blooded earthiness, technical mastery and cultural sophistication.

Eventually I get to Colorno. It's a town where water was power, both real and symbolic, able to provide not only flour but also aristocratic frivolity. This is where the Parma river, the Galasso canal and the Lorno stream all converged. The latter two are often dry now, but in the Middle Ages they fuelled the economy: a "tower of waters" straddled the canal which powered a mill. The nearby hamlet, Sanguigna, is where they sourced the tough dogwood (*Cornus sanguinea*) for mill cogs used here and on the Po. Later, when the Farnese nobles from Parma wanted the fountains of their grand Ducal Palace in Colorno to spew and spray water, that tower was redesigned: the power of the water lifted the water itself to a cistern up top so that it could then flow fast into those fountains. The ochre-brick tower eventually fell into disuse: having been a residential dwelling, it was later an oil press and a chicken coop, but is now simply covered with shrubs, its windows bricked up: a ruin in the middle of a traffic island.

The Ducal Palace still stands, though, an incongruously grandiose building for a small town. It was redesigned in the eighteenth century by a French architect to look like Versailles, and it really does: the vast, cream-coloured building has over four hundred rooms and I count seventy-four windows on the front elevation alone. Many of the fountains and statues have gone, but the gardens are still classy: knee-high hedgerows, an orangery, an arboreal tunnel, an avenue of ancient oaks which have dropped thousands of acorns. The building now houses, among other things, a cookery school and the local library, but before that it was, for a long time, a psychiatric asylum.

It was here that one of the most dramatic power struggles of the late sixteenth and early seventeenth centuries took place. The Duchy of Parma and Piacenza had been created by Pope Paul III for his son, Pierluigi Farnese, in 1545. The Farnese family had no connection with this area, and the local nobles inevitably took against this nepotistic imposition, especially since Pierluigi was a reprobate (he had previously been excommunicated by his own father for alleged murders and rapes). That animosity increased when Pierluigi attempted to end fiscal evasion and force nobles to reside within the city of Piacenza rather than in their own fortified strongholds. The nobles rebelled: in September 1547, Pierluigi was murdered and flung from the window of his new castle in Piacenza. One of the nobles associated with the murder plot was Ferrante Gonzaga, who promptly occupied the city. Pierluigi Farnese's son, Ottavio, eventually took back control of Parma and Piacenza, but the dynasty often appeared besieged by the surrounding powers: by the Gonzaga, the Sforza, the Estensi and so on.

Colorno was a place of strategic importance for the Farnese: not only did it offer access to the River Po, it was also on the border of the duchy's territory with the Gonzaga. But the town had been gifted by Francesco Sforza to the Sanseverino family, from Caiazzo near Napoli, and by 1564, the ruling noble woman of Colorno was Barbara Sanseverino. She was married to a Count from Sala Baganza, but soon gained a reputation for organising extravagant, often carnal, gatherings. In the words of her biographer, Gigliola Fragnito, Sanseverino turned her palace in Colorno into "a kind of 'meeting house' for noble women of easy virtue, for princes and aristocrats... during the carnival she became the director of erotic games". She was the "promoter and protector of licentious meetings".

Sanseverino would also visit Alfonso II at Ferrara for a month of entertainments. "It was an unrestrained, socialite's life," Fragnito writes. In 1573, during her long stay in Rome, one man wrote a letter to a friend that said – with salacious subtlety – "never has there been a princess who has given as much satisfaction as this woman". Sanseverino was suspicious to the Farnese less because of her libidinous parties than her allegiances. One of her frequent visitors at Colorno was Vincenzo Gonzaga. The failure of his marriage to Margherita Farnese (an attempt at pacification between Parma and Mantova) was largely blamed on Sanseverino's soirées. Gonzaga's butler wrote "we do nothing other than dance night and day".

By the 1590s, Pierluigi Farnese's great-grandson, Ranuccio I, was scheming to take control of Colorno. His "Costitutiones" of 1594 were an attempt to increase his fiscal and judicial power over the province's various feudal lords. The duke had financial worries: the costs of constructing Parma's pentagonal citadel were dwarfed by his father's debts of 800,000 ducats incurred during his wars in the Low Countries. Colorno offered rich soil, a prestigious palace, access to the Po and a buffer against the Gonzagas' expansionist ambitions.

Barbara Sanseverino, by then a widow and aware of how endangered her fiefdom was, decided to marry a count from a nearby village. "There's no benefit to being a woman, nor

Fishing on the Delta

Trepponti, Comacchio

The Po and its road-topped bank near Villanova Marchesana

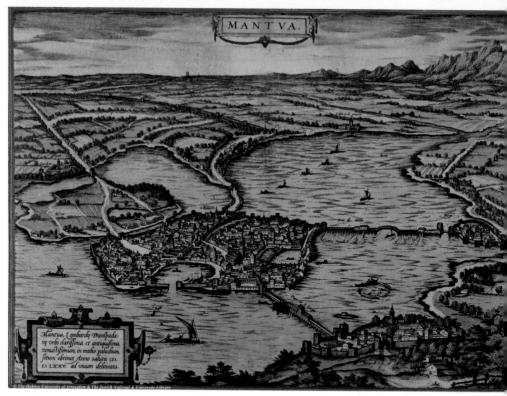

View of Mantova, 1575

A carpet of 'star cucumber' near Gualtieri

'The Island of the Interned' in summer

'The Island of the Interned' in winter (from same position)

The author canoeing with his son

The snow-capped Alps coming into view near Valenza

Explosives used for mining in Monferrato

Looking at the Po and paddy fields beyond from
Rocco delle Donne

Ponte Vecchio, San Mauro Torinese

Laundry along the river (Torino, early twentieth century)

The dry riverbed near Saluzzo

The river and Monviso

Start of the Po valley

The source of the Po
(the painted stone says
'Here the Po is Born')

Buco di Viso

a lady, nowadays," she lamented in a letter to a cardinal. But external events were going against her as her allies passed away: Alfonso II d'Este had died without heirs in 1597, and her nearest protector, the Spanish governor of Milano, Pedro de Azevedo, died in 1610. Sensing his opportunity, Ranuccio declared Sanseverino's inheritance of Colorno illegitimate and a lengthy juridical process began.

Before a decision was reached, Sanseverino and her husband, son and grandson were, with various nobles, arrested and accused of having plotted to kill Ranuccio and his family. Historians are divided as to whether there really was a plot or if it was merely a pretext for the duke to take control of Colorno. But once they were tortured, many confessed to the crime of *laesae maiestatis* – high treason against a sovereign (the only man not to confess died in custody). On 19 May 1612, Barbara Sanseverino, her face covered by a black veil, walked onto the scaffold. She was beheaded in Parma's main square and all her possessions and properties, and those of her fellow accused, fell into the hands of the Farnese family.

It's harder writing about a familiar home than somewhere you're seeing for the first time. And I'm not really sure Parma even justifies inclusion in a book on the Po. Unlike Ferrara and Mantova, it wasn't quite Aquaticus Dux, a ruler of the waters. The city does have two rivers – the Baganza flows into the River Parma just above the Ponte d'Italia – and it, too, used to have *navigli* (canals) criss-crossing the city. But they've almost all been drained, filled in and paved over.

The only water that makes you think you're still part of the Bassa is the fog. That atmospheric humidity is my excuse for holing up in Parma for this Christmas week. I want to understand this murky air, which has been constantly invoked ever since I was on the delta. All the river dwellers eulogise it as some sort of comfort blanket, or a flannel to the brow after the incessant heat of summer. There's something about the air of the Bassa that I've been lectured about, on and off, ever since I first came to Parma half a lifetime ago. Francesco Barilli, a film director from Parma, tells the story of finding himself in a fog so gelatinous that he tried to project a film onto it.

Although the elderly often complain that it's not like the old days, the fog still seems pretty dense to me. In December, in Parma, the air's so wet you could almost wash your face while you walk. It turns everything black and white. I've often felt an affinity with Eric Newby, author of *Love and War in the Apennines*, because he married a woman from the Parma lowlands whose family had been exiled (like my grandfather-in-law's) from Italian territories in what had become Yugoslavia. He wrote that Parma "has a bizarre quality about it, especially in the depths of winter... That's when the thick fog rises from the ditches and canals that irrigate the plain." The city, he said, "becomes an eerie, ghostly place with its church bells clanging out in the now invisible bell-towers".

I used to be, at best, indifferent to fog. Friends here talk longingly of the fogs of their youths and after a glass or two of wine they would start on about its metaphysical properties. I thought it was just them making the most of the marshes where they grew up. But then, one night twenty years ago, a couple of friends took me out into the Bassa on a December night when car headlights were worse for showing the way than the moon. So we rolled along the banks with our heads out of the window, lights off, shouting suggestions to the driver. We were guessing where the road was, and got hopelessly lost, but ended up at a party where someone knew someone else, and we stayed there all night. The fog was still so thick at dawn the sunrise seemed to take two hours.

So I came round to the fog and its potential for offering the unexpected. There's something bawdy about it because it closes in and makes for intimacy and domesticity. I got married in Parma in December and, ever since, I've associated fog with romance. It allows you privacy in open spaces. It makes the nights exciting because you can't see what's coming. And Parma is a city of damp vibrancy: "Closed within her humid bastions", the music critic Bruno Barilli once wrote, "Parma is a maze of alleys, colonnades, burrows and *borghetti* full of passion, violence and generosity."

But although I'm beginning to appreciate the fog, it's hard to say if that's all it is. This windless and industrialised plain has some of the worst air quality in Europe and when you go to the hills in the south you can see a grey, translucent rug hanging over the entirety of Parma and the Pianura Padana beyond. When you're in that air, there's a drunkenness to the light. There are often no shadows. Airflows are only created by the slipstreams of cars and HGVs, speeding up to crossroads. It's muggy and stuffy. "Air, air," Paolo Rumiz wrote about his metaphorical suffocation in Emilia, "there's no air."

Gianni Celati is probably the most eloquent writer on this disquieting atmosphere. In "Conditions of Light along the Via Emilia", he writes about "light exploding in undoing": "Almost permanently suspended on the plain is a bluish and pearly strip according to the seasons. That is the plume in which one lives round here, a plume where every luminosity disperses in innumerable reflections." The explanation he gives is both environmental and pedological, blaming the dust on "the residues of combustion engines, the layers of pulverised asphalt and tyre surfaces, as well as the vapours exhaled from the calcareous and clay-marl soil…"

That lack of freshness in the air is the reason that the rare clear days make citizens of Parma almost elated. On cold February mornings after a snowfall you can finally see the mountains to the south from the city's bridges. I get the impression that that extension of horizons makes people breathe more slowly. Other times, when it rains, the air is rinsed and fresh and the Baganza and Parma rivers are angry with floods. When the rains coincide with snow melts, the rivers crash almost to the apex of all the bridge arches, tangling tree trunks in the brickwork.

But much of the time we just have fog. If nothing else, it makes for good poetry. Giovanni Pascoli, the *fin de siècle* Romagnan poet, wrote a simple ode urging the fog to hide what's far away. His "Nebbia" becomes a celebration of rustic simplicity: the "drab" droplets are asked to insulate the writer from "wanton tears" so that he can appreciate closer imperfections like the valerian-filled cracks in the garden wall. A pair of peaches and apples are sufficient to bring contentment, giving "their suave syrups / to my black bread".

He wants the fog to make the world monochrome once more, not remind him of lost loves but of the last, illuminated final journey:

Nascondi le cose lontane	Hide the far-away things
che vogliono chami e che vada!	That want me to love and be gone.
Ch'io veda là solo quel bianco di strada,	Show me only that white of the lane,
che un giorno ho da fare tra stanco	that I'll travel one day to the contrite
don don di campane.	clang-clang of the tollings.

It's January and I'm on the slim road to Coltaro. Coltaro is where the Taro used to flow into the Po, though that now happens five miles or so upstream.

The static egrets and herons, with their hunched shoulders and cricked necks, look as if they're huddled against the pinching cold. The fog is so solid I can't see the river, only hear it – a play and gurgle of eddies. A thick rope, disappearing into the whiteness, slackens and then tightens again as an unseen boat squeaks.

The sun looks like the moon. There are rows of pollarded trees, their gnarled trunks bulbous and trimmed. Houses are hidden, not that there are many: the odd building comes out of the gauze like a tombstone, but it's mostly fields, ditches and herons. There's one car every quarter of an hour. The word for this atmosphere is *uggioso* – gloomy.

Over the years, the Coltaresi have been the butt of sneers from surrounding villages: they're often called "gypsies", and if you ask what's meant by that, the sneerers will say the Coltaresi have always been smugglers and hustlers. One writer from Parma, in 1950, only half joked when he wrote, "the ancestors of the Coltaresi were sleeping among the reeds while, without doubt, the ancestors of the Sissesi [the next-door town] were already sleeping on sofas". At the time of the Ducato, he wrote, "Coltaro was just a wide swamp".

It's true that from here you could jump into a different jurisdiction fast: it was always on the aquatic fringe of the Duchy of Parma and Piacenza, on a fault line between the Farnese and Pallavicino powers. It meant that these reed beds, thistle hillocks and leaning trunks were good places to unload contraband cargoes. The Coltaresi even call themselves gypsies, but with a slow nod which suggests they're proud of their roots, of their ability to get by alone and without any help from outsiders or the state.

In some ways it's a nothing sort of frontier village, constantly threatened by water and by the authorities. But Coltaro is remarkable because its floodplain has, for centuries, been common land. It once had 300 million square metres of commons, and that subtly changes the feel of the place. Every century or so, the village has to come together to defend the commons, and it has lost a lot of that land over time. But they still have far more river-fronted common-ownership than anywhere else I've seen so far. I grew up in a village of a comparable size to Coltaro and can weigh up pretty accurately what it means for a village of three hundred households to have access to millions of square metres of common land. It completely changes the calibre of human interaction.

These commons came about because of flooding. The story goes that after the Coltaresi helped Sanguigna's Benedictine monastery shore up its river defences in the fifteenth century, the monks beseeched the Bishopric of Parma to grant the Coltaresi *communaliae*, or *comunaglie*. A map from 1588 appears to show the land in question, but the course of the Po has so altered since then it's hard to tell. An ordinance of the Stato Parmense in 1715 recognised that the village's floodplain was theirs, belonging technically to the bishopric but with rights in perpetuity as if the villagers were the true owners. In 1806, Napoleon and his French surveyors confiscated all church lands, and thus also swiped these commons since they were formally still ecclesiastical lands. But the Corsican's widow Maria Luigia – who became Duchess of Parma after the Congress of Vienna – reinstated them on 30 September 1820 in order, she said, to satisfy *le preci* (the imprecations or prayers) of the locals. She recognised that anyone who "had a house in that hamlet and therein made their fire" was allowed to farm in the lands between the *comunello* and the river. It amounted to about a hectare per household: enough of a share in the commons that you would overcome your differences to defend it together.

Mussolini refused to accept the validity of by-laws of previous duchies and bishoprics, and attempted to confiscate them all for the state's demesne. That's how the nearby Mezzani commons disappeared in the 1920s and 1930s as his centurions measured up their floodplains and drew up contracts to sell them off. But the Coltaresi, they say, were tougher. I imagine the regime's notaries and lawyers coming into these lands and being deliberately confused. No map could keep track of the Po, so quite where the land and river met was always a moot point. The villagers were old hands at nudging and banking the waters and could easily have flooded a field to make it disappear when the *gerarchi* came round. Opening their archives and annals, the Coltaresi confused the outsiders with talk of ancient usufructuary rights unrelated to ownership: access to water, to firewood, protection of fishing rights, rights of way, a *livellario* right to pasture, permission to sink a stick to measure depth. The fascist prospectors got lost, perhaps, amid the ever-changing waters and words and, in the end, left matters mostly alone. A third of the commons during Mussolini's *ventennio* fell into private hands – around a million square metres, or roughly 100 hectares. But there remained enough commons – around 200 hectares – to keep Coltaro unified around a cause. Almost three-quarters of a million square metres are now the state's demesne, divided – because of that ever-shifting river – between Emilia-Romagna and Lombardia. The area keeps getting smaller, but 1.3 million square metres are still Coltaro commons.

When you go to Coltaro's floodplain it's not that different from the others: it's planted with perpendicular rows of poplars or else maize for cattle fodder. But when you look closely, you see that the ages of the poplars are different within just a few dozen metres, as if belonging to a different plantation. Look at aerial maps, and that subdivision into tiny patches of land is even clearer. Although each household has the right to roughly a hectare of land – they say it's 10,347 square metres per family – certain areas are worth far more than others: some are on the flooding frontline, or else have privileged access to the water with a nice pier, or are so close to the village that it takes half the effort to get there. So each lot is subdivided into five or six smaller parcels to ensure that no one person has all the best land and another all the worst. It's a patchwork of minuscule holdings and it takes cartographical skill to interpret what's what. Because, in some ways, the commons are now farmed as if they were nothing more than tiny lots of private land. Although there's no ownership as such, it's almost as if there were. When you go to the village hall, they have a huge map of the lands and it looks like a wall-size game of irregular boxes: mosaic-sized chips, thin twigs of a field, barely visible paths.

"In a way, it's real socialism," says the president of the council of ten that manages the lands. Half of that council is elected every year: five councillors one year, five the next, with each serving a two-year term. There are usually about two or three *aspiranti*, those hoping to have their right to land recognised. It's a tall order: nowadays you have to own a house, and to have been resident in the village for ten years. So things move slowly. But it gives the village a continuity which is noticeable as you walk round. The houses look just a bit older, the people a bit younger. Maybe I'm only seeing what I've already read about: one monograph suggested a statistical anomaly in Coltaro in terms of a more stable demographic – the residents are younger, with longer durations of stays and there are more frequent return visits from departees.

I ask the president how it changes the atmosphere of the village. "There's more coming together but there are also," he chuckles wryly, "more arguments." There are always differences of opinion: if an *aspirante* has been renting in the village for seven years, and then buys a house for three, does that give them a right to a plot of land? Does a grandson of a recorded family from the village, who now lives full-time in Rome, have more right than, say, a Sikh dairyman and his family who have rented here for decades? As with all idealisms, the commons keep having to be reinterpreted, recodified and rediscovered. But the president and his council are pretty wise. When they talk about their battles, they're not normally internal but external. The commons council was one of the moving forces behind a 2017 law passed almost unanimously in the Italian parliament which recognised around 2,200 different commons throughout Italy. Coltaro was, once again, in control of its own destiny.

"It's more individualistic now," says the president, attempting to summarise the centuries of evolving use. "Everyone farms their own piece. But this commons is still a curating entity of public interest." Villagers are forced to come together and define what is good for them all as a group. They pool interests – footpaths, machinery, know-how and songs – and defend them against rapacious profiteers. And in doing so they themselves make a small income every year.

It might just be the fog, but Roccabianca is dank: the squat buildings of the petite, colonnaded piazza are grey. The castle is grand, but not in great shape. All the pointing is deteriorating. The lower runs of bricks have fallen away or turned green and cement has been slapped on where someone hasn't had the patience or funds to do the job properly. Ivy has almost reached the top of one of the turrets where you can see scaffolding holding the roof up. But with its grassy moat, and grand towers, it's still strangely stunning. Roccabianca used to be called Arzenoldo, but in the 1450s a local nobleman built this castle for his lover, called Bianca, and the town was renamed.

I'm feeling weary. It's not to do with the season or the climate, but the sense that I'm writing a nature book with very little of the natural world in it. Between 1960 and 2010, the area of agricultural land in the Po's watershed surface diminished from

62 to 43 per cent, a net loss of 1.3 million hectares. Almost the entirety of that lost land was due to the eradication of 1.1 million hectares of permanent and temporary meadows. The consequences are stark. There's no birdsong. In these barren prairies, there are more pylons than trees. There are logistics depots and low-slung factories. I thought that travelling the Po might relieve me of the lack of a garden in my life, but it's only reminding me of it all the more. I occasionally rub the soil from the fields between my fingers and it seems like exhaust dust, dirty and inert.

In recent decades, farming practices in the Pianura Padana have altered radically: since 1982, the cultivation of maize and rice – both water-intensive and heavily fertilised crops – have increased by 47 and 102 per cent respectively. Cattle no longer graze in open grasslands, but are kept indoors, given maize-based feed from hoppers and troughs. (Only cattle whose milk is used for Parmigiano-Reggiano cheese are still fed the traditional alfalfa.) But the greatest change in agriculture is the sudden increase in the number of pigs. There were 1.24 million pigs in the Po basin in 1960; fifty years later there were 6.71 million. But while this whole area is renowned for pork products – for Parma ham, for *culatello* and *salame di Felino* – I've never seen a pig in almost twenty-five years of travelling around Emilia-Romagna. Intensive, industrialised farming means that the animals are caged in concrete warehouses and this has turned the once-prized asset of manure into a waste-disposal problem. Farm animals used to fertilise the soil naturally as they grazed open pastures, but now their nitrogen-rich waste is hosed off the concrete and stored in fat silos as slurry. Due to chemical fertilisers, this land is already drenched in nitrogen: the situation is slightly better than in the 1980s, when the agricultural surplus of nitrogen in the Po basin (which inevitably ended up in groundwater as the soil became saturated) was estimated at 300,000 tonnes per year, but the figure hasn't fallen far in the following decades.

As a result, there are supposed limits on the quantities of slurry that can be distributed per hectare, but the guidelines are often ignored and, with nitrogen highly soluble in water, its distribution has a catastrophic effect on rivers and canals. But it alters the air, too: this hazy atmosphere is partly the result of ammonia, and other nitrogen compounds, that volatise from slurry and fertilisers. The resulting particulate matter (ammonium salts) is one of the causes of Emilia-Romagna's polythene sky.

All around me there's a botanical exuberance that isn't fertility but fertiliser: you see the eutrophication in these drying canals, which are so algaed it looks like you could walk on them. There's an unnatural yellow glow to it now in this unreliable light. The ratio of HGVs to bicycles on these narrow country roads (raised dangerously between deep ditches) is about one hundred to one. Yesterday a lorry had overturned: the contents had spilled out of the back end and the driver was perched up on his cab in that ditch as if he were just setting up a wonky stall. Something is amiss here. Paolo Rumiz wrote about this part of Emilia being "an exhausted land… a horror of vacuity".

Rivers are supposed to help cleanse a bad conscience. I thought hanging out along the Po might be a little like being lowered into the River Jordan, the baptismal waters returning me to my place in creation. But the Po is so dirty and murky it's as if it needs a cleansing more than we do. I can't see any innocence to it. I keep thinking of all those dead conscripts, the oily film, the plastic bags, the sewage. As well as nitrogen, there are worrying levels of chlorides, phenols, phosphates, heavy metals and microplastics in the Po. In the mid-1990s, measurements of the river's pollution revealed that it disbursed into the Adriatic every year an estimated 2,642 kilograms of zinc, 1,154 of copper, 1,312 of lead, 944 of chrome and 243 of arsenic. Much of what people piss all over this wide basin ends up here. Sometimes, after a high weekend in wealthy cities, the levels of benzoylecgonine, a chemical excreted by cocaine users in urine, peaks in these waters. We've turned a source of purity into the recipient of something worse than sewage: the by-product of bingeing. And when I see this river – so often equated with a god – I don't see divinity or something worthier than me, but a scorned cesspit. I, too, scorn it. I look away, and long to get home.

I read recently about a blues harmonica player who says you should listen to the Po, play your harp in front of it and hear it echo. Others say its own sounds are unique, especially when the river is full. One book calls it *il muggito* – the bellowing or lowing: "that animal noise which comes from the depths of Hell. The river is a bull, an ill god that bellows from the innards of the earth." But I just hear growls. I find myself yearning for steepness. I want to stride up a hill and get the view from its summit. I've been tramping for months now and I'm still only about 25 metres above sea level. The river is so wide it's unrelatable. It's as if I'm trying to bond with a slug.

The person who gets me over my gripe with this dull landscape is Giovannino Guareschi. He eulogised the Po, calling it "the only respectable river which exists in Italy". He joked that it really only begins at Piacenza: "respectable rivers develop in the plain because water is stuff which is made for remaining horizontal and only when it is perfectly horizontal does water conserve all its natural dignity. The Niagara Falls are a circus phenomenon, like men who walk on their hands." He relished the stagnancy of the river ("vast, deserted, immobile and silent, more than a river it seems a cemetery of dead waters...") because it suggested solemnity: "the beat of the river's old heart is slow..."

Guareschi was born here, in the tiny hamlet of Fontanelle, in 1908. His family shared a house with the socialist cooperative and, since he was born on 1 May as the workers were celebrating, Giovannino was held aloft on the balcony by Giovanni Faraboli, the socialist leader, and declared a future champion of the cause.

Guareschi's father wasn't good with money: he had been imprisoned for almost two years for unpaid promissory notes and, as a salesman of agricultural machinery to landowners, he often came into conflict with the socialists. Guareschi was only six when the family was forced to sell up – they were bought out by the socialist cooperative – and moved to Parma. In many ways, Guareschi spent his life trying to get back to Fontanelle and his beloved lowlands.

By 1922, the socialist cooperatives in Fontanelle were booming. The overarching "Casa dei Socialisti" had seven food outlets, two textile shops, a wine cellar, a butcher and two cheese factories. They owned, as a collective, 300 hectares of land and were renting another 500, plus 150 hectares of woodland along the Po. They had threshing machines, an electric sawmill, a people's library with 6,000 volumes, a credit union and a construction cooperative. Giovanni Faraboli – that socialist who had lifted up the newborn Guareschi – had created a shared empire. But on 6 August 1922, at 6 a.m., armed Blackshirts arrived in cars and lorries and burned the "red cooperatives" to the ground, including Faraboli's house. They called it, daintily, the *fiammifero livellatore*, the "levelling match". Soon afterwards, Faraboli went into exile in France.

The Guareschi family, too, was forced to move again. Guareschi's father was declared bankrupt in 1925, and Guareschi left the private college, the Convitto Maria Luigia, where he had been tutored by "Za" – Cesare Zavattini. He was fortunate to have good mentors. After he had failed a Latin exam, a priest helped him with his retakes. Zavattini introduced him to newspapers and satirical magazines in Parma and Milano.

By the Second World War, Guareschi was a successful cartoonist. But in 1942 – informed (incorrectly) that his younger brother had died on the Russian front – Guareschi got drunk and shouted obscenities against Mussolini in the silence of the night. He was immediately arrested and conscripted into the army. Refusing to fight for the Germans in 1943, he was sent to a internment camp for Italian soldiers for almost two years. There he tried to entertain other internees with sketches and skits (many of which became part of his bittersweet book, *Diario Clandestino*). Despite returning safely to his parents, wife and children in 1945, he was even more melancholic after the war. As he said in one of his cartoons: "I lived for two years as a prisoner in Germany and now, for the last two years, I'm dying as a free man in Italy."

Guareschi felt that post-war Italy was becoming a dangerous, dark place. It was he who first described Emilia as the "Mexico of Italy" because there were so many killings (often of fascists by partisans) in the post-war years. He campaigned against the "popular front" of Communist and Socialist parties in 1948 and yet, at the same time, called the Christian Democrats "completely cursed". He was against the grain in every way, describing himself as "a Monarchist in a Republic, a right-winger in a country which is moving, decisively and inflexibly, towards the left, a supporter of private enterprise in times of statism, an advocate of unity in a time of regionalism, a supporter of Italianism in a time of anti-nationalism, an intransigent Catholic in a time of Christian Democracy. I haven't been – as it might appear – an independent, but an anarchist. Not a free man, but a subversive."

But it was during those difficult years that Guareschi became globally famous thanks to his amusing Don Camillo tales. He wrote 346 in all and in each the same tough priest is at loggerheads with the irascible communist mayor, Peppone. The characters were clearly modelled on men he knew – possibly the priest who had helped him as a teenager and Faraboli, the socialist with what Guareschi called "the clear and honest face". The short stories became successful films, capturing the cleavage in post-war Italy between Catholic piety and political emancipation. But as well as Don Camillo and Peppone, there were two other characters that gave the deceptively simple stories a metaphysical depth: the crucifix (which speaks to the priest) and "the great river". Like the crucifix for Don Camillo, the river is a pacifying presence: "at the end, the two enemies agree on the essential things because of the broad, eternal breath of the river which cleans the air". Given the unbearable heat of the Bassa in summer, the river was a cooling presence to hotheads: "It's always cold on the riverbanks in the evening, even when it's hot." It wasn't just to do with the temperature, either, but the ethereal beauty of that water. Some of Guareschi's descriptions of it are, as was his style, colloquially lyrical: "the light, blue fog of the night, like a veil of sleep, still glides on the placid waters of the great river. Then the sun pokes out its head from behind the hedge of poplars and starts to throw specks of shining gold on the water and the lark, rising, from the middle of a meadow, goes straight into the sky, leaving behind a thin trench of trills…"

For Guareschi, the river was like a fickle deity that could be both generous and cruel: "the great river sometimes arranges these quirks: it takes land from one side to give it to another. It makes Tizio poorer in order to enrich Caio…" (That mercurial nature of the river – delivering land and taking it away – is evident from the regional boundaries here: the line between Lombardia and Emilia-Romagna doesn't follow the current course of the river, but its old route, so that bureaucratic and aquatic boundaries criss-cross like tangled string.) In Guareschi's stories, the "placid and majestic" river swells and floods; it's a place of attempted suicides, but also a confessor, the recipient – like a deity – of prayers and supplications. Characters go to the riverbank to bare their souls: "words fell on the water which took them far away."

Guareschi knew that this landscape can often seem oddly still and uneventful: "Everything seems immobile in the lowlands and one gets the idea that nothing ever happens along these deserted riverbanks, and that nothing could ever happen inside those red and blue houses with small windows." Appearances were deceptive, though. "Actually, more things happen here than in the mountains or cities because of that blasted sun which gets into the blood of the people. And that red, overgrown moon which isn't the usual, icy moon of other places, but which here also burns and, at night, heats up the brains of the living and the bones of the dead." His fellow "*bassaioli*", he said (his "lowlanders"), were notoriously hot-headed. He called them "*balenghi*" – weird or odd – and relished their eccentricities and struggles which came from being nocturnal: "the beating sun makes people sleep in the day, and the mosquitos keep them awake at night." This was the backdrop, the *mondo piccolo*, which inspired his Don Camillo stories. For Guareschi, it was a constantly inspiring landscape: "in a land like this, you only need to stop on the road and look at a farmhouse drowning in maize and hemp and immediately a story is born."

But his contrariness and principled stubbornness didn't make for an easy life. Having published an article accusing the Christian Democrat prime minister Alcide De Gasperi of having urged the Allies to bomb the outskirts of Rome during the war (the authenticity of the letter, since destroyed, is still contested), Guareschi was sued for libel and imprisoned in Parma for 409 days (from May 1954 to July 1955). He refused to ask for a pardon or appeal the decision. After his release, he gradually fell out with publishers and film producers. He bought a smallholding back in the Bassa and opened a trattoria, but his health was declining. He was seen as an isolated, cantankerous reactionary. Guareschi dismissed Italy's post-war economic miracle as "a hot and dusty wind which smells of cadavers, sex and sewers". But often his scorn was prescient: he called Italian television "a factory of cretins" and scorned the country's linguistic contortionisms: "the only true enemy of our people is rhetoric," he wrote. "Rhetoric makes the masses drunk… and makes them fall into fatal errors." Guareschi saw himself not as a destructive Cassandra, but as an endorsing analyst: "humour," he wrote, "is the acid with which one tests whether the metal which is presented to you as gold really is gold. Humour doesn't destroy; humour reveals what should be destroyed because it's bad. Humour destroys only the ambiguity. It reinforces that which is substantially good."

In 1963, Guareschi was asked to participate in an eccentric documentary in which two famous writers from right and left – he and Pier Paolo Pasolini – were tasked with answering the central question of why modern life is characterised by unhappiness and anxiety. Although Guareschi's contribution is occasionally unsettling (he laments the expulsion of European imperialists from Africa, and his anti-communism and anti-Americanism was far more in evidence than any anti-fascism), he answers that question with more insight than Pasolini: "our unhappiness comes from the freneticism," he said, "of our material pleasures." There was a proto-ecological critique in his analysis: "humanity has rebelled against nature," he said, "and this uncertainty in our future causes our anxiety." For someone writing in the early 1960s, as the rest of the country celebrated an economic miracle, it was a prophetic analysis. As he wrote in one of his last Don Camillo stories: "the earth doesn't betray. It's humanity that has betrayed the earth." "Man is behaving," he wrote, "like someone who has a beautiful peach, but throws away the pulp to gnaw on the nut."

Suffering ill health and scorned by progressive society, Guareschi died in 1968, aged only sixty. Although one of the bestselling Italian authors of the twentieth century, there were only a handful of mourners at his funeral. He was buried with the monarchical version of the Italian flag on his coffin and a bucket of earth was brought from the bed of the River Po and buried alongside him.

I'm almost at Zibello. The riverbank is, for once, frosted hard. No one knows where the name Zibello comes from, whether because it's on a bit of land ever so slightly raised above the floodplains (*gibello*, from *gibbo* – a hump), or from Ghibello (i.e. Ghibelline). But the word only means one thing to most people: *culatello*, the marbled, cured pork from the rump of the pig.

Like so many of these villages, it has been left behind. It still has its houses and fields, even a lovely red-brick fortress with its flared colonnades and proud, oblique flagpoles... but it no longer seems like a village. The Cinema Excelsior is abandoned. Nobody knows what to do with the grand cloisters of the Dominican monastery. When you walk towards the river, you see rusting hoppers and a conveyor belt that leads nowhere. It's desolate in the original sense: alone and abandoned. This is a village which had just over four thousand residents in 1921. At the last census (2011) it had only 1,841.

But in those cloisters they have one of the best museums in the whole region: the museum of peasant culture. The warden enjoys making me guess what all the simple tools he shows me were used for.

"This?" he says, holding up something that looks like a long oar, but with the paddle deeply cupped.

I take hold of it: it's poor wood, clearly not a prized possession.

"A tile-chucker," he says, showing me how the man on the ground would launch the tiles up to the roofer to save traipsing up and down.

He passes me what looks like a glass needle. "*Al ladar*," he says in dialect. I don't understand and shrug. *Il ladro* (the thief) was, he tells me, inserted into the wine barrel to test the taste.

We go through the whole museum like that: every surface is covered with the most basic objects: the large teardrops of desiccated pumpkins, used as containers for water or gunpowder, bags woven with the tough sheaths of corn on the cob, matches made out of hemp dipped in sulphur, the *sciaparói*, wooden wedges used to split willow longitudinally, which was then used to bind brooms, tie up vines and make baskets. There's the *canéli dla pulenta*, a stick for stirring polenta that was also (he moves his head, pretending to duck a blow) used by women to defend themselves.

The genius for simple solutions is apparent everywhere: a one-legged milking stool with a belt so that it could be tied to the waist of milkers and, when the two buckets were full and needed to be carried, the stool didn't need to be picked up, too. There are photographs of thick beams placed in a ditch of cattle manure since it protected them from woodworm. Poverty and resourcefulness created instruments from almost nothing: to thresh wheat, peasants needed a *correggiato*, a flail, but leather was too expensive so they used eel skins. They're tough and twisted, like dried banana peel.

This tiny museum was created by a local doctor, Giuseppe Riccardi. Born in 1915, he witnessed first-hand the ways in which rural life changed rapidly in the twentieth century and he wanted to preserve what he could of the tools and the culture. Most of all, however, he lamented what had happened to the Po. He remembered, he once wrote, "when the waters of the Po were drinkable and when the unchallenged sturgeon of two metres or more, the blue prince of the fish, darted in his depths; when innumerable birds, from the nightingale to the cuckoo, from the goldfinch to the pheasant, lived undisturbed in the Po's reed beds, in his brambles, in the undergrowth". Now, though, he said (writing in 1993), "the river is no more majestic, still less romantic; because, in disciplining his waters, coercing them into slip canals, introducing large-scale, intensive poplar plantations, allowing powerful ploughs and harrows to subvert all the undergrowth of the floodplains, even of the islands, there has been a depopulation of many living creatures both in and out of the water. Now the river is abandoned, deserted... the great river is plagued by serious turmoil and moreover it's humiliated, forced into the degrading role of the great cesspit of Padania."

Every mile or so you come across a grandiose farmhouse. They have different names for them here, but each of the terms exudes a sense of the imposing confidence of the landowner: *casa colonica* (a colonial house), *la grancia* (grain house) or *podere* (which derives from *potere*, "power"). Along one wing they usually have a grand portico called a *barchessa*, a space for storing machinery and the reels of alfalfa fodder. The tiles are often the exact same colour as the bricks – a sort of linen-at-sunset.

Most buildings round here have an aged solidity: billowing columns look like vertical torpedoes. Fortresses have pocked brickwork with, inside, slowly erasing frescos and rusted-up shutters with peeling varnish. Sometimes, inside, they seem like time capsules from previous centuries: there are barrels which, even side-on, are almost two metres tall, wooden ladders covered in cobwebs, tower-top lookouts covered in bird shit but with fat beams and blushing bricks. Nothing seems posed or on display. Things have just been left this way.

Sometimes you see boulevards of pollarded trees so thick they must be close to a hundred years old, but between the rows there's just a grass track, leading nowhere. The faded grandeur comes from the fact that many of these hamlets and villages were once considered "capital cities", with their own fort and chief of police.

And when you meet them, the farmers are just as solid as those buildings, thickset and blunt. In Italian they would be called *burbero/a* – "gruff" or "surly" (in dialect *sgruso/a*). I ask one signora – shaped like a hung ham and wearing an apron stained with either blood or tomato passata – if she has any eggs to sell.

"Who sent you?" she snaps.

When I say no one, she's even more suspicious.

But like the buildings that's just the external pose. When you get talking and the farmer's guard descends, you glimpse the fun behind the façade as you wait for the eggs: a toddler playing with half a dozen kittens in the courtyard, an old man pitchforking hay into the stables, an inexplicably attractive daughter who carries your eggs by gathering them in her jumper. They don't have egg boxes, and they'll break in my pockets, so a family discussion begins about how best to carry them. The old man is grumpy at the prolonged disturbance now, but smiles: "only one way to carry them safely – in your stomach!" So I blag an onion as well and set up my camping stove on the bank above their farmstead. There's nothing to it, but it seems like a feast.

Until the eighteenth century, there were odd exceptions to this flat land. Dotted across the whole of this landscape there were wide plateaus, a few metres higher than the surrounding land, that extended for hundreds of square metres. Farmers had long noticed that the grass on these mounds grew greener and denser, and when they dug down the earth was dark. They tried spreading it on surrounding pastures and it acted as an excellent fertiliser. But they noticed that it contained many bits and bobs: bones, broken plates, fragments of metal and so many spindle whorls that the soil was dubbed "fossil earth" or "cemetery earth". Those shallow hillocks became well-known quarries, with the owners making good money by selling what was thought to be *marna*, or "marl". By the time of the Napoleonic inventory of agricultural resources, in the early nineteenth century, a wagon of "terramarna" (assumed, back then, to be Roman remains) would cost five lire. Within decades, much of the archaeological treasure had gone, simply spread across fields to help the grass grow.

Attitudes changed, however, in the middle of the nineteenth century. In 1854, the waters on Lake Zurich were so low that the remains of a stilt house were seen in Meilen. Publication of Charles Darwin's *On the Origin of Species* persuaded many that human history was far deeper than previously thought, and the Italian Risorgimento encouraged Italian archaeologists to study the country's own ancient artefacts. Attention inevitably turned to those odd, fertile mounds found all along the Padanian plain. In Parma, a professor of natural history and an eighteen-year-old coin enthusiast, Luigi Pigorini, began various digs in nearby villages. What they discovered were Bronze Age settlements which they called (borrowing the vernacular description of the marly soil), "terramare".

These villages were complex irrigation solutions to the aquatic basin of the Po from the middle to recent Bronze Age: the waters from the nearby river, or its tributaries, were diverted to form a moat around a two-hectare rectangle containing stilt houses for up to two hundred people. During excavations, the holes made by the vanished wooden posts looked like the dimples in focaccia. Often those habitations had a hole into which ash, broken plates, fragments of metal and bones were thrown, offering a crucible of Bronze Age refuse: it was a culture that was trading amber, casting bronze, weaving linen, hemp and wool, carving antlers and animal bones and – using sophisticated irrigation channels – cultivating cereals.

Sometimes the agger (the central, raised area within the moat) was as large as 20 hectares containing possibly a thousand people, but usually the terramare were smaller and only two kilometres apart, creating a polycentric, loose confederation of villages. It's estimated that in around 1200 BCE the terramare had, to the north and south of the Po, some 150,000 inhabitants. Soon afterwards, however, the civilisation seems to have collapsed and the settlements were abandoned, possibly because of climatic changes, warfare (there's evidence of burning) or else social disintegration caused by egalitarian societies becoming hierarchical and coercive.

Rome's Prehistorical and Ethnographic Museum is now named after Pigorini, who dedicated his life to understanding these terramare. One of his central theses was that the Padanian plain was settled by Indo-Europeans, possibly amber traders, from the north and that the layout of these villages – with their boundary ditches, perpendicular streets, their internal division into civilian and military areas, and the sophisticated system of wells and shadoofs (distributing water in containers using a rod counterbalanced by weights on the other side of the pivot) – "makes it clear that the terramare are the cradle of Italian civilisation". Pigorini's controversial thesis (and the debate continued for decades) was that Roman civilisation emerged not only from the civilised south, but from what was often dismissed by palaeontologists as "the barbarian north".

Civilisation was often synonymous with deforestation, and it seems certain that the people of the terramare were responsible for the first, systematic clearances in this ancient *silva magna*, the immense forest of the Padanian plain. It was a process which continued for centuries and is still evident in the place names: the tiny village of Le Roncole comes from the medieval Latin *runcare* (to de-wood), and a *roncola* in Italian is a billhook. Roncole is only a T-junction of a hamlet, but it was here that, in 1813, Giuseppe Verdi was born. His father was the owner of the local tavern. There weren't any glasses. Wine was served in a *scüdlén*, a terracotta bowl. The fact that Verdi grew up among the hard-drinking, hard-singing locals is often thought to have influenced his musical development. He had no doubt ample natural talent – he was the church organist at the age of nine – but, as Barilli wrote in his book *Il Paese del melodramma* – "the hostelries were always full of shouts and songs". Barilli's theory was that Verdi was a natural emanation of this land ("his breath has a healthy whiff of onion... and his instincts are full of a primitive vehemence", he wrote), and that this flat part of Parma was uniquely given to the melodrama that Verdi would immortalise: "a turbulent and fearful people [given to] insults, rackets and tumults." Barilli wrote (in prose as relentless as the music it describes) that *Il Trovatore* has "hysterics which give way to tumultuous and blind exuberance, with an extravagance and a fulminating, positive convulsion which is thoroughly Italian...". Verdi himself confirmed that emotional excessiveness, writing to his librettist, Franco Maria Piave, that when he composed "my heart beats faster and tears stream from my eyes".

One usually assumes that emotional melodrama might be stoked by dramatic topographical extremes like mountains or cliffed coastlines, but Guareschi had a theory that it was this "desolately flat land" which gave rise to "such exuberant, romantic music": "look, for example," he said, "at our sunsets, these sunsets which explode suddenly and violently, full of reds, of yellows and unexpected flashes. They explain why, in this land, such an excessive music was born."

In later life, Verdi liked to portray himself as the genius son of illiterate peasants, but the reality was that his parents – in gifting him a spinet and organising his lessons – were active participants in his education, sending him to Busseto, the next-door town, to study. I walk there and enjoy its understated grandeur: there are, as usual, long, colonnaded arcades with – in the semicircle of the arches – signs advertising the café or shop hidden behind. Slim balconies, antique streetlamps and the rust-brick castle make the place seem classy and robust. Verdi came here to study aged ten and lived for eight years with an entrepreneur and landowner, Antonio Barezzi, who used to supply Verdi's father with various liqueurs for his tavern. Barezzi had created a forty-five-strong orchestra and became, for decades, a fatherlike patron to the composer. Verdi fell in love with his daughter, Margherita, and the pair married in 1836.

The impression one gets of Verdi from walking around this small town is of stubbornness. The castle was redesigned in the 1860s to accommodate a stunning opera house, the "Verdi Theatre", but the maestro refused to set foot in it. He avoided Busseto because, after the death of his wife Margherita and their two young children, he lived with the soprano Giuseppina Strepponi and he was irritated by local disapproval of his relationship. As you wander around now, though, everything is a tribute to him: there's Verdi square, with its statue of the seated maestro, and four different museums are dedicated to him within a few miles.

But more than those museums and their sanctified objects – all the napkins, letters, spoons and spinets – it's the music that makes me sense Verdi's spirit. There are many raucous bands inside the spit-and-sawdust bars I'm always drawn to. Often they're of a very different genre to Verdi's classical operas or even to that Mezzani genius, Cantoni, but these bands still have a thirsty exuberance that I enjoy. One "orchestra" is called "a thousand litres", and another – taking its name from the aliases that rogues might give to the police (MePekeBarba) – shouts about how much they want a blond (a "lager"): "I want a lager, I want so many, I want a lager, I want it here. I want a lager, with all its foam, I want a lager, for pity's sake."

∼

The footpaths along the river come and go. Sometimes you're next to the water for a few miles. But then the path peels away and you drop into a hamlet of half a dozen houses. Then there's another diagonal up the bank and you're above the floodplains again and through the skeletal trees you can see the murky water. Every few miles there are depots with a dozen hillocks of grey sand. Sometimes a pump house scissors a bridge, its fat pipes rising and falling through the building. And the other side, away from the river, fields fade into the exhausted fog.

You often feel like you're not getting anywhere, in part because you regularly have to tack back: a wide bend in the river means you spend an hour walking to somewhere only just a stone's throw from where you started. Or else the path peters out and you're on private land and have to turn around. You hardly ever see another human being: sometimes, in the distance, dust rises behind a ploughing tractor, or you wave at the old signora tending her chickens in the scrub of an abandoned farmhouse. But otherwise the world is distant and oddly straight: apart from this meandering, misleading river, the geometry – the telegraph poles, plough lines, conveyor belts and poplar trunks – is as linear as the contrails in the sky.

But rather than frustrated, I'm beginning to trust it. One moment you're remote from civilisation and then, completely unexpectedly, you find yourself in an "antique court", a stone manor with a rose garden and restaurant which must have once belonged, given the name, to the aristocratic Pallavicino family. I had almost turned back because there was only a cemetery and a few flash cars by a building site. But press on, until you're almost at a copse called Il Bosco della Lite (the intriguingly named "Woodland of the Argument") and you can put yesterday's sandwiches away and enjoy everything your budget can afford.

With a full stomach, I decide to make peace with this ugly drain of a river. I read the other day that line from Simone

Weil in *Gravity and Grace*: "It is better to say 'I am suffering' than 'this landscape is ugly'." And so I'm thinking that maybe I should stop grumbling about the state of the river and its wounded edges. I can hardly blame the Po for the surrounding industrialisation, nor the locals for draining the land and feeding themselves and selling the surplus. When I'm by the water, I'm beginning to pity the river, wanting to apologise to the Po, not blame it. I sit in its dry sand, freneticism stilled by this idling bend, and I can hear the water now, or rather its consequences: snagging branches and riffling gravel.

Further on, I see a woman alone on a bench, staring at the Po as if it were the Acheron, the river of woe. I notice that two anglers are whispering to one another. Boats pass, but even the engines sound muffled. In what can often be a noisy country, the volume and pace of these banks are often soft. Zavattini's dialect poem says it well:

Sl'è grand al Po.	The Po is mighty.
Coi ca s'incuntra là	Those who meet there
i sbasa senz'acorzasan la vus,	lower their voices without realising it,
e i arcnòs,	and recognise,
cm'an po' ad malincunia,	with a degree of melancholy,
ca siom dabòn cumpagn.	that we are truly mates.

SIX

Cremona, Piacenza, Pavia and Lomellina

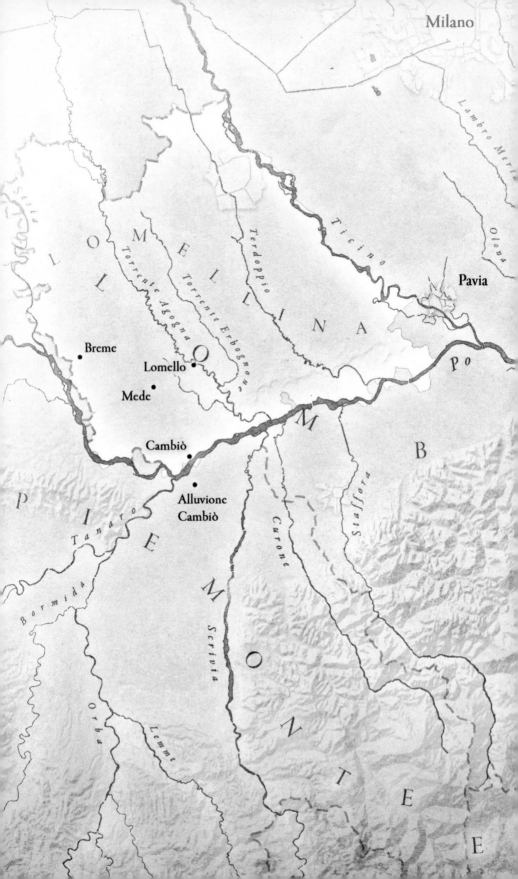

CREMONA, PIACENZA, PAVIA AND LOMELLINA

San Zenone
al Po

Rottofreno

Calendasco

Piacenza

Maleo

Pizzighettone

Caorso

Cremona

Stagno
Lombardo

*Bodrio del
Lazzaretto*

Lambro

Canale della Muzza

Serio

Adda

Oglio

D

R

I

A

R O M A G N A

Torrente Tidone

Trebbia

Torrente Nure

Torrente Rigilo

Chero

Torrente Chiavenna

Torrente Arda

Stirone

L I A

N

W   E

S

| 0 | 10 | 20 |

km

've crossed over to the left bank, into the province of Cremona. This area is notorious for what are called *bodri* or *bugni*: they're sinkhole lakes which dimple the edges of the river, sometimes not even that close to it. They're formed when the river breaks its banks and spills into the farmland, creating what one monograph I read calls "a whirling rotational motion which, literally drilling the ground, ends up producing particular excavations in the shape of an inverted cone, sometimes up to twenty metres deep". Once formed, these *bodri* are often linked to and replenished by the river through aquifers, and they slowly become rare oases in these dusty prairies.

The *bodri* tend to be chilled places but they have an added resonance now that we too (thanks to Covid) are living through a time of contagion. Just outside Stagno Lombardo is the Bodrio del Lazzaretto: this was the isolated spot (a literal lazaret or recluse for quarantine) where the plague-stricken were sent. The presence of fish in the lake presumably gave the ostracised sufferers some hope of surviving their isolation.

It's calm in the winter sunshine. There's a terrapin on a wide, static trunk which rests half in the water. There are coypus with their snouts just above the surface, elegantly floating this way and that. A great reed warbler flits between the willows. Even though it's February, it's so dry that the crispy leaves crack under foot as moorhens sprint across them. For once the sky is an infinite blue, but everything else is a dull brown. I sit and enjoy the scene, hearing splashes and occasional scurrying in the distance. I can understand why the dialect word – *bugno* or *bögn* – is thought to come from *bunia*, the Latin for breadbasket: it seems like a bowl of wholesomeness.

Although floods occasionally create new ponds, these *bodri* are, inevitably, disappearing. In the 1723 land census there were 130. Improved river defences and the hunger for agricultural land mean that there are only about thirty left. Many have been filled in or sucked dry. As you walk around you often see crumbling, tiny pump houses, local imitations of those grand ones three hundred miles downstream. At my back, there are permanent sprinklers all across the fields, their four-inch metal tubes emerging from concrete footings. There are yellow warning signs of underground power cables – 15,000 volts – for bleeding out the water.

Aerial images from here show something strange. All along this side of the river there are great semicircles in the land, arcing for half a mile or more. Fields overlap one another like fish scales. Normally fields are, obviously, more or less rectangular, but here a dozen or so are squeezed into one semicircle after another. Once you've noticed one, you see many more. They're clearly the wider bends of the old course of the river, its banks and its floodplains. Where we impose lines, the river gives voluptuous curves.

I walk the short distance from the *bodrio* to the hamlet of Stagno Lombardo (literally "the Lombard swamp"). I realise, yet again, how little can be secret in this wide-open plain. You can see the next-door village, a mile away; you can even make out a distant bicycle on a raised road, a pick-up bouncing along a dirt track, a stooped coat with an impatient dog.

It doesn't take long to find the Cittadella estate. Behind the brick wall is a grand courtyard and, around the side, the barn looks like the nave of a church, with wooden lancet arches disappearing into the distance. It was here, on 11 November 1887, that the agricultural cooperative of Cittadella was founded. It was the brainchild of an anarchist from Pisa, Giovanni Rossi. An intellectual agitator who used the alias Cardias, Rossi had briefly been in prison and on release moved to Brescia, where he became a vet. Believing private property was "based on theft and deceit", he was fixated on creating an alternative society. He had written a utopian novel (*Un Comune Socialista*) and was convinced that "people who grow up in socialist settlements" would be "the fermentation which makes the dough of the revolution rise. Let's show to unbelievers that a village, a whole commune, can live and thrive, in socialism..." Inspired by a short-lived Irish commune in Co. Clare, Ralahine, which was set up in the early 1830s, and by the Obshchina (the village commons) of Russia, Rossi's cooperative rented 120 hectares, and twenty houses, from an idealistic landlord.

Problems were evident from the start. It was a patrician experiment in which the landowner and intellectuals tried to tell the peasants what was best for them. Women were allowed to attend, but not vote in, meetings. Rossi quickly became disillusioned by what he felt was the conservatism of the locals: "habit is harder to battle and beat," he wrote, "than any other thing." The contractual agreements were actually very generous: members were allowed to keep two-fifths of the silk, a half of each pig and a third of the grain while the cooperative traded the rest on their shared behalf. Using modern agricultural techniques, Cittadella was financially very successful. But the labourers complained about the pooling of the rest of their produce, leading Rossi to inveigh against their "mean and short-sighted egotism". "Here they've socialised the work," he complained, "but they haven't yet socialised business and partnerships."

Rossi decided to bring two socialist families into the village – from the other side of the river – to shore up the ideological foundations of the community, but the outsiders were, inevitably, resented and a whispering campaign (fuelled by an ousted farm steward) began against Rossi. "I've never had such a painful period," he wrote years later. In February 1890 – just over two years after the cooperative was founded – Rossi set sail for South America, where he set up another community in Brazil ("Cecilia", the subject of a Jean-Louis Comolli film).

It's eerie poking around the semi-ruin now. The walled garden, with its brick arches, is crumbling. The rendering has gone on all the terraced houses and their shutters are rotting. The community was wound up shortly after Rossi left, in October 1890, so it was only operative for three years. They rarely seem to last long. The Irish community on which it was based only lasted two, and Cecilia, again, just three. The enthusiastic landowner who had leased the land to the community later wrote of communes: "they are experiments from which, in my opinion, it is impossible to derive any positive experience. I don't know if Rossi is also now cured of the illusion."

Others were even harsher: the anarchist Errico Malatesta said that he "deplored" what Rossi had, twice, attempted, comparing both communalism and emigration to "desertion in the face of the enemy", a form of escapism whereas "the duty of revolutionaries is to make every effort to help the poor understand that poverty exists there as well as here and that the remedy, if they want it, can be found staying where they are and rebelling against the government and the bosses". These criticisms – from both the realist and outflanking-idealist sides – are very familiar. But I still can't help myself being drawn to these fleeting incarnations of communalism and wondering if the world isn't improved by people going against the tide and, rather than privatising the shared, trying to share the private.

The Po is unusual because 65 per cent of its entire watershed is designated as lowlands. It doesn't cascade through canyons and isn't, except near its source, hemmed in by hills or mountains; it flows through soggy lands that are barely above the river's surface, sometimes even below it. As a result, many settlements have names which celebrate fleeting dryness or altitude, like

"Buonemerse" (roughly, "well-emerged lands"). The Po spilt over its confines so regularly that few cities dared be right next to it. But Cremona is an exception, nestling just to the north-east of one of its generous bends. There's also a port, an egg-shaped basin just off the river which was supposed to be connected to Milano by a canal, although it was never finished.

Cremona is a city made famous by its luthiers – Amati, Guarnieri and, most famously, Stradivari. Even today as you walk around the cobbled streets, there are many workshops and boutiques where violins are made and sold. The hourglass shapes of their fronts and backs hang in windows and on walls. They're so thin they look like crisps. Some already have oblique "f" holes drawn on the wood in light pencil leaning away from the centre bout (the side bites out of the crisp). Dozens of concave pegs, split or chipped, are thrown into boxes of rejects under the workbenches. More than a hundred luthiers still work in Cremona, a city which has frequently revolutionised music. Claudio Monteverdi, the sixteenth/seventeenth-century composer and pioneer of opera, was born here, though he later moved to Mantova to be "musical maestro" at the court of Vincenzo Gonzaga (Barbara Sanseverino's friend). He broke with medieval polyphony and wrote what is considered one of the first operas, *L'Orfeo*. Mina, one of the great singers of the post-war years, grew up here. Her 1965 song "Brava" is vertiginously fast, a boastful display of the virtuosity for which this city is famous.

With its thirteenth-century bell tower, its crenellated palazzi and half-marble baptistry, Cremona is a stunning place. As you walk round, you often see – carved into the cream-coloured stone or stitched into the heraldic flags – a vertical arm holding a ball. The story goes that the city used to have to pay a tribute of a five-kilogram gold ball to the Holy Roman Emperor. Tired of this fiscal extortion, in the late eleventh century the city asked Giovanni Baldesio (now known in dialect as "Zanén de la Bàla", "Giovanni of the ball") to fight off Enrico IV (some sources say he fought a duel with Enrico's son) and rid the city of this burden. Baldesio won the contest and the city was freed of its costly dues. "*Fortitudo mea in brachio*" the city's motto now recites: "my strength is in my arm".

But as soon as you leave that glittering centre and head back towards the river, you're dwarfed by its heavy industry: the oil refinery and steelworks. Then, suddenly, you're lost in the woodlands along the water, and it's as if you've covered a few centuries in the space of five minutes. The sky is clear and for the first time on this journey I can see, to the north-west, the creamy peaks of the distant Alps.

This stretch of river was the site of one of the most notorious battles of the "Lombardy wars", fought between the Venetian Republic and the Duchy of Milano between 1423 and 1454. In June 1431, the Battle of Cremona saw thirty-seven Venetian galleons face off against fifty-six Milanese galleys. The Venetians might have won had one of their commanders (a former mercenary for the Milanese, Francesco Bussone, nicknamed "Carmagnola") not ignored appeals for assistance. The Venetians were routed, losing much of their fleet and seeing around ten thousand men either killed or captured. Carmagnola (his nickname came from the town on the Po, where he was from) was tried for treason and beheaded in May 1432.

I cross the river again, onto the right bank, and come to Monticelli d'Ongina with its grand Pallavicino-Casali castle, cracked and smeared with cement. There's a sagging badminton net in the grassy, waterless moat.

I've been waiting to get here, to the "isola Serafini", for weeks because this is where the Po is cut in half: this stretch of the river used to be omega-shaped, but in 1958 a channel was cut, and a hydroelectric dam constructed, creating an island as the channel completed the omega's circle. It was an engineering operation which had a devastating effect upstream. Sturgeon, eel and grey mullet could no longer pass beyond this point. Only in 2017 was a "fish ladder" constructed at a cost of €4.8 million: it now zigzags across the dam, allowing fish to pass – all, that is, except that familiar catfish which is supposed to be captured and exterminated.

It's an odd break in the flow of the river. At the moment, the downstream side of the dam has very low water. There are wide expanses of grey sand with wading birds. But a sign warns visitors of possible flood waves from the "hydraulic operations" and the water must sometimes be much higher as there are bundles of dead leaves and straw caught about seven or eight metres above the current level. Long flags of that light green plastic used to wrap bales of hay flap high above me.

You can hear the constant whine of a chainsaw and the groans of dumper trucks piled high with sand and gravel. I've read that between 1975 and 1985, almost 12 million cubic metres of lithoidal material (stones, pebbles and so on) were extracted from the Po every year. Between Cremona and Boretto, the riverbed was lowered by, on average, five metres, thus increasing its speed and erosive potential. I follow the Adda, one of the Po's largest tributaries, for half a day. Many of the roads here are just gravel tracks from one farm or hamlet to the next. There's a particular smell here of manure and damp and sand. "*Il lezzo fa il lazzo*", one local says to me: "the stench makes the jest" or perhaps "the party".

Irrigation ditches and channels run along the side of the fields, often blocked at one end with a gate called a *paratoia*. Now they're usually made of metal, but in the old days were little more than long wooden boards, like a wide cricket bat. Every estate round here used to have a *camparo*, the land warden, whose main role was the opening and closing of the gates, drawing what water was needed and moving on what wasn't. The Adda used to attract gold hunters (one document from 1061 reserves the right of the emperor to the proceeds of *aurilavatione* – "gold washing"), and it's thought that some of the gold the Cremonesi used to pay in tribute came from these clear waters.

I walk around the small towns. Pizzighettone has fat, grassy city walls and only one square tower survives from the old castle where the French king, François I, was once imprisoned after the Battle of Pavia in 1525. Its bridge over the Adda leads to Maleo, with its crenellated Palazzo Trecchi behind locked gates. Just south of here is one of the tightest loops of the Po (the name Corno, a tiny hamlet here, comes from the Latin for loop). From the apex of that sharp bend the river looks more like a lake with a slim island in the middle. That *pialassa* – the give and take of the delta – is just as evident here, with the river offering up its treasures or else eradicating whole settlements. Noceto was a small hamlet of, according to the 1809 census, 550 people. But the floods of 1839 and 1841 completely destroyed the village, wiping out the wooden shacks and the few brick buildings. They say that during droughts you can still see the remains of bricks in the silt and at night you can hear the tolling of the hamlet's sunken bell. What did survive was the wooden statue of San Michele, which floated downstream and is now brought back to the river in a procession every summer.

The river offers up other reminders of mortality. There's an area here called I Morti della Porchera ("the dead of the piggery"). Legend has it that in the mid-eighteenth century pigs started digging up human remains with their snouts in these floodplains. The corpses appeared to be those of foreign soldiers, possibly fatalities of the War of Austrian Succession or of the plague, who had either been hastily buried here or else had just washed up and sunk into the silt. A cross and later a small chapel were erected on the site which remains a source of ghoulish stories for local children.

The relationship between the river and religion is always interesting. When it's threatening to trespass on land, the water is treated as a sinner called to order by the clergy. Guido Conti tells the story of the time (back in the sixth century) when Sabino, the Bishop of Piacenza, was told by his deacon that the Po was flooding church lands. "Go and say to the river," Sabino said sternly, "the bishop has ordered you to calm down and return to your bed." The command was written down and the paper thrown in the river which obediently slunk away to its usual place.

In the modern era there are plenty of photographs of church crucifixes and saints being dipped in the water to allay the flooding, the priest's cassock being held by deacons to make sure he doesn't fall in face first. But at other times, rather than being a miscreant, the river is portrayed as a deity, either providential or vengeful. That is the other recurrent image of the Po through history – an omnipotent, Old Testament tyrant. It was whimsical, one day gifting gold, fish, firewood, gravel and even cadavers, but the next flooding farmlands, destroying crops and homes and claiming lives. What I didn't expect is that the river-as-god motif, so common through history and literature, also holds in our era of ecological crisis: scorned and ignored, it has been reduced to an obstacle. We no longer believe in the myths about the Po, that it is generous, fickle and awful. Like T. S. Eliot's river in *The Dry Salvages*, this "strong brown god" is "almost forgotten". And, like all things scorned, it has retreated. The river hasn't disappeared, of course, but it is in some ways vanishing, its droughts a "reminder / of what men choose to forget".

After the floods of the autumn, I'm amazed now by how low the water is. It's not yet spring, and there's already what people are referring to as "a potential hydrological crisis". When I set out I expected that the Po might contain fewer fish, or more pollutants, but not that the actual river itself might be slimming. It has barely rained here all through the winter, and farmers are now forced to draw on the river's waters, via canals and pump houses. But even those canals are now dry. In one village I walk through, there's a noticeboard which lists *le asciutte* ("the dried-ups"), with a table of all the irrigation channels which, drawing on the Po, are now "partially" or "totally" dried and listing the dates on which it is forbidden to draw water.

I ask a jovial villager to explain the implications of all these dried-up canals, and he chortles. "It means," he says, "that at night you see silhouettes scurrying to open and shut the sluice gates." Even now, in February, the water is so scarce that people are fighting over it. The hydrometric level of the river is currently -2.66 metres, which is around the level measured last August, at the height of summer. One agricultural union, Coldiretti, says that the river's flow is below a thousand cubic metres a second, 24 per cent less than the seasonal average. It's obvious to the naked eye: even on the upstream side of the dam you see long stretches of grey sand where the river has receded. The tributaries and runnels I pass are even thinner, often just ribbons taking up less than a tenth of their gravel beds.

I cross the river easily according to what interests me on one bank or the other. A few seconds and I'm over. But it never used to be so easy, and I'm slowly beginning to appreciate how one side can be – in its food, farming, dialects and habits – drastically different from the other. A river, after all, is where the word rival comes from. The contrasts are particularly marked on the stretch I'm now travelling. On the left bank it's very rustic. There's no big city near, and it's called, derisively,

"Magozia" ("yokel-land") by those on the right. Those who believe in progress would say that the right bank is centuries ahead: there's the white nuclear power station of Caorso (now decommissioned), the forest of chimneys as you crawl through industrialised Piacenza, the vast Amazon depot nestling in the crook of major motorways.

Piacenza has always been an important intersection: right next to the Po, it also sits on the old Via Emilia, connecting Rimini to Bologna and Milano, as well on the ancient Via Postumia, which linked the port of Genova to Aquileia in the far north-east of the country. So it was a regular place for imperial assemblies to resolve contentious issues. In the mid-twelfth century, Frederick Barbarossa was attempting to reassert his sovereignty over the increasingly wealthy municipalities of northern Italy, particularly Mediolanum (Milano). Barbarossa's "Constitutio de Regalibus", announced at the Second Diet of Roncaglia in November 1158, just outside Piacenza, decreed that all rivers and streams were *Viae Regiae* – property of the sovereign. Frederick didn't mince his words: dues were listed as "the 'arimannie' [the tributes due from the *arimanno*, a freeman], the public ways, the navigable rivers and those from which are derived navigable canals, the ports, the tributes which arise from the banks of the river... the levies commonly known as *telonei* [tariffs], the moneys... the *angarie* [work-in-kind]... the income from fishing and salt-flats..." The paragraph is long enough to leave the reader in no doubt that the emperor wanted the lot. Whoever controlled the water always knew it was a source of wealth.

The cities of northern Italy were unwilling to cede their newfound power and wealth to the emperor and within a decade, in November 1167, five major cities – Milano, Lodi, Piacenza, Parma and Ferrara – had created the "Lega Lombarda", swearing an oath of allegiance at the Abbey of Pontida. Within months, that alliance increased to thirty cities. Almost every important municipality of northern Italy – with the exception of Pavia and Como – joined the League and, in 1176, it won a decisive battle against Barbarossa at Legnano, north of Milano. The subsequent peace signed in Konstanz in 1183 makes amusing reading, with Barbarossa trying to reclaim his authority even as he gave away his powers:

> Although we should and could severely punish your crimes, nevertheless we prefer to govern in peace. In the name of the Holy Trinity, We Frederick, by the grace of God Emperor of the Romans, therefore concede to you, cities of the League, the regal rights [to impose taxes, mint coins and administer justice] and your statues forever... within the cities you can continue everything as you have done until now, without our interdiction...

The symbolism of that opposition to outside interference was revisited in the 1980s and 1990s by Umberto Bossi as he created the Northern League, a political party that called for secession from the rest of the peninsula. The Northern League had an annual festival at Pontida (where the 1176 oath had been signed), and was nicknamed *carroccio*, the four-wheeled, standard-bearing carriage of an Italian free city which became an icon of the military victory at Legnano. Bossi and his followers called their imagined country "Padania", a name taken from Padus, the old word for the River Po. Bossi used to travel to the Po's source and take a phial of its waters across the whole plain as a symbol that his fiefdom was the drainage basin of this river. Even now, long after Bossi's political eclipse, people often ask me if I'm a *leghista* when I tell them I'm travelling to the source.

The Diet of Roncaglia and its repercussions showed how important control of the river was for the incomes of those in power. Dues were paid on everything that moved, on all the *staie* or *moggi* ("bushels") of salt, wine, flour, livestock and all the rest. The river also offered plum positions in the civil service: the Capitano Ducale or, later, the Capitano della Darsena (of "the dock"). Taxation on land in the floodplains was contentious because the size of a person's landmass was constantly being eroded or added to by the hairpinning water. Sometimes a village even found itself, after the river had shifted, on the other side of the water: there's a place a few miles upstream of here called "Alluvione Cambiò", meaning basically "Flood Changed".

A mile or two west of Piacenza you come to the Trebbia river. A wide, wooded tributary, it's here that Hannibal, in December 218 BC during the Second Punic War, defeated the Roman army. It's said that, having reached Italy through Spain and France, he used his famous elephants to curb the speed of the Po, and allow his laden army to cross the river. It may be apocryphal, but there is now, beside the main road which runs alongside the Trebbia, a large sculpture of an elephant in memory of the battle. A local hamlet, too, is called Rottofreno because, according to legend, it was here that the bit (the *freno* or *morso*) of Hannibal's horse broke (*rotto*).

This area is where they used to grow and sell willow rods for supporting vines and vegetables. But the vineyards all use concrete posts now, and vegetables are held up by bamboo canes bought in garden centres. You sometimes see an old willow tree in a farmyard, but the coppicing of great plantations is long since finished.

I stay the night in one of those farms which seems out of time: chickens roam around the courtyard and it smells of woodsmoke and manure. The sky is turning dark orange and the clouds are candyfloss pink.

A few elderly men and women pass along the lane on bicycles. There's a brightly illuminated fishing lake and bar the other side of the field, and you can hear the guffaws of young men. Behind them, to the south, the Apennines are turning black, beginning to converge with the Alps in the north as I get closer to Monviso. Now that I can see the dark silhouettes of the Lesima and Penice mountains to the south, I'm absurdly relieved. After all the walking and wading, the paddling and peddling I'm still, here, only around 60 metres above sea level. But within a week or two I'll start the ascent, slowly at first, but the river will narrow and rise and I'll finally leave this immense plain behind.

For the next two days I cycle from one village castle to the next. Calendasco's is chickpea-beige and has been so absorbed into its agricultural surroundings that it's now just part of a tumbledown farmyard. I cross the river and ride to Chignolo, where the castle looks more like a grand villa and has a lawyer's brassy plate on the closed gate. At Belgioioso, the castle is covered with scaffolding that looks like it's been there for years.

I'm often reminded how rare that role of tavern host has become. When you hear people in Santa Vittoria or Roccabianca talk about a "host", it sounds like they're describing a man or woman who was like a confessor and counsellor, a cross between a GP and a priest. But now the bars are run by people completely unconnected to this land. That's not a complaint about immigration, but about culinary authenticity. In one bar I ask what cheeses there are. "Just tall cheese," the "host" says, holding her hands far apart, one above the other. She ducks under the counter and pulls out a long orange block that looks like a gate post.

I pass on the cheese and wander to San Zenone al Po. This small village was the birthplace of Gianni Brera, one of Italy's most admired journalists of the twentieth century. He invented perfect nicknames for a generation of footballers and coined an entire lexicon to describe aspects of the sport. But, having been born by the banks of the Po, he frequently tried to explain what the river meant to him. "It isn't really a river," he wrote, "but a drain at the bottom of the immense hull of Padania." He called it a *sentina*, a bilge or cesspit. Much of his life was spent trying to put into words what the river meant to the villagers who grew up so close to it that they could hear it at night: "it stretches out like a python," he once wrote, "now lazy, now infuriated."

But the metaphor Brera kept returning to was that of the drunken and unpredictable father, generous or scary according to his mood: he called the river "Padre Po" (a pun, perhaps, on the celebrated Capuchin friar Padre Pio), "a drunken father with an evil bellyful". That, he explained, was why "us river-dwellers hate our father": "the current smacks drunkenly from one side to the other: it corrodes and impoverishes, it deposits and makes rich."

Brera's birthplace was once on the other side of the river, on the right bank, until in the late fourteenth or early fifteenth century flooding caused the river to flow south and leave San Zenone al Po on the left bank, deprived of its rich fields. You can still see, in aerial photographs, the long arc the river used to flow along until it chose the straighter line. Perhaps because of that ancient change, Brera wrote that "riverside life is characterised by precariousness". The "cantankerous common father" of the Po creates, he wrote, "an atavistic, I would say biological, fear in Padanians. Their great river growls and wanders like a blindman from one side to the other. Noisy and sinister thuds occur. Whoever cultivates land along the riverbanks feels inside the anxiety of those who are having their bread removed." Brera calls the river (something you hear repeated in every village) *un fiume traditore*, a "traitorous" or "backstabbing river". The figures bear him out: in 1968 the flooding of the Po caused 72 deaths; in 1994, 68 lost their lives and in 2000, 44.

The village itself is a quiet, rustic place. Even the houses in the middle of the village have old barns which form courtyards and stables. It's the last settlement on the slim Olona, a Po tributary that's now only a few metres from joining that drunken father. I follow it and am soon at the roar of a sluice gate which grates the Olona into white foam. There's star-cucumber everywhere, hanging like fat cobwebs from the trees. I walk through a poplar plantation and come across one of those happily hillbilly sites: there are pallet armchairs, rattan sofas and a blue table-tennis table. The bar – a Portakabin floating on a pontoon – is 20 degrees off horizontal because the water is so low.

There's a young guy hanging out with his girlfriend. A few skiffs are moored to the pontoon and I ask if he's got one I can borrow. We agree that I'll leave my bike as a deposit but, looking at the boat, the bike might be worth more: its paint is flaking, the rowlocks are rusty and the transom is spongy on top. But he fills up the outboard motor and reckons I'll be in Pavia in an hour or so.

It's a lovely jaunt. When you're this low to the water, the trees and banks hide civilisation and you feel like a wild man again. Only the odd water or bell tower pokes above the willows and alders to puncture the fantasy. Occasionally a fallen tree has snagged in the riverbed, and a bare branch sticks out of the water like the arm of a drowning man.

A butterfly flits in front of the boat, bouncing to the other side. There are tangles of driftwood caught up in overhanging branches or sandbanks, and families of mallards gather in the protected lee.

Sandy flats emerge from the water, some covered in tall grass where ash herons and cormorants are crouching. One hydrometer I pass reads -2.8 metres. In the last serious floods, in 2000, the water was 7.9 metres above zero, so almost 11 metres above where it is today. The concrete cubes, dumped along the banks to stop erosion of these two-metre-high sand cliffs, are all exposed.

Quite soon I can see the double diagonals of the Ponte della

Becca. The kilometre-long bridge straddles both the Po and its left-bank tributary, the Ticino, and as I approach I can see clearly the difference between the two. The Po is, as ever, silty and murky whereas the Ticino – with its waters coming from Lake Maggiore – is so clear you can see the individual pebbles of its bed a metre or two below the surface.

I bear right, travelling up the tributary. The whole atmosphere of the river is different: it's smaller, and more humane somehow. There's a man in rubber dungarees thigh-deep in water with a rod. I pass houseboats with colourful murals: huge paintings of fish, or sandy, wooded islands and naked women. I'm briefly leaving the Po partly because I've always wanted to see Pavia, but also because this detour was an integral part of the Po's navigation route. When the Naviglio Pavese was constructed, between 1812 and 1819, the Po was finally connected to Milano (almost precisely due north of here).

Within a few minutes you can see the cupola and lantern of the Duomo in the distance above the trees. Then, as the river tacks left, the layers of the city come into view: the ruin of the 1926 concrete hangar for seaplanes and the sloping city walls topped by a boulevard of beeches. On the left are the coloured houses of Borgo Ticino – all different heights and hues, with neat gardens rolling towards the water where there are tarp-covered boats. Straight ahead is the city's famous covered bridge. It looks, deliberately, like a monastic cloister pulled into a line. There's a small chapel in the middle.

I tie up the boat on a pontoon at the edge of a park and wander into the city. History is deep here. Pavia lays claim to being the symbolic site of the fall of the Roman Empire. In 476, at what was then called Ticinum, the "Barbarian" statesman Odoacer besieged and killed Oreste, a Roman general who had appointed his sixteen-year-old son – Romulus Augustus – emperor. Odoacer was, probably, a Hun (his father had worked for the more famous Attila), and Gianni Brera was convinced that the word Po derived from the Hun word (from Mongol) for swamp, marsh or river.

From 572 to 774, Pavia was the capital of the Lombard kingdom. Columbanus, the Irish missionary, was welcomed here in 612 and given lands in the Trebbia valley, in Bobbio, by the king and queen. When the city was conquered by Charlemagne, the Romanesque Basilica of San Michele was used to crown seven Holy Roman Emperors as, also, Kings of Italy (including the power-grabbing Frederick Barbarossa). Another church holds the mortal remains of St Augustine. It's the sort of city where even the graffiti is highbrow: on one wall someone has spray-painted in Latin a quotation from Augustine *ama et fac quod vis* ("love and do what you will").

The Duomo itself, a red-brick building from the outside, is white inside. When I admit to one of the guides that I'm struggling to date the architectural period, she chuckles: "they started the building in 1488 and finished in 1898!" Just outside the Duomo is the stump of the Torre Civica. Built in the eleventh century, it inexplicably collapsed without warning at just before 9 a.m. on 17 March 1989, raining down 8,000 cubic metres of brick on the streets below. Four people were killed.

Pavia used to be called the city of a hundred towers, and around sixty still survive. Many have been absorbed into churches and other buildings, but half a dozen stand alone, square, brick testaments to human one-upmanship. I follow my nose and end up in the *broletto*, the petite courtyard where public meetings were once held. I wander to the stately Visconti castle – each side of the quadrangle is 150 metres, although one wing is missing – and back to the boat along the tree-lined canal with its old warehouses backing onto the water.

I head home facing the blue hills of the "Oltrepò Pavese", that part of the province of Pavia which is the "other side of the Po". It's a region known for its excellent wines. Thanks to its marly soil, it grows more Pinot Nero grapes than any other region outside Champagne. This Ponte della Becca was originally constructed (out of boats) to be able to move the grapes and wine to Pavia, and I wonder if its original name was actually "Ponte Bacco", of Bacchus, rather than (more likely) named after the Italian for woodcock, *beccaccia*.

If you know where to look when the water's low, you can see the ancient remains of old, flooded settlements like Sparvara and Borgofranco: they're just lumps of mortar in the river now. Precariousness was a way of life this close to the river. It wasn't just that the village could go under, but that new lands would emerge, and surrounding villages would go to war to claim the rights to emerging soils. The annals talk of a ferocious feud between Valenza and Frascarolo over the rights to a new island in the middle of the river. Another nearby village, Guazzora, solved potential disputes by decreeing that all new lands belonged to the local nobility, no one else. Each stretch of the river has its own dialect to capture this promiscuity of the Po, lying in one bed, then the next. It was like his *droit du rive*: *Al Po al va 'nté cal vò*, they say round here: "the Po goes where it wants."

It's hard to conceive of the river's rampancy because right now the Po seems, for the first time in my journey, shallow and narrow. It's cutting up into the first rapids, no bigger than meringues. I'm blissed out by it. Maybe it's just the season – the spring sky is a deep blue – or because things are getting easier. Occasionally, from the left bank, I can see a whole horizon of snow-capped Alps, even the equilateral peak of Monviso.

The colours of this floodplain make you tipsy: pinky flat-peas, purple sprays of cow vetch, blue love-in-a-mist sitting almost surprised on its bed of bouncy green string. There are larkspur purples and even the weeds, the bindweed and thistles, seem brave and beautiful.

Dozens of turquoise dragonflies hover and scram. A pair of flirting meadow browns bounce along, animal spirits leading me along this thin cut between nettles, horseweeds and goldenrods. It's 25 degrees and it's snowing: the sky is thick with poplar wool – *pappi dei pioppi* – that creates drifts in the green alleys.

I hear a clang between my sneezing. I think it's a church bell, probably for a funeral. But then there are other bells, odd tones and getting closer. I suddenly realise that about seventy-five steers have stormed the floodplain, about a third wearing large bells on leather necklaces as wide as your thigh. Now they're loving the vetch and you can hear their crunching beneath the lowing and banging. I climb up the bank and watch them for a while, entranced by the hypnotic noise.

I wander on to Valenza. It's a town famous for its goldsmiths and jewellers. It wasn't just the Po that attracted gold prospectors but also, they say, the River Orba, a few kilometres south of here, near Alessandria. As you walk around town, gold is obviously the theme: there are gold traders, fashion shops called "ingot", many jewellers and metalworkers. And as you cut away back to the river there's a black cube in the landscape, surrounded by about two hundred cars: the European HQ of Bulgari, the jewellery conglomerate.

The next day I walk towards Bozzole. Slowly the sounds become softer. There's a constant hiss, but it's hard to know if it's the water or the wind in the creamy spills of the robinia. The aspen's sound is different. Their whitish leaves sound like those little rapids: an almost inaudible sashaying which gives the tree its name: *Populus tremula.*

There are one or two other people around. Three caravans are parked up between tyre towers, solar panels and IBCs (those thousand-litre plastic cubes for storing water). Barking Alsatians are chained to poplars. From one well-hedged hideout, an old lady is staring at me from her deckchair while a handkerchiefed head bounces between the runner beans.

It's different this side of the water. Lusher, perhaps, certainly more hilly. That hiss isn't just the Po or the trees, but all the tributaries which cascade into it from the steep hills to my left, the river's right. They're the first inclines I've seen this whole journey.

Quite soon there's a bridge off to my right. It's narrow and the traffic on it is heavy, but I want to get into Lomellina so I cross over. This is rice country. By chance I've arrived at the perfect time: the waters of the paddy fields mirror the sky but are also just beginning to show a haze of green. Egrets pick their way through it, pincering up worms and tadpoles. This area has the sweet smell of elderflower mixed with the stench of the seaside at low tide. It's high spring now and, after weeks of rain, the vegetation is bursting. Some of the fields have a diagonal line, a trench the width of a shoe box. This *acquaiolo* creates an even distribution of the water across the field.

About two-thirds of these fields are rice, the rest is wheat. Renata Viganò captured the colours of these Lomellina fields in her 1952 pamphlet, *Mondine*: "there's the red-gold to the wheat – here the grain isn't blond as ours is, but has a Titianesque violence, a flame on the ears – and then there's the blue-green of the paddy fields..." She was being uncharacteristically lyrical, but she captures the shimmering vibrancy of these fields, all the tissue-paper poppies and cornflowers. Overhead photographs often resemble tulip plantations, all radically different colours: silver, red, gold. But at ground level it's more subtle, an array of whispering shades depending on where you stand.

Lomellina is one of those territories that even most Italians haven't heard of. An area of land about 1,200 square kilometres, with about 200,000 inhabitants, it's defined by four waterways: the Cavour Canal to the north, the Sesia river to the west, the Po to the south and the Ticino to the east. Its heyday was around a thousand years ago, when the main route between the Lombard glories of Torino and Pavia was through what was then dense, damp forests. There's so much moisture in the soil that a well, in dialect, is called a *surbia* – an absorber. The most well-heeled travellers crossed the River Sesia at Cozzo, headed south to Breme Abbey, then to the Provost's castle at Sartirana, to Lomello – the town which gives this land its name – and onwards to Ticinum (Pavia).

There were important monasteries on that route: Lucedio, Pobietto, Breme and Acqualunga. They oversaw the construction of hundreds of canals and ditches and effectively turned themselves into the central banks for the local currency: water. Controlling the flow and the access put them in a position of power because flowing water was needed to drive mills, to water livestock, to wash clothes and irrigate fields. Monasteries sometimes farmed the land themselves – employing a grangerius, the head of the grange – or else offered their waters to local peasants in return for up to a sixth of their harvest. Rice began to be cultivated here by monasteries in the fifteenth century since it was the ideal crop for these often sodden lands: "rice is born in water", a local saying goes, "and dies in wine".

Rice cultivation really only took off, however, with the construction of the canal which closes Lomellina to the north. Built in the mid-1860s, the Cavour Canal – between Chivasso and Novara, to the north of the Po – meant that paddy fields now had a controllable, countable source of water. The canal was designed by an unsung hero of the Risorgimento, Carlo Noè, who back in 1859 had flooded the area between the Dora Baltea and Sesia rivers to impede the Austrians' advance during the War of Independence that led to a united Italy. Noè's canal is 82 kilometres long, with 101 bridges and 210 siphons drawing off the Po's waters and distributing them across over 300,000 hectares. The speed of completion, despite engineering complexities, was a symbol of the new nation's confidence. "In little more than a century," wrote the agronomist Salvatore Pugliese in 1927, "a vast country that was largely uncultivated, sparsely populated and covered with scrub, has turned into a very fertile region, rich in inhabitants."

Rice quickly came to dominate agriculture after the canal's construction. At the beginning of the nineteenth century, only 6 per cent of this region was involved in rice production. By 2000 it was 61 per cent. Italian cultivars became famous, named after a bureaucrat in the National Rice Organisation (Carnaroli, which is often used for risotto), an agronomist (Marchetti) or a place (Arborio, another type used for risotto). Historically, it was a labour-intensive crop that required manual weeding and, as usual when thousands of low-skilled labourers are employed, estates were desperate to minimise their costs. A 1903 report from the Milano Labour Office found that here, in Pobietto, daily wages varied from one lira sixty to one lira ninety in return for ten hours' work. To put that L.1.60–1.90 into perspective, one bridge tariff record, from ten years earlier, suggests that it cost L.0.05 just to cross a Po bridge on foot. Being poor is always expensive.

Photographs from the late nineteenth and early twentieth centuries show men acting almost as armed guards to the weeding women, called *mondine*. A man stands on the bank with a scythe in hand, whetstone in the horn on his belt. He surfs on the mud, riding a wooden plank drawn by a horse, raking the flooded mounds level with its iron rudders underneath, a process called *slottatura*. The rider stood astride the plank and shouted orders to the horse and the women.

All the interviews with former *mondine* mention *miseria*: the poverty or wretchedness. The women were bent over all day with their legs and forearms in the water. Being away from their homes for forty days gave the weeders' work a sense of grim, Lenten suffering. They lived in improvised dormitories in stables and barns, using *scartocci* (corn on the cob's parchment envelope) as mattresses. They washed in ditches, ponds or at public taps. Provisions were meagre: most days it was only rice and beans. There was sometimes a *pietanza*, the mercy victuals of 100 grams of bread a week, 100 of cheese and 150 of jam. Occasionally they trapped a duck, or a few frogs, and had a stew (having to hide the cooking smell from the gangmaster).

They squelched barefoot through fields which had last year's wheat stubble in the muddy mix, its sharp spears cutting soles and snapping nails. They were prey to horseflies, mosquitos and leeches. Grass snakes and frogs were no danger, but many didn't like the slithering animals which became concentrated in one section as the lines of weeders – there were normally twelve to sixteen in each line – converged. Sometimes a farmhand would appear with a wooden barrel and the *mondine* would slake their thirst by all sharing a diminutive pewter mug.

The *mondine* culture is celebrated by many as a cradle of socialist ardour and moving musical defiance, a time in which women banded together and fought for their rights. Because of their songs they were often nicknamed *rane*, "frogs" – a nickname which, like most, sounds derisive or admiring depending on who used it. Singing bent over wasn't ideal, but they did it, they said, to warm themselves up when, at 5 a.m., they started working in the cold water, or towards lunch to quieten their stomachs which had only had a half-glass of milk for breakfast. The music was a sort of Lombardia-blues, borrowing from folk, socialist, soldier and partisan songs, almost all in a minor key and with a febrile soprano that usually slides up and down to find the right note. Recordings from ethnomusicologists were often made in the field, and you can hear the splash as the line of women advance and retreat through the water. There's something almost bagpipey to the tight, whining sound: a male drone joins from the sidelines, or a woman sustains a high note for bar after bar. Some songs have the oompah of an accordion, but mostly they're dull lamentations, sung bent over as voices bounced off the water. Despite the caustic tone of the songs, they were encouraged by the gangmasters as they were thought to diminish gossip and increase productivity by maintaining a rhythm to the work.

"*O cara mamma vienimi incontro*" goes one song: "Oh dear mother come to me". In "Hear the Frogs That Sing", they urge their lovers, and parents, not to cry that they had gone away to this hardship. But as well as laments for those they loved, there were faster, stampier songs for those they didn't: "Shut it, shut it, husband mine" or "I'm the *mondina* and I'm exploited". Quite a few of the songs allude to the battle for an eight-hour day. Unions were formed (called Leagues) and there were fatalities during strikes. Renata Viganò was inspired to write *Mondine* by the death of Maria Margotti, aged thirty-four. Already a widow, Margotti was killed during a protest against strike breakers' brutality in May 1949. "On one side is hunger," Viganò wrote, "and on the other side is a piece of bread. In between is slavery."

Back home, gossip was rife about these women who worked in distant paddy fields with their legs exposed and who returned home not only with a few hundred lire and bags of rice but also with new ideas about rights and wages. Those who hadn't left gossiped about what romantic stories might have taken place in those forty days and, in the 1950s, films glamorised the strife, mixing up hard farming with a crime story (in *Riso Amaro*) or a love story (*La Risaia*). But it's strange wandering around now as the fields are completely empty. Pesticides and tractors have replaced the songs. In Valeggio, vines and creepers have covered the turrets of the castle, so you can only work out its rough shape from the bushes hiding it. The paint you still see on stable doors – "Women's Dormitory" – is fading from red to cracked pink. It's the same story in Scaldasole, where only the roof of a square turret pokes out above the greenery. Windows are empty. Castles have become farm courtyards and farm courtyards have become car parks.

But the locals' insouciance towards architectural demise gives Lomellina an odd restfulness. There are narrow, cobbled alleys with high brick walls which snake between the forts and the bars. It's very different from Emilia: the villages are narrower, more hidden or sheltered. In the middle of the villages are football pitches and mini cinemas. And there's certainly civic pride: houses have certificates if they've been repainted brightly and are considered "chromatically requalified". One brick flue from a demolished furnace teeters over a sports ground. Another bends like a banana next to a fenced-off ruin.

The ancient monasteries have mostly been converted to farms called *grance* (granges for the grains), so you sometimes chance upon a modern agricultural operation with unexpectedly ancient quadrangles and cloisters. In summer women used to work the rice in these courtyards, using a *ventilabro* – like a cupped oar – to throw it in the air to separate the grain from the husk. They would rake it back and forth, attempting to dry it in this notoriously moist location. The big estates had industrialised driers, because any humidity reduced the price. Those who weren't desperate for payback on their investment would store the rice in great silos until the price rose in winter.

The poor, meanwhile, caught what they could. As the fields were drained in August, the frog catchers trawled the remaining damp spaces with a small frog attached to a stick to attract the others. As the frog catcher put the captured animals in his bag he broke their legs to keep them there. There were fish, too, and anglers carried tiny amounts of explosives which they cracked in an iron pestle to scare off those rival anglers, the herons. As autumn turned to winter there were other means of making small change. In these low-lying lands, there were many frost pockets. Running water was no good for making ice but the *roggie* – the steep, low ditches – frequently had an inch or two of ice in late November or early December. The peasants said you had to get the ice in the ice rooms by the day of the Immaculate Conception, 8 December, or else it was hopeless. Soon after that the days started getting longer. So those who were scratching a living would go round cracking the surface of the drainage channels in late autumn, bringing the packed sheets of ice to the underground iceries of the old monasteries.

The complexity of water distribution in this rice-growing area reminds me how much it is a resource which is shared rather than hoarded. To ensure a fair distribution of both costs and water there are over a thousand irrigation consortia in Piemonte alone, covering overall around half a million hectares of land. Water enforces associationism because it's neither constant nor, normally, static: although we try to control them, flows are erratic and water's inevitable movement means that neighbours have to come to tricky accords. One rice grower I talk to, who rents around a hundred hectares, tells me that the flow across his land, from now until mid-August, is around 300 litres of water per second. I ask him to repeat this as it sounds absurd, so he takes me to a bridge over a bullet-straight canal: the water, three metres wide, is flowing at about the speed of a sprinter. Other channels and ditches cross his land, cascading onto his fields when he opens the sluice gates and then flowing onwards onto the farms beyond his. It means the rice growers are all connected and rely on those who use the water before them not to contaminate the currency. It's similar to the key challenge faced by Aipo, the Inter-regional Agency for the River Po, which is persuading different legislative regions to reach agreements for the benefit of the whole river.

In his excellent book *Water: A Biography*, Giulio Boccaletti traces how democracy in the ancient world was, in part, driven by the need to "develop institutions to manage the consequences of a sedentary life in a world of moving water...". Water became an element through which citizenship was defined, with the state mediating between the demands of individual liberty and the public good. Notions of citizenship, its rights and responsibilities, are still refracted through water. Many peasants had to fight for the right to *samboira*, a concession to use waters from midday on Saturday to midday on Sunday when it wasn't required for the irrigation and milling operations of the large estates. It led to fights and endless legal actions because the water for irrigation was vital in those dry summer months when millers were working full time grinding wheat, barley, chestnuts, chickpeas, rye and oats. That communal nature of water management is apparent in many villages where you see the remains of washhouses: open-air structures with low walls sloping at 45 degrees towards the wet centre. Many have been demolished, but the occasional ruin reminds me of how much more we used to share both chores and resources. Dirty laundry used always to be public because there was no other place to wash it.

SEVEN

Monferrato and Torino

MONFERRATO AND TORINO

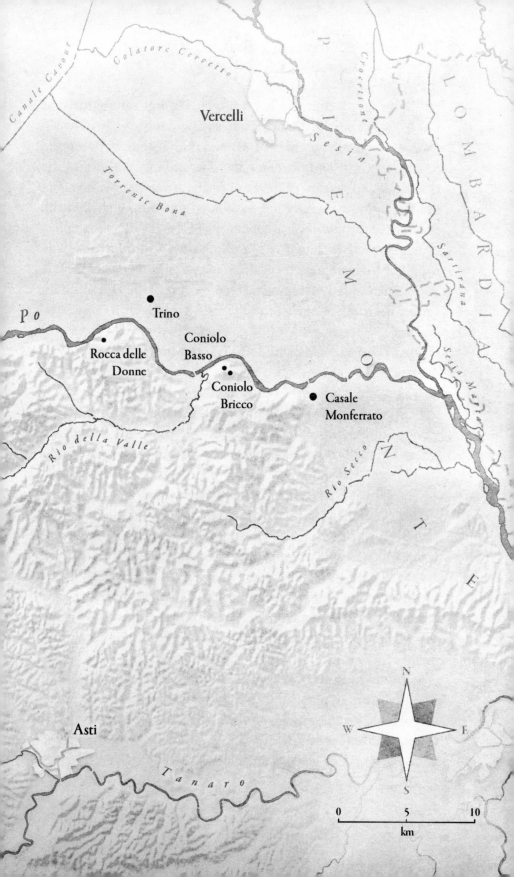

C asale Monferrato is a genteel city, but for centuries it was a fortified marquisate sitting dangerously between the powerful cities of Milano and Torino, between the Sforza, Visconti and Savoia clans. The old city walls, and the casemates and ravelins of the great castle, are almost overhanging the Po. By now the city has expanded north, too, so that the river slices through it.

Legend has it that this area, known as Monferrato, was founded because of a love affair in the mid-tenth century. A young man called Aleramo was at the court of the Holy Roman Emperor, Otto I, in Aachen, and fell in love with Otto's daughter, Adelasia. The couple eloped to Albenga (between Nice and Genova) and had seven children. The red and white of the city's coat of arms echoes, it is said, the colour of the horses that Aleramo and Adelasia rode during their elopement. Years later the city of Brescia rebelled against the emperor and Aleramo came to the rescue. He was reconciled with his wife's father who offered him all the lands between the Po and the Tanaro rivers that he could cover on a horse in three days.

The dynasty Aleramo founded, known as the Aleramici, became militarily important in the Middle Ages. During the Crusades, one marquis, Corrado, even became, briefly, King of Jerusalem before he was murdered there in 1192. The marquisate eventually fell into the Gonzagas' hands through marriage to the niece of the last, son-less marquis. As well as murdering the late marquis's illegitimate son, the Gonzagas also boosted the city's defences, expanding the castle's fortifications and putting down rebellions.

It's a town famous for strange things: for its expertise in refrigeration engineering, for an asbestos factory which is responsible for hundreds of local deaths and for biscuits called *krumiri*. *Crumiro* is the word for a scab or blackleg, often come across in workers' leaflets and speeches during strikes. It comes from the name of the Saharan tribe the Khumir, who opposed French occupation in the nineteenth century and who were thus deemed to be "barbarians". The serrated, boomerang-shaped biscuits (supposed to commemorate the bushy moustaches of King Vittorio Emanuele II) were presumably called *krumiri* simply because the name sounded exotic.

In many ways, this first part of Piemonte is chocolate-box beautiful: as soon as you leave the one-field floodplain, the dirt roads and gravel tracks hairpin into the hills to the south of the river and you find yourself in a landscape that looks more like a wet Tuscany: avenues of vines follow the contours, slender towers emerge from a cluster of houses on the horizon, still-green wheat fields roll lazily into one another, grand drives are lined with cypresses.

But cycling through the villages, I become aware of something different. Some of the towers turn out to be mine shafts: square and tall, but windowless. Narrow, terraced cottages remind me of Welsh holidays with my grandparents: nineteenth-century rows that can only be miners' barracks. I'm not pedalling fast, but I soon lose count of all the ventilation shafts and pit-heads I see in the middle of the wheat.

The reason for these mines, I discover, was marl. This impure argillaceous limestone had been used as mortar in stone and brick constructions ever since Roman times and much of Casale Monferrato, including its grand fortress, was built using marl from Coniolo, a small village just above the Po. The abandoned flues and furnaces I see around here were used to cook up the limestone that was also used to build the new railway network around Torino and Casale Monferrato.

In the mid-nineteenth century, chemists had proved that this pale rock, abundant under these vineyards, was the perfect mixer to make "natural cement" thanks to its high content of iron oxide. It was less prone to problems with water, and open-shaft mines began to appear. By 1846, there were eleven in Coniolo alone, each turning the landscape a sickly grey. It was like a gold rush: over the course of the second half of the nineteenth century, business boomed, and railways, weigh stations, pit shafts and storage bays spread across the nearby hills. There were five bridges or elementary rigs over the Po in this one arc, allowing the rock to reach Morano sul Po, the other side, where it was crushed, processed and floated downstream to the fast-growing cities to the east. This part of Piemonte was also developing ever-faster ways to extract minerals and rocks through the use of dynamite: Ascanio Sobrero, born in Casale Monferrato, spent much of his professional life researching explosives, and his discovery of nitroglycerine (after working with Alfred Nobel in Torino) enabled marl mines to increase production exponentially. Suddenly there weren't just a few metres of tunnels, but whole kilometres chasing veins in all directions.

Coniolo was perched just above the river. The steep walk from riverside to church only took five minutes at most. In 1901, the village's marquis, Evasio Fassati, granted mining rights to an industrialist for one thousand lire per year. The mining here was ruthless because transport costs were negligible. Coniolo was directly in front of Morano sul Po, with its vast depots on the flat side of the river. But by 1904, some villagers were noticing problems. Glass "spies" were attached to walls, and many pinged as the mortar pulled them apart. The village bell tower, standing at 14.5 metres, was measured to be 30 centimetres off vertical. The marquis noticed that his 25-metre-deep well was broken in two places. The mining was clearly causing subsidence.

The marquis, Fassati, started legal proceedings against the mining entrepreneur from across the water, Francesco Bertone. Bertone had become so wealthy he made an offer for seventy of the houses in the village. The marquis, of course, refused to sell, though his estate quickly passed to Bertone after an intermediary purchase. By 1911, many of the villagers were slowly dismantling their houses and taking the bricks and stones another kilometre or two up the hill. They were creating Coniolo Bricco (higher Coniolo). Even there, on the higher land, another thirteen houses had to be abandoned.

They heard and saw what happened to their old village: once or twice a week another wall or roof down there fell to the ground. As the world went to war, their streets, church, barns and manor all gradually subsided and disappeared. By the time those soldiers returned from the First World War, Coniolo had gone: it had been turned into a quarry, and Coniolo Bricco had replaced it. But they still kept dying in the mines because, unlike agricultural work, it wasn't seasonal. Mining offered a year-round wage, and so anyone who could brave it became a miner in spite of the risks: two miners, a fifty-one-year-old and a fourteen-year-old, died in 1923. Another died in 1929, and three more in 1933. But when you cycle around here there's no evidence of any of that. The remains of the village lie under a woodland. All you can see are bridge plinths and teleferique loading bays poking out amid the oaks.

As I'm walking along this soggy floodplain of mugwort, Japanese knotweed and elderflower copses, I hear clanging bells again. The shepherd at the front is walking slowly with a stick. He's seen and ignored me. The flock keeps coming – about seven hundred sheep, two hundred goats and a dozen donkeys. There's another shepherd at the back who looks like the twin of the first.

"*Disturbo?*" I ask as I walk towards him.

He shakes his head.

Lori is from Biella and has, he says, almost a thousand animals here. He's moving them through this floodplain, up and down to munch it clean before taking them up into the hills in high summer.

We talk figures. He says he slaughters some four hundred and fifty animals a year, and gets around €2–2.5 per kilo of lamb. Given that each animal probably gives him twenty kilos of meat, that means around €16–22K of meat that the brothers sell. I ask what other income he has, and he shrugs: a bit of goat meat for specialised markets, bit of milk, the fleeces.

I tell him how I used to get flustered looking after a flock of twenty sheep and that he seems very chilled with a thousand animals. He smiles: "where are they going to go?"

I'm at Rocca delle Donne, "the women's fortress". Apart from bridge crossings, it's the first time I've seen the Po from far above. From up here I can see the river for dozens of miles: it's straightish towards Casale heading east, but to the west it bends left and right towards Torino and the Alps like a stereotypical serpent.

Very little is known about this notorious nunnery which, perched right above the river on the edge of a steep hill, became another stronghold to control and tax merchandise travelling up and down the Po. The nunnery was suppressed in 1492 by Pope Alexander VI, who accused the abbess and her nuns of "unruly behaviour". I like to think it was their strength, more than their morals, that concerned the authorities. There's something very evocative in this place name – "the women's fortress" – but the only remaining buildings have become ochre-stoned homes and whatever went on here is long forgotten.

On the other bank, amid the shining rice fields and roads, there's a patch of green that looks like moss on the chequered sea. The greenery is vast and its outline oddly linear. Its footprint is far bigger than the nearby town, Trino, and from up here – through the binoculars – it looks slightly raised. (Later I look at maps which show that the 575-hectare woodland sits a slight bump of 50 metres above sea level which, on that flat left bank, is akin to being mountainous.) The cut-off south-east corner suggests agricultural encroachment. This is – it's a bit of a mouthful – the "Bosco delle sorti della partecipanza" ("the woodland of the fates of participation" or perhaps just "the woodland of chance").

It's an easy drop down into Trino, zigzagging down the hill and over the busy bridge. The woodland's HQ is a courtyard with tractors, planks spaced apart for seasoning, men in green overalls and a small weigh station. The yard entrance is marked by a pediment announcing, next to a stone crest, "Partecipanza dei Boschi".

The leader is called "the first conservator": Ivano is a small man who is briskly bilingual, talking in dialect to the men and scholarly Italian to me. He has the same surname as many of the "participants" of this woodland: Ferraroti. The historian sitting in on our interview, himself a former "first conservator", is an unrelated Ferraroti. Participation in this woodland is by inheritance alone, and back in 1275, when it was founded, the village didn't have many surnames.

The woodland was a gift to the people of Trino from the Marquis of Monferrato, Guglielmo the Great, in gratitude for their taking his side in the war against the Vercellesi to the north. It's a woodland which appears both an example of the purest communalism but also, at the same time, of immovable traditionalism. Left-wingers in the early twentieth century wrote about it as "a collectivist society par excellence" and as "a concrete example of communism". But it is also exclusionary in a way unthinkable in our era: because one's lot is passed on exclusively by inheritance, only about one-tenth of the town's current population owns a share in the woodland (roughly 750 out of 7,437). At present there are, in all, 1,376 participants, although almost half are considered *foresi* (dialect for out-of-towners) and therefore benefit only from one *quartarolo* (felling patch) instead of two. Like many long-running communities, the "woodland of the fates" has developed its own language which makes it appear, to outsiders, both poetic and mildly incomprehensible. They call the tallest trees, those which aren't felled, *le quinte*, the "backstage" or "wings", because they're the trees that create the great spectacle.

One of the things I find most intriguing about this wise project is that, for all the idealism, at its centre is pure chance: lots are drawn to assign every participant's felling allocation, hence the name of the woodland. That lot drawing is a Sunday morning pageant that takes place in November, and so usually involves wine and joviality. A grand sheet lists the names of all those who have requested to be entered in the draw so that they can be assigned their share of the take. Seven leaders take turns to draw from their seven urns the names of every single participant. If you have two *quartaroli*, one will be on the sunrise side of the woodland, one on the sunset side of the felling area. You have until the end of March to fell, and until the end of April to clear. Thousands of waist-high, wrist-wide sticks mark the perfect rectangles for the participants. But being a naturally regenerated, deciduous woodland, there are differences between felling sections: sometimes the *quartarolo* might contain only around three tonnes of timber, but if your draw is good you might be close to eighteen or nineteen tonnes. A large area is set aside for those who draw a poor lot (with an estimate of less than three tonnes) and who are thus able to supplement their own harvest with some timber from another common area. As with everything about the Bosco, it's been thoroughly thought through.

By now it's a truism in western political thought that holding land communally is deleterious. Ever since the 1968 publication of Garrett Hardin's "The Tragedy of the Commons", privateers have pontificated about how collectivism dissolves and dissipates resources. But here are 575 hectares which, over almost eight centuries, tell a radically different story. Bruno Ferraroti, the historian, tells me: "there's always been this desire and capacity to hold to our rules. Our ancestors always made it clear that, even in difficult periods, the woodland itself had a value. No one has ever profiteered." That's not quite true: the Bosco sold 157 hectares in 1593, and fourteen in 1868, but on the whole it has remained absolutely faithful to its founding vision. It has even acquired a further 40 hectares in the last thirty years.

But the preservation isn't just about the surface area. Here you get a faint inkling, for the first time, of what this landscape looked like in the Middle Ages. There are species and sizes of trees I've never seen in northern Italy. I admire the grey, corkscrewing bark of hornbeam copses, and Ivano tells me how cobblers still come here to source hornbeam timber to make their most resilient heels. There are, of course, hazels, elms, cherries, maples and alder, but there's high forest, too, some of the "standards" (the fully-grown trees surrounded by coppiced areas) being almost 30 metres tall. In each hectare of the take, between around fifty and a hundred trees are excluded from felling, both the largest trees and the chosen *matricine* (saplings). The forestry management is all best practice: brash (the tangles of unwanted branches) protects the coppice and, eventually, turns to mulch. The non-native trees – the robinia and red oaks – are slowly being eliminated in favour of the natives.

It's not only the trees that make this place different. I see a glossy ibis, dipping its bent beak into a marshy edge. The understorey is all quaking sedge, wood anemones, comfrey, marsh marigolds, hairy hazelworts and butcher's-broom. The only hint that all isn't quite natural are the notched and painted sticks that identify the rectangular cutting areas. This used to be a sacred wood: the nearby hamlet is called Lucedio, probably an evolution from Lucus Dei – God's Woodland – and it's hard here not to sense a refraction of light which takes you into a deeper dimension, at one with other beings.

Not that participation has always been open to all. Although women could inherit the right to participate, as early as 1493 that share could be forcibly purchased by the Bosco for 180 florins. By 1528, female participation was being bought for 200 florins and in 1904 the going rate was 141 lire. Women were excluded not only due to prejudices about their inadequacy for forestry work, but for two subtler reasons: to ensure that population growth wouldn't dilute each share, and to encourage male residency in the town in those centuries which were renowned for invasions and incursions from rival marquisates. The result was that, in 1903, of 1,036 participants, there were only forty-one women; and in 1957, when the number of participants was at a record 1,639, there were only 190. So as well as the collectivist ideals of the space, it's also the stark traditionalism that strikes you: the same surnames go on through the centuries and a surname from Torino, let alone from outside Italy, is seen by some as a dilution of Trinesi blood.

But they have a sternness that I find hard not to admire: any participant responsible for damage or theft is excluded from the woodland for ten years. And it has modernised. Its new rule book of 38 Articles (agreed in July 2014) now allows for inheritance from both male and female lines. Two *quartaroli* are now set aside for local schools and four for public buildings. It's a solid operation and, understandably, they take themselves seriously: Bruno shows me their most ancient parchments and describes how the statutes have evolved over centuries. He laments the difficulties of the woodland now having to negotiate with the "Piemontese Park of the Po" quango. Funding is being reduced at a time in which participation in the Bosco is worth ever less: firewood is devalued because it's hardly used now for heating and cooking, so the woodland increasingly rents out areas to commercial operations which harvest wood for floorboards and prestige furniture. There are some, the excluded Trinesi, who don't think that this "pooling of private interests" should receive public funding anyway, so the woodland is repeatedly having to justify its existence. There are hydrological challenges, too, since the hundreds of thousands of hectares of paddy fields siphon off water resources. Like all large collectivist entities, the Bosco della Partecipanza is constantly negotiating and evolving.

And at the heart of it is luck. The woodland still uses its Latin description on official documents: "Partecipantia Nemorum Tridini Quae Sortes Vocantur" – "the Trinese's participant glades known as the fates". Being a "woodland of the fates" gives it a sense of destiny, as if it was meant to be. It's a reflection on human greed that this randomness has preserved the environment better than deliberate intervention and rationality. For centuries Trinesi have entrusted to luck a central role in the distribution of their precious timber and I like to think it's because, back in the thirteenth century, they trusted both each other and nature's generosity. Perhaps that's my romanticist's take, but it seems clear that chance can reduce that recurrent problem in communalism – a perception of unfairness. It's hard to complain you've been hard done by when resource assignation is purely down to chance.

I'm conscious that I've been looking at the river from all directions bar one. I've flipped regularly from left to right bank and, most of the day, have been facing the current as I journey upstream. But I haven't looked back, towards the sea. Now that the walk is just beginning to go uphill, I'm pondering the water's direction much more. And I'm still asking myself why I'm going "the wrong way" in the first place. I know I would never have embarked on this exploration downhill but am now curious about why not. Perhaps it's something to do with water as a metaphor for conformism, ever obedient to the pull of gravity. The great oral historian and partisan Nuto Revelli struggled after the war to understand the "agnostic attitude" of his Cunese compatriots towards the partisans. One senses his reserved bewilderment that relatively few gave active help to the partisans and their cause. His explanation was that "our peasant is prudent and never or almost never goes against the current". To prove the point, he quotes a local proverb: "'*l'acqua enta sempre lasela 'ndé 'n tel bas'*" – "water must always be allowed to go downwards".

It's probably my reluctance to go with the flow that made me instinctively journey from delta to source. Given the journey has been almost horizontal thus far, it's not been that much harder, but it's definitely an odd choice and I'm noticing it more now as the river slowly begins to ripple and the footpaths are no longer always horizontal. So I'm trying to understand why I'm going in this direction. Perhaps there's an aloofness or arrogance in me, or simply a longing to go solo after years of communal living (as a family we lived in a micro-community for eight years, meaning that a dozen of us shared every meal). But I also enjoy the extra effort of going against the current. I like the ache in the arms when I'm canoeing and in the legs when I'm walking, knowing that the reward is up there, in those mountains where the river slims to nothing. Most of all, I want to save the best till last, and the smaller the Po becomes, the more I appreciate its unexpected fragility.

With every few miles, the river is shallower, too. It's still more than a metre deep in places, but there are more patches in which it stretches over gravelly inclines and it bubbles as if you've chucked salt into boiling water. Sometimes I can't get a purchase with the paddle now as it scrapes on the riverbed. So I do something I hadn't planned on doing. I'm reluctant less because of the repetition than the narrative inconsistency, but I turn the boat around. I go with the flow.

Immediately the river feels different. Those cubes and offcuts of concrete which are always piled on the outside of the river are suddenly a real nuisance. Blocked by those lumps, the river slowly goes deeper that side, sucking the sand from under the blocks so that they gradually tumble further into the water. The regular edges of the cubes stick out now, so that you have to stand in the boat to see what's coming. When the water pushes you wide, among the fallen trunks and the concrete blocks, you inevitably snare the prow. The current pushes down on the starboard side and the wide-open canoe takes on water fast, and before you know it you're having to lean over the other edge to compensate. There's nothing dangerous in it, but the thoughtlessness of that concrete dumping – when trees could do a far better job to remediate erosion and flooding – is riling.

You can see more, though, because much of the time you're just drifting, idly nudging the craft away from where it might snag on the gravel. When the river straightens there are cliffs, two or three metres of vertical, dense sand pocked with hundreds of holes. This is where the *gruccione*, the European bee-eater, hides out. Sometimes you just see its copper and yellow head poking out, scanning for insects to snatch from the air. Those holes go back a few metres into the sand, protecting the birds' eggs from predators.

The tributaries here are so different from this direction and you can see how they affect the master. The Orco tinkles in from the left, its waters very shallow and clear, but the Po soon absorbs it and goes back to its habitual grey murk. A bit later, the Dora Baltea bombs round the corner from the left, and the current is sharper and much colder. In between, much of the river's water is drawn off by the beginning of the Cavour Canal.

I carry the boat over the slippery rocks, among the freshwater mussels, and plonk it down on the far side of the weir.

But the familiar detritus of human stupidity is everywhere: a shoe, an orange table-tennis ball, a paint bucket bobbing like a coracle, two blue and orange Nerf-gun bullets. I'm only seeing a fraction of what academics have already measured: in one three-month period in 2018, 220 kilograms of rubbish were pulled from the Po at Pontelagoscuro, of which 92.6 were plastics. One 2020 study revealed that the number of microplastics found in a cubic metre of Po water oscillated between two and eight items. It doesn't sound like much until one remembers that the river has a daily flow rate of between 50 and 80 million cubic metres. Trees filter the refuse, the ensnared driftwood in their high branches acting like colanders capturing the plastics. The salad leaves of plastic go two or three metres up the tree, to wherever the river has shrugged them off in recent months. But I wonder about what's not visible, too: environmental health scientists have calculated that the total loads of antibiotics carried by the river (predominantly ciprofloxacin, ofloxacin, lincomycin and vancomycin) rose, in one sampling site, to as much as 5.8 kilograms of active ingredients per day.

It's early summer now and there are crescents of white stones forming beaches on the inside of the bends. The melancholy dissipates when you wander around: a fallen trunk has created a long bench, slightly lower on one side so even those with short legs can get up. It looks designed for an all-age group. I sit on it, eat some of yesterday's cake and watch the bee-eater's aerial battles.

Between Chivasso and Torino, the river is squeezed between converging main roads. When there's no bike path next to the river, I find myself weaving across dual carriageways. The Po is stretched shallow now on white stones, and as it shrinks it leaves tiny fish in ponds created by fly-tipped concrete and snagged trunks. They won't last a week if it stays this hot.

A bushy maple is hanging on in the dry gravel, its trunk thick as a child's thigh. Its wafery leaves are aglow with the afternoon sun. I can see the Basilica of Superga on the hill up to the left, the first sign that I'm almost in Torino.

But the denser the industrialisation, the sweeter the hippie spots in riverside clearings. One – with a wooden sign calling itself *teatro fuori* ("outside theatre") – has seats, books, costumes and sayings. One of the handwritten signs urges travellers to listen to the river, so I walk the dozen paces to the beach through Japanese knotweed. Suddenly you can hear rapids. The noise is the same but constantly different, like brushing chains. It's a relief to think that the river finally has a drop (I'm still, incredibly, only at 230 metres above sea level). But I can see no rapids. They sound so close, but all the water is shallow and almost stagnant and the sound, it slowly becomes obvious, is coming from above me: the clapping leaves of the poplars.

The bridge to my left is a hydroelectric dam with little water to fuel it, but it does change the water: upstream of the dam, the river is static and dark green. You can see dark puffs of weeds freckling the surface. As the river turns west, I peel away, drawn by the shouts and clacks of a pétanque pit. I follow the straight canal which comes off the river a kilometre upstream and into a suburb that used to be called "oltre-Stura" ("the far side of the Stura", one of Torino's four rivers).

What happens next is strange. Ever since Chivasso I've felt I'm moving among modern, square blocks of houses and factories, and here – right in the midst of Torino's industrialised east – is a hamlet that looks more like something from a film set. Some alleys are too narrow for cars, and the buildings create little piazzas which are anything but square. It seems to be a century or two older than everything that surrounds it. It's called Bertolla, a *borgo* that began to boom in the mid-nineteenth century after the city council of Torino took action, in 1860, against what it called "unsanitary, inconvenient and dangerous sites": that legislation meant that the city's laundry – usually done on the banks of the Po in what is now the city centre, in the suburbs of Moschino and Vanchiglia – began to move to Bertolla five miles away. It became a *borgo* with almost only one profession.

"In Bertolla," a friend says to me, "if you just put your finger in the ground you would find water." Every house, I'm told, used to have its own *bealera*, a waterway: the men went to collect their clients' laundry on Monday morning, dropping off at the same time the previous week's wash. The women did the hard work: bending over a *scagn*, a wooden board, and scrubbing all day on their knees. When you read the memoirs, the women often talk of the pain of the caustic soda in their cuts, caused by splinters, ice and blisters.

It's strange, talking to the elderly here, how basic but resourceful the process was: they used to put the cuttings from vineyards at the bottom of the large wash buckets because they were strong, didn't stain and the short twigs lifted the laundry off the bottom to make sure it didn't plug the hole when they needed to drain the bucket. They sourced offcuts from sawmills and carpenters to fire the ovens which heated the water. Women made cushions from straw to protect their knees. One local historian writes about the white sheets, hung on iron cables in the meadows below Superga, moving "like butterflies": "they stopped, then took off again with the wind which first just moved the lower hems a little and then puffed them up more, before they wilted and went inert."

But things changed quickly after the war. The 1,290-metre canal I have just left was opened in 1953 and two years later mains water arrived. Within a generation, most people had their own washing machines and Bertolla's canals were slowly filled in. The men with carts reinvented themselves as *teracin*, the gravel luggers who helped lay the foundations for the city's post-war expansion by taking whatever they could from the riverbanks.

Torino is shaped a bit like a chestnut: the east-south-east edge of the city is slightly concave where it butts up against the hills and, at their feet, the Po. The city's three other rivers flow into it from the west, first – as I come to them – the Stura, then the Dora and Sangone. I sometimes get confused between these Torino tributaries of the Po. There are nine different rivers called "Stura" in Italy (it comes from the Occitan *estura*). And there's more than one Dora, the next tributary to hit the Po in Torino. As a name for a "water course", Dora has echoes throughout Europe: in the Douro in Portugal, the Durance in France and the surname Doria in Liguria (the equivalent, perhaps, of "Waterman"). "La Dora" also sounds different because it's feminine unlike the ever-masculine Po. But, strangely, Torino isn't a city which sits astride its rivers, like London or Paris. Its rivers were defences, more moats than thoroughfares. The city walls were in the middle of all four waterways: west of the Po, south of the Stura and Dora, and north of the Sangone.

The first one I come to, the Stura Lanzo, is often blamed for much of the muck that flows into the Po, although it's hard to know if those comments are due to prejudice about an old riverfront encampment of two thousand immigrants. But the Stura is also a river which bares its secrets, with Pliocene trunks, about one to three metres across, now emerging jagged from the disappearing water. These are the remains of the Glyptostrobus trees, ancient swamp conifers. They've resisted for millions of years thanks to clay being impenetrable to oxygen and halting decomposition. Now, due to erosion and dehydration, they're exposed, worn each year by currents and air so that, like so much else, what has survived through aeons will be quickly eroded in our own lifetimes. The privilege of seeing their rusty-black shapes only reminds me how we have unwittingly exposed them.

I go back to the Po and follow the dark footpath under the cool of an avenue of lime trees. The ground appears completely covered in yellowish sawdust – the dry leaves, fruits and seed pods which have dropped from the limes. Walkers, joggers and cyclists create mini explosions as they crunch them. At the confluence with the Dora Riparia I bear right, following this murky tributary up through the city centre and the old industrial quarter of the city. The Dora had more of a drop than the Po and was used for centuries to power the city's mills.

It was the Torino's high water table and accessible acquifers that, in part, gave the city its greatest military triumph. A "great well" had been constructed at the centre of Torino's citadel between 1565 and 1567. It had two staircases, a metre and a half wide, that circled down opposite walls so that animals could descend the 22 metres, draw water and then ascend the other side. The pentagonal fortress in which it was housed stood at the south-western edge of the small, walled city. There were sixteen "royal bastions" in all, each jagged protrusion having sub-ravelins so that the whole city, in maps, looks like a stretched circular saw. It was a fortification structure pioneered by the Italians in the fifteenth and sixteenth centuries and came to be known as "trace italienne". After the invention of cannon, a traditional ring-shaped fortification was no longer viable: it offered an easy target and had blind spots, areas under the ramparts where a castle's attackers couldn't be fired upon. A low-lying, pointed star (with thick, brick walls which shattered less than stone) reduced the vulnerability to cannon and meant that defenders' fire could now reach all areas outside the fortifications.

Duke Vittorio Amedeo II of Savoia was thirty-five at the outbreak of the War of Spanish Succession (1701–14). That war to decide who was rightful heir to the late Charles II of Spain's vast territories pitted the Habsburgs and the English against Louis XIV's France and the newly crowned Philip of Anjou, Charles II's appointed heir. Vittorio Amedeo II was an ally of the French: he was married to Anne of Orleans, and between 1701 and 1703 Savoyard troops fought alongside the Franco-Spanish troops in Lombardia. But his duchy – straddling lands from Chambéry to Torino – was a tiny state compared to the French in the west and the Spanish in the east, in Milano. Vittorio Amedeo was suspicious that his French allies were hoping to annex his duchy and began correspondence with his cousin, Eugenio, who was commanding imperial troops. Perhaps the French got wind of this secret contact with the enemy because on 29 September 1703 around 4,500 of Vittorio Amedeo's troops (five of his ten regular regiments) were disarmed and arrested at San Benedetto Po on orders of Louis XIV. The duke considered the act such an affront that, on 7 October that year, he declared war on both France and Spain.

So began a race to reach Torino. One by one, all Vittorio Amedeo II's cities were taken or abandoned. French forces moved into Montemélian, Nice, Asti, Susa, Ivrea, Bard and Vercelli. Only Verrua – that fortress above the Po, to the east of the city – held out for far longer than expected, surviving a six-month winter siege until it, too, fell in April 1705. After that, French and imperial troops marched towards Torino in almost parallel lines from the Veneto and Romagna: the former north of the Po and the latter to the south of it. Eugenio's army crossed the Po at Carmagnola, making contact at last with the Savoyard troops. The imperial and Savoyard army now numbered almost 30,000 men. Including the extra-mural suburbs of the Po and the Balôn, there were around 40,000 inhabitants of Torino, their numbers suddenly swollen by this influx of troops, miners, farmers and livestock. Only the hills immediately outside the city, on the far side of the Po, were still in Savoyard hands.

In some ways the siege of Torino laid many of the symbolic foundations for the Risorgimento. Here was the Savoyard dynasty fighting against foreign invaders. There was much myth building in retellings of this famous siege: there was an eclipse of the sun in May 1706, an ominous sign for the "Sun King" of France... and the Taurus constellation, symbol of the city of Torino, was seen in the sky that night. Previously anonymous citizens were lionised for leading the defence and the attack.

French hesitation had given the Savoia a year to improve its defences before the siege began in earnest in May 1706. The strategic genius of the defenders of Torino was to exploit what might have been a weakness: the low-lying nature of this city. The citadel facing the French was unlike traditional fortresses because it had deliberately been built not up, but down. "It was almost invisible," writes one historian. It sat low to the earth, its zigzag walls and multiple trenches impossible to scout from the deforested plains in the west where the French were camped and exposed. Fourteen kilometres of tunnels were dug by the Savoyard troops and the maps of them look like magnified snowflakes extending towards the enemy. There were two sets of tunnels, the higher around seven metres below the surface, the lower just above the water table at around 14 metres. The city's defenders could hear French troops and locate their cannon by the simple sonic test of buckets of water or rice on a drum placed in those long tunnels. They positioned explosives under where they calculated the French artillery was, backfilled the tunnel and lit the fuse. It was a successful strategy: by August 1706, the 44,000 French troops had been reduced to 27,000. The mines killed around two hundred French troops on one day alone.

The French launched many attacks and, on the night of 29 August, managed to penetrate into the entrance of the tunnels. Two young men rushed to lock the doors to give them time to blow the access tunnel, but the younger man preparing the fuse was so nervous he couldn't light it. The legend goes that the other man, Pietro Micca, scolded him – "you're slower than a day without bread" – and told him to save himself. Micca then lit a deliberately short fuse, sprinted away and, along with all the invading French troops, died in the explosion. Micca was quickly idolised in patriotic retellings of the story, his name invoked over the following two centuries to promote a sense of Italian heroism and self-sacrifice.

In early September the duke and his cousin inspected the enemy from the crest of the Superga hillside. "They're already half defeated," Eugenio allegedly said, looking at the diminished French forces. Five days later, Savoyard and Imperial troops attacked the French. On the night of 5 September, a young woman offered to lead them inside the Pianezza castle through a series of tunnels she knew. The castle was taken, and French officers, cannon and two million francs were captured. On 7 September, the Battle of Torino led to the liberation of the city, and the ducal forces used the rivers Dora and Stura as traps for the retreating enemy. The French were driven out of Piemonte having lost, in all, around 30,000 men.

"The consequences of the battle of Torino were immediate and momentous," writes Geoffrey Symcox, Vittorio Amedeo's biographer. "Piemonte was freed from the invader and the survival of the Savoyard state was assured. The state of Milano and the Duchy of Mantova soon passed to the Habsburgs, whose dominion was to last a century and a half."

The Peace of Utrecht that ended the War of Spanish Succession in 1713 granted Vittorio Amedeo the Spanish Kingdom of Sicily. The House of Savoia was now a royal family and the Superga hilltop was given a regal basilica, designed by the same Sicilian baroque architect, Filippo Juvarra, who also transformed much of the city. Territories in Lombardia and Monferrato were absorbed into the Savoia state, as were the Protestant areas of the Pragelato and Pellice valleys (to the west and south-west of the city). A *bucintoro* – a grand, gold-plated gondola – was commissioned so that the newly regal family could enjoy pleasure trips along the Po.

Partly in revenge for that French defeat, when Napoleon swept into Torino almost a century later his troops began dismantling its defences and today very little of the citadel is visible. The main keep is intact, but all the rest, like the city walls, has since disappeared. Its principal remains are underground: one can still walk through a few kilometres of those tunnels, narrow brick burrows which are cool compared to the summer above. They were used as air-raid shelters in the Second World War and only after the war, in October 1958, was the exact location of "the Pietro Micca staircase" discovered by an army general from Torino.

Vittorio Amedeo himself had a melancholic old age. Although his city now had a court and he a crown, his firstborn son died of smallpox in 1715. Three years later, the Spanish invaded Sicily and, in the peace settlement, Vittorio was forced to accept what was considered the lesser island of Sardegna. He retired from public life and abdicated in favour of his other son... but then changed his mind and endeavoured, in his sixties, to make a comeback, renouncing his own abdication. His son promptly imprisoned him and, allegedly going mad, he eventually died a prisoner. "By a profound irony," Symcox writes, "Vittorio Amedeo was destroyed by the power of the state that he had done so much to create. In a last mad gesture he tried fumblingly to overthrow the structure of authority that he himself had established, forcing the new keepers of that sovereign power, whom he had trained in his own ideal of ruthless duty, to crush him."

That night I go to a party with a friend. We drink beer sitting in the Ginzburg Gardens looking at the illuminated Murazzi. The Murazzi are the stone quays that run north and south of the city's central bridge on the river's left bank: they have oblique staircases running down to the water and were originally designed as riverside warehouses, workshops and storage depots. An entire suburb, Moschino, was cleared to make way for these "big walls". Mudbanks and fishermen's shacks were paved over, but slowly even this wide riverfront fell into disuse. By the 1970s the Murazzi were being used, partly, as a city-centre car wash.

In the late Eighties and early Nineties, though, they became, according to Marco, my friend and a regular DJ there, "our little Côte d'Azur or Ibiza". Along that quarter-mile of slab-like riverside real estate, nightclubs sprung up: Giancarlo's, Csoa, Lega dei Furiosi, Doctor Sax and others.

"This is a city which has pretty clearly marked social divisions," says Marco, "but all were equal in the Murazzi. There were Ferraris and bicycles, punks and the well dressed." There were clubs for all sorts of musical tastes – grunge, trip hop, house, techno – but, he says, everyone came together. "It was a feeling of incredible freedom. We don't have the symbolism of a river like the Americans, all that 'going down to the river...' stuff, but here, in the Murazzi, the river really did take us away. Well, the drugs too," he shakes his head sheepishly, "but there was this sense of possibility, of getting away from everything. And then," he smiles, "you were home in ten minutes."

It was an area that soon became notorious. It already had a reputation – "you knew what you were going to if you went down there," Marco says – but deaths, drug dealing and arrests made it appear like a stain on the city centre. Attempts to clean up the clubs meant they became less edgy and more appealing to blander fashionistas, and eventually accusations of abuse of permits and disturbance of the peace effectively, in 2012–13, ended the era of the Po's most transgressive, hedonistic space.

The next day I travel out of the city along the cycle path towards Moncalieri. There are many rowing clubs here, and every minute or two a slim vessel speeds past, the backs of the oars slapping the water.

Under the Isabella bridge there's a saxophonist, his raspy rehearsal bouncing off the arches, the walkway and the water. A slim bridge takes me over the Sangone tributary, and once you're past the castles and the parks, the joggers and cyclists thin out. The path becomes sandier, squeezed between the green Po and the city's golf course.

As often happens, the two sides of the river are now very different. On the far side, the hills look green: you can see sports clubs covered in wisteria, hydrangeas and camellias. You can hear the tennis balls bouncing off the raquets. Grand villas are hidden among the maples and magnolias. But this side, there are multiple railway tracks, dual carriageways and the old Fiat factories.

Another bridge brings me to Moncalieri, the brick castle that used to defend the southern edge of the city's stretch of the river. At the top of a steep path through the Sunday market, its dimensions are immense: it has four square towers, five storeys high, with the main gate framed by smaller, circular ones. Many of the rooms are, as was the tradition among the Savoia, derivatives of Chinese decorations, full of black lacquer, gold leaf, lilies, pagodas and stylised waterfalls. But the view from high up is dispiriting: you can't see the Alps anymore for all the smog, only mile after mile of tower blocks and power lines. The luxuriant curves of the Po are completely hidden.

EIGHT

Towards Saluzzo

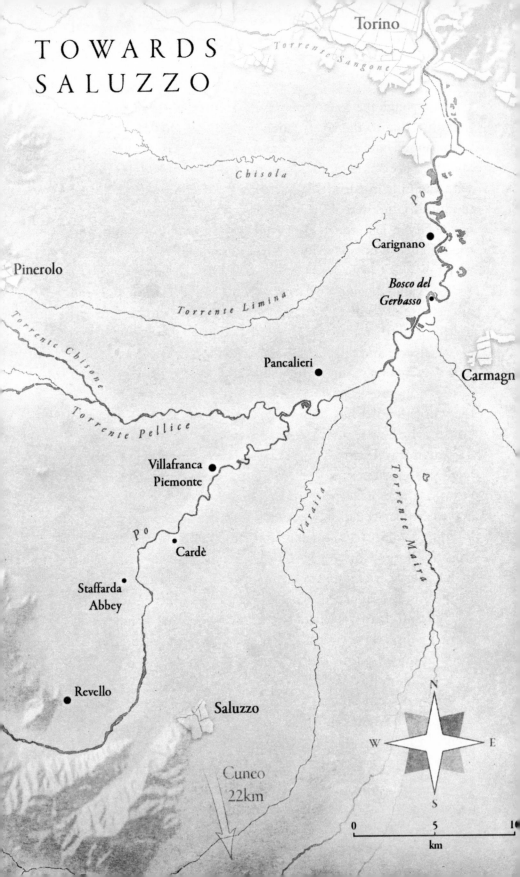

TOWARDS
SALUZZO

Torino

Torrente Sangone

Chisola

Po

Pinerolo

Carignano

Bosco del Gerbasso

Torrente Limina

Torrente Chisone

Carmagn

Pancalieri

Torrente Pellice

Villafranca
Piemonte

Varaita

Torrente Maira

Po

Cardè

Staffarda
Abbey

Revello

Saluzzo

Cuneo
22km

N

W   E

S

0   5   1

km

pass through the concrete landscape with slightly gritted teeth, apologising to the river which appears as squashed as I am. The handlebars can hardly get through the narrow bottlenecks, and the wheels skid on the sand and broken ramps. After flirting with the hills in Monferrato, I thought I was about to hit the mountains, but here it's grimly flat again. When you do get out of the city at last, the fields are all maize plantations and main roads. There's no space by the river now, so I try and find my way towards Carmagnola.

I see a man digging with a plastic bucket and spade in the sand at the base of some crumbling buildings. The sand has vertical holes with little mounds where it has clearly been excavated by insects. I stop and talk to him. He's an entomologist looking for a rare fly he once found when he lived here, for ten years, back in the Noughties. He says he can't believe the speed at which the whole hamlet has been abandoned. It used to be flats and houses which were used by commuters heading to Villastellone, Carignano or Torino. It was classy and gentle, he says: there were young Metasequoias, an ancient mill, barns and stables. Now they're mostly gone – the trees in tornados, the mill is static and the roofs are falling in on both agricultural and residential buildings. Apart from the marquis's central "palace" itself, the whole of Borgo Cornalese is returning to nature. Figs, which like their roots restricted in stone, now frame and invade the ruins. Fat beams and smashed tiles lie on the fenced-off courtyards.

The church tower rings the hour twice: three rings, five-minute pause, three rings. "It does that," says the entomologist, "so that the labourers in the fields, if they miscounted the first time, could be sure the second."

As usual, I have to switch dictionaries every few days. Here a cluster of houses is called *tetti* (roofs) and land measurements aren't in hectares or acres (*biolche*) but in "days" (*giornate*, which is the same principle: like an acre, it was the area that could be ploughed by a man and an ox in a day). But as you look at the fields, there are no animals or humans. "This is a biological crime scene," the entomologist says. "It's a form of violence against nature." His indignation is not only the fact that "maize isn't even native", it's that all these maize prairies are genetically programmed not to do what nature intended: the cob remains completely closed, not shedding seed but just maximising rough feed for cattle so we can eat beef whenever we want. No other species get a look in.

"Nature has its own laws," he says, "and they're quite easy to understand." He points at the sky, now full of rollercoasting swallows. "Cows equal flies equal swallows," he says. "But interrupt the food chain, plant only one crop, protected by pesticides, and this is what you get." He shakes his head at the tall, tough maize.

I push on to the Po Morta, another "dead" lake created by the river's retreat. The hand-painted sign by the green chain-link fence says the lake is now a private members' club. Two old men sit on a bench with a single crutch leaning on the bench between them. There are more brick ruins around: a village oven is now overgrown, the earth piled almost to its mouth. A tall tower at La Gorra – looking thirteenth or fourteenth century – now has a concrete lean-to and sits in the middle of a tractor-filled courtyard.

Then I come to the Gerbasso woodland and immediately the melancholy lifts again. It was created in the mid-1980s by a visionary ichthyologist (a fish studier) called Gianni. A modest man, he credits an ecologically minded mayor from that era for going along with the idea of creating a refuge for wildlife that was as close as possible to being a recreation of the vast *silva magna*, the great forest of the Po basin. Both the lot-drawing woodland in Trino and, closer, the Merlin wood in Caramagna offered examples to follow, and slowly the woodland swamp took shape. If you go there now it's taken over by non-humans: a frog tiddlywinks across the path, there are wild boar scratching in a clearing and dogwood rubbing up against the alder. The orchid-like flowers of spotted snapweed bob above its green leaves.

There's a lot of water round here. Some of the lakes are disused quarries, others are forgotten river courses. Both are fuller than the river itself now, which trickles over stones under the scorching sun. Bushy saplings are fluffing up in the dry gravel. The river is maybe 15 metres across now and percussional, like coins jangling in a pocket.

This space is charming because it's both tended and ignored. There are wooden signs here and there (like the untranslatable *sentiero ragazzabile*) but at the same time butterfly larvae hang on threads in the middle of the paths as if no one has been this way for weeks. The track keeps peeling away from the river then back to it, so that you get glimpses of the Po from different angles: it bends fast into the bank and sounds deeper as it slowly crumbles off rock, then stretches out on the straight and becomes quieter again.

With that vast power station at its mouth, the river has felt mildly vulnerable ever since I started this journey. But now it's as if the Po is disappearing. Not just because I'm going the wrong way and it's obviously slimming, but because much of what the river has been, for millennia, is now gone. The grayling, which like oxygenated, fast-flowing water, are rarities now. There's either not enough water or it's not *acqua dolce*, freshwater. "We've got massive problems," Gianni tells me. "Purification plants don't work because they're costly to run. And even if they did, they use outdated technology from thirty or forty years ago. Our lifestyles are ever-more devastating." Nitrogen, phosphates, algae and gravel extraction have almost completely eradicated what used to be regular species on this stretch of the river: the marble trout, otters and bittern.

His lament overlaps with those of so many people I speak to along the Po: that land use has radically altered in the space of a single lifetime. Round these parts, oil used to come from walnuts, but now olive oil is transported hundreds of miles. "You're lucky if it even comes from Italy," says someone else who has joined in the conversation... and before you know it an ecological lament twists into a nationalist rant.

Few people outside Piemonte know where Carmagnola is. The name is vaguely familiar to Italian schoolchildren thanks to Alessandro Manzoni's 1820 tragedy about the famous Count of Carmagnola (beheaded by the Venetians for possible betrayal after that Battle of Pavia). But this town of around 30,000 people, immediately south of Torino, means little to people today. For much of the early modern era, though, Carmagnola was at the centre of a vital military trade. The earliest records of hemp in Carmagnola date from the fourteenth century, when the nearby Abbey of Casanova purchased hemp for habits, bell pulls and agricultural rope and reins. Rich in the water required to rot hemp canes and enable the removal of its tough fibres, the town became one of the capitals of European rope- and sail-making. The cannabis plant was so associated with Piemonte that it even (possibly) gave its name to one of its regions, Canavese.

Hemp cultivation was a fast, though arduous, process. The hardy plants grew in dense forests in the fields, easily reaching three or four metres in one season. The females, which produced seed for oil and for flour, were left to grow longer, but the male stalks were cut down in early autumn as they began to yellow. Voluminous with foliage, they were left to soak in water for 7–12 days. Stones were used to weigh down fat, long bundles in ditches, ponds, lakes and rivers. The poorest peasants used dew, which meant the whole process took three times as long.

This process of maceration was stinky, as rotting vegetation always is. But eventually the hard green stalk turned mushy and the orangey-blond fibres could be drawn from the lightweight woody stalk. That remaining wood was often all the women got paid for this separation work, taking the balsa-like stalks home for baking (although now, being spongy and undense, that wood is being rediscovered as insulation in green buildings). Any leftover canes were used, along with vines and willows, to make or repair the long rope-making arcades.

Once extracted, the fibres were thrown onto iron combs upended on workbenches: all day the men would yank the tangles through the ever-thinner teeth, until eventually they had combed manes of ochre fibre. Spinners then drew the bundles out, pinching, twisting and feeding it, as a wheel operated by a child reeled the yarn in. To make ropes rather than fibre or string, the women would do the same walk the other way, back to the start of the arcade but now twining four or eight cords into one. The wheel kept twisting tighter and once the rope was densely coiled and stopped, they raked it with metal chains which had been dumped in boiling water to stop them freezing. The hemp cord became almost glassy with the smears of wet metal and was then placed in cold water to wash it ochre again and shrink it even tighter.

There was always a connection between the river and hemp: not just because water was needed for maceration, but because hemp was also, like horsehair, used to caulk boats. Those boats required rope, too, for sails and moorings. Military suppliers came to Carmagnola to source the wick for firing the new *archibugio* guns which had become common in the fifteenth and sixteenth centuries. Soaked in saltpetre, this wick became effectively the match to fire the ball from the muzzle. The fibre invariably provided the foundation for the country's great paintings: the sturdy cloth was called a canvas (*canovaccio*) because it was derived from the cannabis plant.

There were eighteen cord-makers in Carmagnola and its immediate vicinity in 1665. Rope was ordered in bulk by naval powers like the Genovan Republic and the French and Savoyard monarchs, who sent their bursars to the *antichi bastioni* – the long, covered marketplace of this one-product town. The demand was for all dimensions and purposes: for dragging cannon, reins for cavalry mounts, laces for boots.

Rinaldo Comba's studies of medieval Piemonte have shown how important the region was as a textile power. Silk production in the mulberry groves was the most lucrative industry, and hemp was always the poorer, working person's cloth. Tailors made up for hemp's roughness by dying it brightly and farm clothing began to look like a slack soldier's uniform with red stripes or green trim. That's probably why Carmagnola hemp became iconic in the French Revolution, a symbol of egalitarian authenticity and paramilitary organisation. The "Carmagnole" waistcoat became, in France, the uniform of the sans-culottes militias, giving rise to a bouncy, anti-aristocracy song of the same name, with its bloodthirsty lyrics about relishing the sound of the cannon.

There's almost nothing now to remind you of that industry. The arcades of the market are still there, but of the forty or so rope-making arcades only one survives and it's a micro-museum. Closer to the river, there are fleeting clues to that culture. I sometimes see holes in the older stables and barns. The smaller ones much higher up were for birds, so the peasants could take an egg or two from the nest. But the lower, square holes just above head height were for inserting poles on which the fibres could dry after maceration. Empty sockets are all that's left.

The story of the decline of hemp is a sad one: in 1882, the town had sixty-six hemp workshops and even three decades later, in 1910, 25 tonnes of rope were being sold every week. Between the two world wars, Italy still produced around 20 per cent of global hemp production. But in the second half of the twentieth century, hemp cultivation almost completely vanished. Unable to compete with cheap cotton and, increasingly, petrol-based polymers like polyester, polypropylene and nylon, hemp seemed outdated. Although there's no record of *Cannabis sativa* being used as a psychoactive substance in Piemonte prior to the twentieth century (the plants used for hemp had only trace levels of tetrahydrocannabinol, or THC, the psychoactive constituent of cannabis), its reputation as a narcotic was being touted by prohibitionists, who lobbied for its legal suppression.

There are still, in Italy, around 1,500 hectares dedicated to hemp production, but that's just 1.4 per cent of the area under cultivation one hundred years ago. But in some ways this small town in Piemonte is still the capital of that culture. Two of the EU's ten recognised *Cannabis sativa* varieties for agricultural use are from here (Carmagnola B and Carmagnola Selezionata). Carmagnola is where Assocanapa – the umbrella organisation bringing together seven hundred or so Italian hemp farmers – is based.

There's an almost evangelical zeal to proponents of hemp. Once they have dispelled fears around drug use, farmers long to tell you about all the uses for the plant: for clothing, construction (hempcrete), cosmetics, nutrition (both seeds and oils), for medicine and drinks (aromatic teas and liqueurs). As everywhere else, Italy has an intensifying debate on the legalisation or decriminalisation of cannabis. But whereas in many nations such a move might seem radical, here it would, in some ways, be simply restorative.

A little further upstream is a smaller village, Pancalieri. It, too, sits low – its name comes from *piano calante*, the "waning plain". A river, the Pancaliera, runs through it and under the red-brick mill. They also used to make hemp cords here, but in the mid-nineteenth century another product took over.

"All these lands are children of the water," says Sara, who is showing me around. "There's even a field here called "*le rive*" ["the shores"]. It means the earth is silty."

Sara is the fifth generation of the Chialva family to produce mint essence and is keen to explain how this soil allows peppermint to thrive. "When you touch the earth it creates all this dust, like golden wisps, because this was the old bed of the Po." It's this vital pedoclimate that makes Pancalieri ideal for growing medicinal herbs and oils, especially mint that requires soil both clayey and siliceous. The soil has to offer both moisture and drainage.

Peppermint was introduced here only in the mid- to late-nineteenth century from Mitcham, in Surrey. There, by the banks of the River Wardle, lavender and mint meadows were cultivated for toiletries and food. I read online that the crest of the local football team, Tooting and Mitcham, still boasts the lavender flower. When investors and chemists saw the profitability of Mitcham, they began looking for other locations in Europe and they ended up in Pancalieri. Torino had long been a capital of Italian chemistry and the distillation of mint oil was simple. The soil around the rivers – not just beside the Po, but also the Pellice, the Varaita and the Maira rivers – appeared ideal.

By the 1920s, there were seventy distilleries in and around this town, with some 600 hectares under cultivation. When you look through photographs of labourers involved in the production of rice and hemp, they're often frowning at the camera, looking exhausted and stern. But the mint growers look far more relaxed, perhaps because the plant was so simple to spread: *Mentha piperita* grew without difficulty and regenerated itself through energetic roots which speedily hunted for moister soil.

The amount of menthol gleaned from these bushes, though, was tiny (roughly a four-hundredth of the overall weight of a harvested plant). The distilleries had to be the size of a wine cellar to boil tonnes of peppermint and cool the absorbed oil and separate it from the water again.

"It was like the hull of a ship," says Sara, showing me the Chialva plant: fires were lit under circular basins which contained 500 litres of water and a maze of glass tubes then drew it off and cooled it. The resulting oil, less dense than water, is still scooped off by hand. It's not green either, but more straw-yellow, almost buttery. Today the process takes just under two hours.

There are still twenty mint growers and four distilleries in this area, producing just over half of all Italy's entire mint essence. Chialva's main client, the nearby confectionery giant Ferrero, buys around ten tonnes of her mint oil every year for its Tic Tacs. But the growers in this still-flat and baking plain have diversified. They supply medicinal oils from sage, melissa, camomile and poppies, making their fields so pastel that they draw almost too many photographers.

Here the fields look so much fluffier and healthier than the maize regiments: there's a blur of insects in the papery cups of the poppies. Chalky wings bounce above orange, red and yellow petals. The mint fields are mauvish now, the leaves with reddish veins below the flowers.

But although these plantations smell good, the odour's not as strong as you would expect. "The stronger mint is, the less it is appreciated," explains Sara. She is scornful of the overpowering mint flavour we expect from toothpastes and sweets, and says that the greenness of the mint drinks is all additives. The real colour – and she gives me a bottle of mint syrup and one of mint liqueur – is barely less transparent than water.

～

Just before the bridge into Villafranca you can drop back next to the river. The sandy cycle path cuts through stands of bamboo five or six metres tall. Odd sculptures make the place playful if a little spooky: there are baby dolls nailed to a trunk, but one or two have come unstuck at the head, so they hang upside down like a brace of baby heretics with nails through their ankles.

The river is clear but dotted with golf greens of algae. Freshwater weeds below are being dragged almost horizontal in the riffles. It's so slender now. It's late July and the river's now only between 8 and 15 metres wide. You often lose sight of it among the maize and artemisia. Hairy islands – tufts of green on white stone – emerge in the middle. At the edges there are often fallen trunks, their half-sunken canopies now providing shelter for waders drilling for food. In the steep bunkers there are sand martins and, bouncing in the undergrowth, white wagtails. A frog loops from one verge to the other again.

I come to the bridge at Cardè. The land here was so untended that it was an area mostly known as a woodland of thistles (*cardi*). Its buildings, like the brick basilica you see as soon as you turn into town, are small but elegant.

From around here all the photographs and postcards show Monviso's snowy, triangular peak only about 30 kilometres away. They say that iconic summit was the inspiration for the Paramount Pictures logo, but there are similarly symmetrical peaks in Utah and Peru which claim the same. Today the Pianura haze is low and I can't see Monviso, only Monte Bracco in the foreground. It looks exactly like the profile of a sleeping gorilla.

It's a straight road with HGVs speeding past. Large brown silos – shaped like giant yurts – ferment waste for biogas production. In the distance, I can see the spire I've yearned for ever since I read about it a year ago. It surmounts Staffarda Abbey, the second Cistercian monastery in Italy, founded in the twelfth century as an offshoot of Tiglieto in Liguria.

The monks were granted the soggy fields (*farda*) at the foot of Monte Bricco by the Marquis of Saluzzo. Like all those other monasteries along the Po, the surrounding lands were quickly drained and the buildings laid out in striking harmony with both nature and scripture: the variety of the columns (of the 260 columns, none are the same) imitated creation's variety. The thirty-three steps up to the monks' dormitory were a reminder of Jesus' earthly years.

It's not, though, quite what I expected. Some of the sterner, ecclesiastical buildings have been drastically altered, given a white rendering or brick buttresses. It's a higgledy-piggledy mixture of austerity, abandonment and modern usage. This place survives thanks to hospitality, a bar and hotel offering comfort in the Abbey's guest quarters. There's even a tobacconist.

In the vaulted, open marketplace of Piazza Roma there are only a couple of tourists and two cyclists drinking beer. Next door, the other side of the stream with its coypus and ducklings, is a working farm with a white cockerel strutting the courtyard. It's as if animals are a bit more tolerated here: a roost of two thousand or so greater and lesser mouse-eared bats hangs from the monastery's calidarium (the warm room). You can smell their guano, and hear constant squeaks, as they settle down for the day.

That warm room is where monks used to melt animal fat to soften up their sandals. Everywhere else was unheated. Only the sick were permitted meat or wine. In the barrel-vaulted workshop, the monks used to spin, weave, tan leather, carve and make paper. They cultivated rice and, when it was outlawed by the Dukes of Savoia for disseminating malaria, they allegedly hid the grains in the hems of their habits. There are many similar legends: the metre-long fishbone in the cloisters is said to belong to the "prodigious fish" that was sent to the monks during a famous famine when their lands were so flooded their crops had failed.

The water channels in the courtyard are dry and the chapter house is held up by improvised wooden beams. The refectory was sacked and burned by French troops in 1690, so although the footprint is the same, its replacement is slightly different. The internal ditches in the building, used to wash plates and hands, are long gone.

Many writers over the years have alluded to the deliberate similarity between the abbey's steeple and the peak of Monviso: the mountain was deliberately mirrored because it was considered halfway between earth and heaven. Monviso and that spire were reminders to Cistercians that (as Hildegard of Bingen would write) they had within themselves both sky and earth, they were constantly veering between the pull of flesh and the weightless freedom of purity. That contrast is still felt: the abbey is in the Pianura Padana – I can't believe that, after all this, I'm still only just over 250 metres above sea level – but only about 30 kilometres away is a mountain that tops out at almost 4,000 metres.

Hildegard wrote of the ability of constructor monks to raise buildings which could vibrate like a finely tuned musical instrument. And here the stones, bricks and beams do create peaceful harmonies. It comes from deliberate asymmetry: even in the church the columns are staggered and irregular. Access is through a door not in the middle of the wall, with steps not centred on the door. The splays of the windows are all different. That might be the result of bad repair jobs over the centuries (monastic life ended here in 1750), but a former parish priest here, Carlo Peano, urged the visitor to see that oddness as intended: "In Staffarda one feels at ease, attuned to the dimension of this construction which is measured in an almost symphonic way and is ultimately tuned to the human one." The eyes are drawn through that irregularity to the only place you can rest with true symmetry, the altar with its repeating trilogies.

It's a calm diversion from the river. The cloisters are part-building site but the double columns are slender and spaced perfectly to allow visitors to sit and reflect. I envy these men the stark bareness of their lives. The idea of deliberately interrupting rest to sing psalms is unimaginable to most of us. The notion of reneging on pleasures, voice, even our own will, to serve an abbot and God seems epically foreign. And while I'm in this monastic setting, I'm thinking about what Guido Ceronetti wrote about the Po. He was the one of the few writers to Christianise the river, imagining it as "a logos which makes water". It's a body of water which acts as a truth bringer about our own dirtiness: "a carnal figure, a suffering, living Word" that absorbs our pollution, our refuse, our guilt and our idiocies.

By the time I get back to the river, though, it's bone-dry. I can't find it. It must be here somewhere between these stones and rising saplings. I walk to the far bank across the low-slung scrub but there's no sign of it. As I scramble around the undergrowth, laughing at how improbable it is to mislay the Po, I disturb a black man who has set up a tarpaulin tent here. There's lots of labour here for fruit-picking in the vast orchards and vineyards, and he tells me he's waiting for a call. He's from Nigeria and it's a relief to speak English for ten minutes. We talk about football and blueberry prices. It's all piecework here, he says. There's no hourly wage, just a fixed price per full punnet. Almost all the pickers are immigrants.

Later I see a farmer and ask him about the river. He tells me it sinks underground in this short stretch during the summer months. He's standing by an idling tractor which is powering a pump disgorging dozens of gallons a minute into his ripening maize field. His cobs are now showing off their burgundy tufts. Water's gushing out as he tells me about his well and I suddenly feel disconsolate at this drenching of fields with rare water by burning diesel to grow genetically modified maize to feed cattle

so we can all have as much dairy and meat as we demand...
and all the while the Po is dry and we wonder why there aren't
any fish. The monks wouldn't have lived like this.

I push on, the battle-beat of the cicadas echoing my chuggling
bike chain. Slowly the maize gives way to fields of fruit.

Twenty years ago there was a kiwi rush here. The demand was
so great, especially from British supermarkets, that hundreds
of hectares were given over to lines of kiwi plantations, each
tree looping its circular leaves over the hairy eggs. But there's
less money in them now, and they're slowly being replaced
by other fruit trees, especially apples. There are spiky green
chestnuts and low, netted blueberry plantations. The water use
is still high: at the end of every long row is a cistern to soak
the whole line.

Once over the bridge above an absent Po, the road slowly
begins to climb up to Saluzzo. This was, between 1125 and
1548, the stronghold of the Marquisate of Saluzzo, the
famous signoria of the Del Vasto dynasty which was forever
attempting to defend its territories from incursions by France
and Savoia. When you look at maps from the Middle Ages, the
marquisate is a small button between the encircling Savoyard
dukes and French kings: each pretending to offer protection
while casting a jealous eye over the marquisate's fertile plains,
castles and mountain passes. The Saluzzo marquises leaned
more to the French than to the Savoia, but were often not
provided with the promised French troops, and over centuries
the Saluzzo territories were besieged, occupied and sacked by
both sides.

Possibly because its ruling family died out so long ago, Saluzzo
seems a hilltop time capsule. Architecturally it's not unsullied,
but there is none of the Baroque overlay here that there is in

Torino. The grandest buildings all pre-date the seventeenth century. It's steep and nothing is perpendicular or parallel until you get to the Castiglia, the fortress, at Saluzzo's summit. It has stolid brick walls with small, deeply inset windows and it looks just like what it later became, a prison.

From here you can understand the strategic importance of Saluzzo. This hillside redoubt looks both ways: to the mountains in the west, and to the plain in the east, now misty in the early morning sun. Pointing through that haze you can see the rock of the town of Cavour emerging like a lumpy pyramid. The river is flowing almost precisely north–south now, and the far side of the valley you can see the marquisate's other stronghold, Revello.

So much here reminds you of the river: the Cavassa family were long-time vicars-general of the Del Vasto family, and their symbol was the chub (*cavedano*) which used to swim upstream to this point. The fish adorns their coats of arms and the grand entrance to their Renaissance palace spells out their uncompromising motto: "Droit Quoi Qu'il Soit" – "straight ahead whatever the cost".

It's as if many of the thin threads of this river journey meet here: as you walk up the hill you pass – in a square which is really just the meeting place of cobbled staircases, terraces and colonnades – the home of Silvio Pellico, the man who wrote *My Prisons* after incarceration in Spielberg. The distance between my two meetings with Pellico, here and way back in Frattesina – reminds me how much the river must have played a role in the Risorgimento: it was the ribbon between divided duchies and mini states. Pellico's brother was a shareholder in one of the earliest Po steamships, the *Eridano*, which journeyed between Pavia and Trieste in the 1820s, and Pellico's connection to the Po was commemorated in his eulogy to Saluzzo:

Ma nessuna di grazia armonìa tacque,	But none silenced your graceful quarters,
O Saluzzo, in tue rocce e in tue colline,	Saluzzo, hearing harmony in your rocks and hills,
E ne' tuoi campi e in tue purissim'acque.	In your fields and your pristine waters.

Pellico isn't a great poet. If there's a cliché to be had, he goes for it: the *colline* (hills) are inevitably "divine" or else *dolci* (sweet). But his evocation of the *immensa valle opima* (that "immense plump valley") over which he gazed and travelled suggests that his nationalist dream was manured by the Pianura Padana. The Po became, for him, like a knotted cord on a monk's habit: holding together the cloth and symbolising sacred vows.

Considering how small it is, Saluzzo reverberates surprisingly throughout Italian literature. Tommaso III became Marquis of Saluzzo during his incarceration by the Duke of Savoia between February 1394 and May 1396. Over those two years of detention, he wrote his *Book of the Errant Knight* in French, a sprawling compendium of stories, mostly about love and its betrayals. He, like Pellico, eulogised his lost homeland and especially his prairies' generous, clean waters: "celle eaue qui est si clere" ("that water that is so clear"). His terse proverbs are fun, too, and echo that connection between Monviso (which he called "Mont Visoul") and devotion, between aspiration and reality: "Qui plus hault monte qu'il ne doit, de plus hault chiet qu'il ne croit" ("He who climbs higher than he should, will fall further than he knows"). Tommaso was released in May 1396 after the second of four instalments of the 22,500 gold florin ransom had been paid to Savoia. But the two local powers continued to fight, and in 1413, Savoyard troops entered Saluzzo and forced the Del Vasto family to become their vassals.

Boccaccio, too, wrote about Saluzzo in the last book of *The Decameron*. The Griselda story (also told by Petrarch and Tommaso III) is about meanness and constancy. It describes the marriage between a fictional Marquis Gualtieri of Saluzzo and his commoner wife, Griselda. Gualtieri treats her abominably to test her loyalty. Griselda's children are removed, she is criticised and reminded of her inferiority. The long-suffering Griselda meekly accepts all these humiliations: "My lord, do with me as you think best for your own honour and peace of mind, for I shall rest content whatever you decide..."

Later he takes away their son, but she is adamantly obedient: "My lord, look to your own comfort, see that you fulfil your wishes, and spare no thought for me, since nothing brings me pleasure unless it pleases you." Then he decides he is going to put aside his wife and take another and Griselda, of course, meekly accepts his wishes. That subjugation is deliberately troubling because it's a story that parodies the whims of feudal tyrants. But it's also an attempt to make a serious egalitarian point. Boccaccio's story is a riposte to Andreas Capellanus's *De Amore*, a twelfth-century treatise which claimed that only the upper classes were capable of love. After the twist in Boccaccio's story, with the revelation that it's just a cruel game to test Griselda's patience, both protagonists are enlightened and described with the same adjective: *savissima/o* (very wise). There's an equality in that repeated adjective, despite the "intolerable" injustice. The noble accepts that he's the ignoble one, and admits he has been "cruel and unjust and bestial": "*ti punsi e trafissi*" he admits to his wife: "I punched and pierced you." The moral of Boccaccio's story is that "celestial spirits may sometimes descend as much into the houses of the poor as into the royal palaces of men who would be better employed as swineherds than as rulers".

The other notorious romance about Saluzzo is the exact inverse. Girolamo Parabosco's sixteenth-century yarn seems to be going very jauntily until, suddenly, it turns into splatter-literature. The Piacenza-born writer and madrigal composer Parabosco wrote his "I Diporti" as amusements and his Briseida tragedy is both enjoyably verbose and brutally short. Briseida is the only daughter of a Marquis Ludovico of Monferrato, amply eulogised as "a man truly so wise, fair and courteous", with such "virtues and valour" that "his people held him in reverence and love as if they were adoring something divine". The symmetry of the story requires that the son of the nearby Marquis of Saluzzo, called Gasparo, was equally immaculate: "a very valorous knight, handsome, wise, he was kind and prudent beyond measure."

Gasparo falls in love with Briseida and commissions his valet, Rinconetto, to write out his forlorn love letter and destroy the evidence of its delivery (hacking his horse into a thousand pieces): "Entertain my spirit with the hope of a kind reply... out of that extreme affection and reverence that I bear for your beauty and virtue, let me be worthy of four words..." The descriptions of Briseida's heart on receipt of this letter are long, but her reply is dismissive and terse:

> Gasparo, your boldness has been truly great, which at the same time makes you worthy of eternal hatred and inestimable love ... I cannot help feeling sorry for you and call myself above all outraged...

But believing in his love, she forgives him. She bids him obey the orders of Monica, the deliverer of her letter. Thus Briseida and Gasparo meet in secret and share a night with "extreme contentment and delight". They promise to meet again, but the following night her father, Ludovico, returns from his hunting trip and discovers Gasparo. The lover is beheaded and his head delivered to Briseida. She takes it, wrapped in white cloth, to Gasparo's father, the Marquis of Saluzzo:

Here is the fruit of thy seed, which thou hast guarded so well. This is the head of your son... I, not yet satiated with the damage of such wicked offspring, come to satiate myself in your pain...

The marquis's grief is so great that he – with a thousand stabs which recall the butchered horse – tore into her "with fury and force".

By the time of Parabosco's story, the Del Vasto dynasty had died out and these popular stories – unrelated in reality to the town at all – filled the narrative vacuum. But the true stories of that dynasty are almost as fantastical. Ludovico II and his second wife were the last of the great power couples of this capital. Ludovico acceded to power in 1475 and one of his earliest achievements was his most memorable. In 1478, he opened negotiations with the neighbouring powers of Provence and the Dauphiné, and their respective overlords, René of Anjou and Louis XV of France, to bore a tunnel through Monviso at 2,882 metres above sea level.

The tunnel was an economic imperative more than a military one. The Genovan Republic maintained a monopoly on the sale of salt in the north-west of the Italian peninsula and enjoyed abundant revenues through the application of the unpopular *gabella*, the salt tax. It's possible that Piemonte's most famous dish – the steaming, anchovy-flavoured bagna càuda ("hot bath") – got its name from smugglers who used to hide contraband (hot) salt under the fish.

The Marquis of Saluzzo was eager to find alternative access to this vital mineral. The quickest way was over the Alps to the salt producers in Aigues-Mortes (the "dead waters") and Étang de Berre, either side of the Rhône delta. But Monviso and its sister peaks were impassable for most of the year. And so, in the florid words of one nineteenth-century Saluzzo historian:

The provident prince observed that at that time it was a long and uncomfortable journey to transport goods and above all salt, from France to the lands of the Marquisate; that moreover it was necessary to pass through Monginevro or Moncenisio, roads that belonged to foreign States and remained closed to the people in times of war, and on which they had to pay heavy and many duties. Therefore he thought that it would not be impossible, by means of a tunnel to be dug in the bosom of the Viso, to open for the Po valley a new and more comfortable way, shorter and running through his own domain.

Ludovico was proposing to go under the Colle delle Traversette (the "crossing pass") using fires, boiling water, vinegar and pickaxes to crack through the fissile rock. As well as importing salt, he was hoping to export rice, fruit and walnut oil to France all year round. It would also provide his military with a far more reliable supply route from his French ally, as well as a retreat from this dangerously dead-ended valley for himself and his infantry if the need ever arose.

The eventual agreement split the 12,000-florin costs between the Marquisate of Saluzzo and the Parliament of Grenoble. Ludovico was given concessions to purchase, annually, 5,300 terracotta pots of salt from the Étang de Berre and 10,600 from the Étang de Lavalduc (taxed at eight florins for every hundred pots). The tunnel – which became known as the Buco di Viso or Pertuis du Viso – took two summers to complete, but by 1480 there was a lumpy, slightly off-line tunnel linking the Po valley to what are now the French territories of Queyras and Briançon. It was originally around 100 metres long, but due to the erosion of the peak's sides, its length is now only around 75 metres. It was eight foot high and ten wide, just enough for a loaded mule to pass through.

The tunnel briefly revolutionised both trade and military strategy in this region. The customs office of Revello, the marquisate's military stronghold the other side of the slimming plain, recorded 20,000 annual sacks of salt in the early 1480s. Ludovico used the tunnel to escape in 1486 when the Duke of Savoia, yet again, overran his mini state. He took back his marquisate thanks to French intervention, but was then forced to honour his military obligations to the French by fighting the Spanish all over the Italian peninsula. He was rarely in Saluzzo. His first wife died and, to cement his over-the-Alps alliance, in 1493 the fifty-two-year-old took Marguerite de Foix-Candale, aged nineteen, as his bride.

The story of their marriage is brief but productive: Ludovico died in 1504 having seen Marguerite bear the Saluzzo dynasty five male heirs. As with Parabosco's story, though, just as a happy ending appeared probable (with five male heirs, the continuance of the Del Vasto signoria appeared certain) the dynasty destroyed itself. Many local historians have blamed Marguerite who became, they say, a matriarchal tyrant: as regent to her firstborn Michele Antonio, aged only nine at his father's death, Marguerite enjoyed unrivalled power. Centuries later she was described by one historian, infected perhaps by misogynistic fears, as a "haughty and fearsome woman". Her name and face even graced the coins from Carmagnola mint which erased Ludovico and showed only her profile: "Tutrix and Curatrix" it said: "tutor and curator". As years went by, it was said that Francesco Cavassa (of the famous "straight ahead" family with the chub fish symbol) was her lover.

As he grew up, Michele Antonio showed little interest in affairs of state, preferring war and conquest in foreign fields. He died, like his father, fighting for the French in the Kingdom of Napoli. During his adventures, Marguerite had imprisoned her second son, Giovanni Ludovico, in Verzuolo castle for three years, but on hearing of his brother's demise Giovanni Ludovico marched on Saluzzo and killed Francesco Cavassa. Suddenly vulnerable, Marguerite looked for protection from the French king. He summoned Giovanni Ludovico, imprisoned him, and made his brother, Francesco, the marquis.

It begins to sound like a soap opera in its umpteenth series now: Francesco of Saluzzo decided, in 1536, to join the Spanish cause against the French. The French king released Giovanni Ludovico and encouraged him to take power. But the slow-witted Giovanni was captured by his younger brother Francesco, who was, however, killed in the siege of Carmagnola. And so their youngest brother, Gabriele, becomes marquis. But he, too, is betrayed and fed a poisoned melon in 1548. At this point, Giovanni Ludovico is the last Del Vasto left standing, since one of the five sons had died in infancy. Three times imprisoned and three times released, Giovanni Ludovico takes the marquisate just as it becomes meaningless: France annexes Saluzzo and, years later, offers an annual payment for the acquisition. With Giovanni Ludovico's death in 1563, the Del Vasto dynasty, too, dies out.

Revello stands opposite Saluzzo as the river sickles around orchards. The town became part of the Saluzzo Marquisate in 1215, meaning that the dynasty controlled both sides of the valley. A castle used to stand here at the top of the hill, but, having been sacked in 1642, it fell into ruin.

As you slowly walk up the wooded hill, past the town's aqueduct, chapels and blackberry clusters, you can still see sections of the ramparts between the 20-metre-high bamboo stands. It's hot and humid, but as you stand in the embrasures, and put your face up to the cobwebbed arrowslits, you can feel the rush of cooler air.

You can see the course of the river a few miles away, hugging the hills to the south. It looks so different from the Bassa now: rather than uninterrupted fields, there are small orchards and so many polytunnels that the land often looks white. Cypresses stand like hairy needles and as the ground rises into these hills, vineyards fill every clearing between the trees and the houses.

Revello was, in some ways, the operative centre of the Saluzzo state: this was a military, rather than courtly, castle and it was, with the customs house in the town below, a frontier town for trade. Water, too, was plentiful, crashing down the edges of Monte Bracco and powering the nuns' millstone in the town. It was that bit closer to France in an emergency, too. Marguerite preferred staying here as she fought her sons and watched them fight. This is where, they say, her partner-in-power, Francesco Cavassa, was imprisoned and killed, fed a plate of poisoned beans.

From here on, the Po finally has a valley instead of a plain. The hills hem it in on both sides and I can, at last, approach the Stone King.

NINE

Stone King

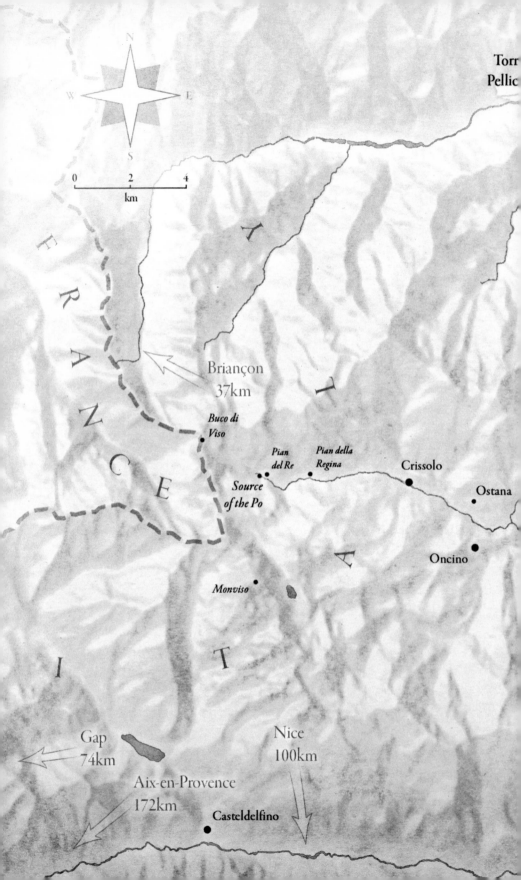

Torr
Pellic

N
W   E
S

0   2   4
km

F R A N C E

Briançon
37km

*Buco di
Viso*

*Pian
del Re*   *Pian della
Regina*

Crissolo

Ostana

*Source
of the Po*

Oncino

Monviso

I T A

I   T

Gap
74km

Nice
100km

Aix-en-Provence
172km

Casteldelfino

Torrente Pellice

erna

Barge

Paesana

Rifreddo

Po

● Martiniana Po

STONE KING

The landscape is subtly changing. As you leave Saluzzo, you come to a street and small suburb called Creusa. It's a sign of how close Genova and Liguria are. *Crêuza* in Ligurian dialect means a walled and paved path which runs along the hills and mountains. Often millennia old, they enable access and trade even in floods and snow. It was a dialect word given global recognition by Fabrizio De André's great 1980s album, *Crêuza de Mä*: the title song evoked the steep, coastal alleys and included the shrill voices of the women hawking fish.

But "creusa" is also a word which is connected to river courses: in certain Lombard dialects *croesus* means a stream, or its stony bed. In Piemontese dialect *creus* means deep. So in some ways these meandering paths, paved with rocks and sunk so low in the ground that the hiker is sometimes only visible from the shoulders up, imitate riverbeds. Designed to keep out water, they also, twisting through the landscape, echo the aquatic course from which they take their name.

The stone is strange to see, too. Ever since the delta, the majority of castles, towers, churches and abbeys have been, thanks to the muddy plains, made of red brick. Roofs have been the same shade, their curved tiles coming from the same source. But now, as the road begins to ascend, the houses are made of stone and rock. The roofs are particularly different: the tiles here are inch-thick, square stones laid diagonally to the roofline. Light grey like the sky and around a metre square, they make the houses seemed crouched, hunched together in villages against this unpredictable climate.

These tiles are sliced from Luserna stone. They're called "lose". When you look on a map, there are many hamlets and villages near here that owe their name to this quartz and feldspar rock: Lose, Monte Losetta, Luserna. And when you're on the main roads around here you see, every quarter of a mile, a quarry and stone-splitting operation, the "lose" piled up on pallets for the next roof repair or newbuild.

The changing building materials are just the first sign that you're entering an unusual territory: the Cottian Alps. The name comes from the first-century tribal leader Cozio, who was given prefectorial status by Claudius, before his royal line was extinguished under Nero. It's an area that has always seemed to be different. Just like the delta, at the other end of the river, this tough topography attracted those who needed to escape crown courts or papal inquisitions. Berber shepherds, the descendants of Saracen incursions in the Mediterranean in the ninth and tenth centuries, sometimes settled here (the North African influences are common, found in both place names and dances like the bacchuber). One of France's most famous bandits, Louis Mandrin, was from the Dauphiné: these mountains were ideal for someone smuggling luxuries across borders at a time when tax collectors were often unregulated, roaming profiteers.

The pull of the Cottian Alps was, for many, a question of survival. In the twelfth and thirteenth centuries, various poverty movements inspired by the Bible began renouncing ecclesiastical power and wealth. The Umiliati was a religious order, mainly centred on Lombardia, which was declared heretical by Pope Lucio III in 1184. The Apostolici were similar: founded by Gherardino Segalelli in Parma, the movement rejected priestly intervention and private ownership, leading to inevitable suppression and the burning of Segalelli in Parma in 1300. Fra Dolcino (scorned by Dante and eulogised by Dario Fo) was one of Segalleli's followers. He, too, was burned as a heretic in 1307. That suppression ensured that these "pauperistic", proto-Protestant movements were largely eradicated in the Padanian plain, but they survived in these austere mountains. Peter of Bruys, the twelfth-century religious leader, retreated here with his "heretical" followers. So, too, did many of the "Poor of

Lyon" as the early followers of Peter Waldo (or Pierre Vaudès) were known before they were labelled "Valdesi" or, in English, "Waldensians".

That accumulation of outcasts, retreating from or rejected by mainstream orthodoxies and dogmas, contributed to the emergence of an extraordinary semi-independent enclave. The long history of the Republic (or Federation) of the Escartons is hardly known in Piemonte, let alone in the English-speaking world. But for many centuries, this federation appears to have been a wise alliance of inventive mountain dwellers. The area was small, straddling both modern-day France and Italy: the capital of the four (later five) compartments was Briançon and the Federation's pear-shaped borders narrowed to the south-west, just reaching Casteldelfino, below Monviso. The majority of the "Italian" part of the Federation was further north, around Pragelato ("frozen pastures"), Oulx and Sestrières.

The name "Escartons" derives from the way they would "divide" (*éscarter*) their own revenues: twice a year representatives of each village went to Briançon *pour faire l'éscart*, to disburse their surplus. The first documentary evidence of this fiscal freedom is a recognition of liberty in 1244 by Guigues VII, the Dauphin of Vienne (on the Rhône, just south of Lyon). A century later, on 29 May 1343, his descendant Humbert II signed the "Grande Charte" which recognised and codified the rights of the Escartons. Humbert renounced "comital taxes, levies on meat and on fires [family homes], and on the inhabitants..."

There were thirty-eight articles to that Grand Charter, and reading the document it's striking how egalitarian it was. Article one recognises equal status between men and women for hereditary rights: "... des deux sexes". The Escartons were permitted to create their own civil and penal laws and nominate their own officials, including a *mansia* for public order. They controlled their own waters, fountains, streets, woods and ovens and weren't only trading wool, meat and wood, but also – thanks to gold and silver mines in Mentoulles and Pragelato – precious metals. The Escartons could take any water they needed from "béals, canaux et conduits" and no feudal lord would be allowed to raid the mountains for wood. They were responsible for their own *corvées* ("chores"). Every hamlet could nominate its own teachers and educators.

In 1349, six years after that Great Charter, and following the death of his son which left him without an heir, Humbert retreated to a monastery and sold his lands to Philip VI of Valois, the French king – a more powerful though far more remote monarch. A financial burden was placed on the Escartons but it was very light: an annual tribute, payable on 2 February, was set at 4,000 gold ducats (equivalent today to about €400,000 which, divided by roughly 45,000 inhabitants, worked out at a little under €9 a head per annum).

The Escartons were a pre-modern association in which power was uncentred, but somehow shared. Historians who have written about this enclave have tended, not surprisingly, to be interested in its egalitarianism and its autonomy from ideological and fiscal impositions. "Each Escarton," the late historian Alex Berton wrote, "is therefore a grouping of communities in a given region, with the task of essentially carrying out the distribution of the general expenses of peace and defence pertaining to local life. Lacking, or unable to rely on, a central power, the Escarton thus became a collective organisation of mutual assistance, at the service of the most desperate cases of each associated community." Historians excited by the proto-anarchic Federation have called it a "Republic" and seen it as a last expression of autonomous social order before the inevitable annexation by nation states. One writer evokes "a sparkling air of freedom nourished by the distance from the seigneurial powers". The Federation does sound, in some ways, proto-socialist: in a mutual accord between the

Escartons from 1382, they avow: *se uno di noi cade, ecco l'altro che lo sorregge* – "if one falls, the other supports him". There was a provision that if repayment of debts was impossible, they would be erased.

After the Reformation, more religious refugees found their way to these mountains. Europe's wars of religion drove many Protestant minorities into these ravines and villages. The Vassy massacre in 1562 and the St Bartholomew's Day massacre in 1572 had forced many Huguenots, French Protestants, to emigrate into safer enclaves. As many as 6,000 Waldensians are said to have been killed in the Calabrian massacres of May–June 1561 (the lower estimates suggest 1,700 victims), and it was inevitable that survivors would return to their Alpine origins and hide. "In the Escartons," Daniele Pepino writes, "the Waldensians became evermore numerous and were considered inhabitants in every sense, so much so that mayors often intervened to save them on the occasion of inquests and trials."

The heyday of the Escartons was possibly in the early seventeenth century. The French Edict of Nantes (1598) diminished the persecution of Huguenots, and one of their own, the Duke of Lesdiguières, was appointed governor of the Delfiné. There was a degree of religious toleration on the Savoyard side, too, with the 1561 Peace of Cavour offering recognition of the rights of Waldensians to preach within prescribed boundaries. These religious outlaws were still seen as bandits: their word for an elder or uncle (*barba*) became a synonym, among Catholic opponents, for bandit or partisan (*barbetto* in the regional dialect). Their tabernacles were scorned as agricultural outbuildings (*ciabàs* – a term which, like many insults, was adopted by the insulted who were proud to worship in a hut or shed).

That truce was brutally broken in 1655. The widowed Savoyard duchess Madama Cristina (nicknamed Madama Reale) was the aunt of Louis XIV, widow of Vittorio Amedeo

I, and sister-in-law of the beheaded Charles Stuart. Against the backdrop of warfare between France and Spain, Madama Reale's brothers-in-law, Maurizio and Tommaso, saw an alliance with Spain as a way to seize the duchy. Perhaps because her regency required a display of martial prowess and ideological cohesion, she decided to shore up her French allegiance by punishing the "Lusernesi" (as the Waldensians were also known). The Waldensian historian Giorgio Tourn called what followed "a pogrom". One eyewitness, a French Huguenot officer, described people "massacred, dismembered, hanged, burned and violated... I saw men murdered in cold blood, and women, aged persons and young children miserably done to death." Refugees now flowed in the opposite direction to a century before, back from the Valli Valdesi to the Delphiné. Since the deaths occurred in Holy Week, the slaughter was called, in Italian, the *Pasque Piemontesi*, the Piemontese Easters.

The ferocity of the Easter massacres had been publicised by those pushing for an alliance of Protestant powers. Oliver Cromwell decreed 14 June 1655 a day of fasting, humiliation and prayer. He despatched an emissary to Torino accompanied by an indignant letter in Latin penned by John Milton: "The fired houses which are yet smoking, the torn limbs, and ground defiled with blood... Heaven itself seems astonished at the cries of dying men, and the very earth to blush." Later, he wrote his indignant sonnet about the killings, "On the late massacre in Piedmont":

Avenge, O Lord, thy slaughter'd saints, whose bones
Lie scatter'd on the Alpine mountains cold;
Ev'n them who kept thy truth so pure of old,
When all our fathers worshipt stocks and stones...

A peace of sorts was agreed at Pinerolo in August 1655. But this was a one-sided ceasefire with Madama Reale conceding only "patents of pardons". The Valdesi would still be excluded from Luserna and Lusernetta, and not allowed to worship in what was becoming their capital, Torre. A citadel was speedily built above the town.

The money raised in England for the Valdesi amounted to £38,097. Not all of it reached them, but there was money to reacquire land, rebuild houses and, inevitably, rearm. A guerrilla war lasted for the next decade. Two Waldensian captains took up arms. The typical weapons were surprise and a long billhook or machete called a *beidana*. One of the guerrilla commanders was killed but the other, Giosuè Gianavello (or Janavel) fought on, even writing a military manual about insurgent strategies:

> The first duty to which you must commit yourselves is that of maintaining the union among you; that the Lord's shepherds be required to accompany their flock, day and night, so that they may be surrounded with honour and respect as befits the servants of the Lord on earth; that they not be permitted to expose themselves to danger in combat but devote themselves to praying to God and encouraging the combatants, consoling the dying and providing for the rescue of the wounded and families in need.

That it was an asymmetric, religious war gave his manual a sense of divine destiny:

> Today the enemy's force consists of bombs, cannons, grenades, artillery fire, cavalry; all this should not frighten you; after one or two clashes the dragoons, who look like devils, will be stopped by God-fearing people who fight for His cause.

In February 1664, the "Patents of Torino" was signed. Gianavello was excluded from the pardons and lived out his life as an innkeeper in Geneva.

A distrustful peace lasted only another two decades. The Counter-Reformation was becoming, in Tourn's words, "not a religious hypothesis but an ideology of absolute authority". Catholic monarchs and dukes were attempting to stitch back the severed ideology of *cuius regio eius religio* – that subjects must adopt the religion of their ruler. Louis XIV saw spiritual defection as an augury for political separation: with their emphasis on individual conscience and elected courts, the Calvinists appeared democratic, if not anti-monarchical. Louis' Edict of Fontainebleau (October 1685) is better known as the "revocation of the Edict of Nantes", ending altogether the crown's grudging tolerance of Huguenots.

Vittorio Amedeo II, that famously on/off ally of the French, followed suit. His decree of January 1686 banned Waldensian worship, ordered their churches be demolished and forced pastors and schoolmasters to leave the country within fifteen days. To ensure that no Protestant stragglers could enter his territory, Louis XIV despatched around 10,000 troops under the command of General Catinat.

By then, the guerrilla leader of the Waldensians was Henri Arnaud. He had been born in the Delphiné to a Huguenot father and a Waldensian mother, settling in Torre in 1656. Arnaud was well travelled and was both pastor and soldier: he had studied theology in Geneva and had been a soldier in the Dutch army of William of Orange. But it was an uneven fight. The ill-armed 2,500 men under Arnaud were routed. Of a population of 14,000, between 1,600 and 2,000 died; 8,500 Valdesi were taken prisoner. They were marched to Carmagnola or sold to neighbouring powers. Pastors and schoolmasters were imprisoned with their families in the Torino citadel. Those who abjured were sent to populate the Vercellese swamps.

Eventually, in the late winter of 1687, Vittorio Amedeo allowed the Waldensians to leave his territories once and for all. Of those

8,500 prisoners, now only 3,845 were still alive. The majority accepted exile and they were accompanied over the mountains to Geneva by Savoyard officers. "As the bedraggled refugees, ill-clad, frost-bitten, weak from imprisonment and Alpine cold, reached the boundary of the city-state of Geneva," writes Prescot Stephens in his readable history of the Waldensians, "they found a crowd of citizens and magistrates waiting to greet them, among whom were Henri Arnaud and Gianavello, now aged 70." Arnaud described the refugees as "moving skeletons".

The exile didn't last long. The formation of the League of Augsburg, uniting powers threatened by the expansionist ambitions of France, and the accession of William and Mary to the English throne in the Glorious Revolution of 1688, appeared to offer the Waldensians an opportunity. In August 1689, 900 Valdesi troops decided to force their way home: they set sail in secret, in fifteen boats, from the Swiss side of Lake Geneva. Alongside the charismatic, impulsive Henri Arnaud, a Huguenot officer from the Dauphiné was chosen as military commander. With muskets, armour and funds provided by William of Orange, whom Arnaud had met in person in the Netherlands in 1688, the Valdesi were often able to pay for their safe passage from one town to the next, but at Salbertrand the only means across the fast-flowing Dora was the narrow bridge with a strong encampment of French troops on the other side. The lack of any other options, or a belief in their divinely appointed invincibility following prayers led by Arnaud, persuaded the Waldensian and Huguenot troops to storm the bridge. Surprised by their audacity, the French commander fled with his troops in disarray.

The Waldensians pushed on through the San Martino valley, through Ghigo and over the Julien pass towards Bobbio. But they were repeatedly bogged down in skirmishes. Already reduced to around six hundred men, the departure of the Huguenot commander and his men left Arnaud with only around four hundred troops. The French, wanting both to exterminate the guerrillas and keep an eye on their unreliable Savoyard ally, Vittorio Amedeo, deployed 18,000 men to the Cottian Alps.

Arnaud and his hungry men spent the winter of 1689–90 encamped around the peak of the "four teeth", on the defensive summit of Balsiglia. When the French attack took place it was, as with that battle in Polesella, the climate which changed the outcome of the battle between Catinat and Arnaud. In Waldensian mythology, the troops were singing Psalm 68 ("Let God arise, let his enemies be scattered") as they watched the French approach the steep sides of the mountain. With a suddenness common at this altitude, rain and mist swept around the mountain, soaking the French gunpowder. The Waldensians rolled boulders down the mountainside, their concealed muskets picking off the first French assault before they emerged to chase the retreating French to Pinerolo.

With a counter-attack inevitable, Arnaud retreated to a summit called Pan di Zucchero (the "Sugar-bread" peak). They were surrounded on all sides by the French cannons but a sudden descent of mist meant the attack was postponed until the next day. But at sunrise, the Waldensians had vanished, led down a mountain path in silence by one of their captains who was from Balsiglia. Even after that absurd escape, they had nowhere to go. Harried, as ever, by both the French and the Savoyard troops, the Waldensians had little hope of anything other than more bloodshed.

As Arnaud approached Angrogna, just below Torre, ducal emissaries seemed to offer hope. They informed Arnaud that Vittorio Amedeo had joined the League of Augsburg and was offering the Waldensians a truce and exchange of prisoners. The pastors and schoolmasters imprisoned in the Torino citadel were released and the Waldensians, only a few hundred to begin with, settled once again into their valleys. Vittorio Amedeo issued an

Edict of Toleration. Arnaud lived another thirty years, writing memoirs ("The Return") which added to the legend of his Garibaldi-esque heroism.

Torre Pellice is a sort of capital, the centre of the Chiesa Valdese. Despite being a small town, there's a large museum and an art gallery. And it's oddly un-Italian – more Swiss and, certainly, more Anglophone. The museum is full of tributes and memories of Canadian or English patrons who donated money to, as well as prayers for and scholarship about, this besieged minority. There are more pubs than usual. The bookshops have titles in English and, since the Waldensians have set up an admired refugee resettlement, the small town is visibly more multi-cultural than many Alpine resorts.

There's a plaque, in one of the main squares, to Edmondo De Amicis. A syrupy prose stylist, he wrote part of *Alle Porte d'Italia* (a romanticised, first-person travel book) here and describes quite well that sense of otherness you feel: "a little Switzerland in Italy... almost entirely gathered and encamped in a vast, square fortress of wooded and steep mountains, including the high Po valley, the frontier with the Delphiné and the Susa valley." He used the intriguing adjective *anguste* (narrow or stifling) to describe these ravines which disappear into the peaks: "those valleys are so deep," he wrote, "so dark, so humid, so crowded with vegetation, that when you enter and leave them, you seem to pass suddenly from daytime to night-time and from night-time to daytime, and you are seized by a chill at every turn."

That chill he refers to isn't only due to temperature, but also to a knowledge that so many battles and guerrilla ambushes took place in these gorges and gullies. Because of the Waldensians' persecution, separation and enforced itinerancy, they often compared themselves to the suffering tribes of Israel. Arnaud, the military leader, spoke of these valleys as "our little Canaan" and the Duchy of Savoia as the "desert". In his history, he quotes Psalm 129: "greatly have they afflicted me from my youth, yet they have not prevailed against me." Alexis Muston, the Waldensian pastor and historian of Protestantism, called his work on these valleys "The Israel of the Alps", a comparison he borrowed from Peter Boyer's much earlier "The history of the Vaudois": "Of all the people that ever have been," Boyer wrote in 1692, "from the Creation of the world till our times, there is none except the ancient people of the Jews, whose History contains so many wonders as this of the Vaudois of Piemont."

The Valdesi are, in many ways, my tribe in Italy and it's hard not to be drawn into the emotional story of devout underdogs and their identification with the Old Testament travails of Israel. But the part of their history I struggle most with is its glorification of martial victories. One of the Waldensians' earliest debates was whether they were to remain non-violent, as had many of the Anabaptist movements with whom they enjoyed personal and theological links, or whether they were warriors, in both a terrestrial as well as a spiritual sense. When I look at the statue of Arnaud in Torre now, long-haired and with his sword drawn, he looks far more like a soldier than a pastor: the Bible is under his tunic and behind the belt, but the sword is drawn.

The Italian side of the Escartons came to an end with the Treaty of Utrecht in 1713. Having survived the siege of Torino and then bested the French, Vittorio Amedeo II demanded a boundary review, pushing his territories all the way "aux eaux pendantes", to the Alpine watershed. It cut off a vital limb from the Escartons. Those "ceded valleys" were granted a recognition of greatly reduced rights in 1737 by Vittorio Amedeo's son, but they were now part of the Kingdom of Savoia. "Little by little," the historian Alex Berton wrote, "the ceded valleys took on the physiognomy of a Lilliputian state." The French side of the Escartons endured until the French Revolution when all privileges from Royalist regime were extinguished. The last assembly of the "Grande Escartoun" was in 1791.

One thing the river has taught me is that its route always negates easy delineation or structural simplicity. At the outset, I had naively expected that the river would offer precision: its course, I thought, would be clear. But the delta was a blur, radically altered by human intervention so that land emerged from the waters and the waters trespassed on the land. On that long trudge through the Bassa there were faint traces of ancient offshoots of the Po dozens of miles from its current bed. But I still hoped that here, so close to the source and where three kids can hold hands across the river's shallow breadth, there would be clarity. Now, at last, I thought, the Po would gift me simplicity because, in the high Alps, there's no doubt about its location. Yet even here I'm seeing only ambiguities. In some ways, boundaries are as smudged here as they were at the delta. Here I had expected the end of Italy, but it's really the beginning of an area renowned for its cross-border, cross-Alpine alliance. The Occitan poet Frédéric Mistral wrote of the brotherhood created around this mountain:

Ami, nosti parlà soun touti dous rouman,	Friends, our native tongues are both romance,
pouden nous dire fraire e nous toucà la man:	and we can call ourselves siblings and shake on it:
toun Po, la mieu Durenço,	your Po, my Durance,
ma touti dous d'un soulet mount,	yet both from a single mountain
von abeurà l'un lou Piemount,	from which drink Piemonte
e l'autro la Prouvenço.	and Provence.

Despite being a sharp boundary between nation states, Monviso is seen not as divisive but as a well, the meeting point of two rivers. It's as if, rather than ending, the Po simply continues underground.

By the time Mistral was writing, the absorption of these semi-autonomous mountains into rival nation states had brought about linguistic loss, especially on the Italian side. Whereas Occitan was spoken across southern France, there were only Italian Occitan speakers in these villages right by the border. At Crissolo an informal Occitan "school" – called the Escolo dóu Po – was founded in 1961 to treasure the vanishing language and remind inhabitants that this area looks, linguistically, west as well as east. The fact that there are three variant, dialect spellings for that school show how much this piemontese *patuà* ("patois") was fluid, as uncontained by orthographical conformity as water is by a sieve.

Even the simplest words (like "the") sound more French than Italian now: *lou* has replaced *il* on the roadside metal maps I'm staring at to find my way. As always with minority languages, there were attempts to cherish it and remind Italians in the Cottian Alps that their scorned dialect wasn't just a folkloric eccentricity but actually a noble language of troubadours and fine storytellers. But there was a melancholy about these attempts at preservation because the language, at least this side of Monviso, appeared close to extinction: Giacomo Bellone, the Italian Occitan poet, compared the vanishing language to the landscape here, addressing her as "paura maire" ("poor mother"):

… velha 'scó un chabòt	… old as a mountain lodge
plen d'ortias	full of nettles
lhi uelhs secs	eyes dry
'scó un valon sens aiga…	as a stream without water…

He describes the mother's children descending into the plains "for a scrap of companionship".

That slow dispersal of inhabitants into the plains is very evident here. Some of the towns have shrunk so much in a century that they're no longer, properly speaking, even towns: in the 1921 census, Paesana counted 8,405 inhabitants; by 2011, it was down to less than three thousand. Rittana, in the province of Cuneo, had 1,411 inhabitants in 1901. Now it has, officially, only 135.

Their gradual disappearance was chronicled and lamented by Nuto Revelli in his extraordinary oral histories of these mountain communities. Interviewing those born in the late nineteenth and early twentieth centuries, Revelli revealed a mountain existence that was often brutal: children aged eight or nine were rented as shepherds in the summer months, going up into the distant peaks for a few lire. Many husbands went to Argentina, America and, particularly, France. As a consequence, the most famous love song of the time was "la Barbiera", in which a man begs a left-behind wife to shave his beard (the man making the request turns out, of course, to be her unrecognised husband).

The First World War stole the lives of many young men in these mountains, but the Russian campaign in the Second was far worse: the 4th Alpine Division from Cuneo in the winter of 1942–3 counted around 18,000 soldiers. After the Russians attacked their positions around Rossoch in January 1943, only 1,607 men survived to return to Italy. Revelli was from Cuneo, but was attached to another division and survived the horrors of the Russian campaign. He later became a partisan in these mountains and, after the war, was drawn to the widowed wives and mourning mothers (perhaps his best book was *L'Anello forte*, "the strong link", which sifts through thousands of hours of very frank interviews with women). Like that other veteran of the Russian fiasco, Mario Rigoni Stern, Revelli wrote about both the stupidity of the Russian campaign and its effects on these remote mountain communities. "In the Maira, Varaita and Po valleys," he wrote in *Il Mondo dei vinti* ("the world of the defeated") "the situations and problems repeat themselves with a dramatic monotony. Communities fray, schools close, the post office is only present in the larger towns. The isolation grows day after day."

In an attempt to capture what these villages were like before their post-war evacuations, Revelli conducted long, informal interviews for decades. What emerges from his books is a world of utter poverty and drudgery. "We came up from zero and today we're still at zero," says one. The curtness of the complaints, rarely containing self-pity but only cynicism, is always striking: "Money makes money," says another, "lice make lice." The details are revealing: how each child had to bring a stick to school to heat the spartan room. Luxury was having a lasagne made with pig's blood. Coffee was made only from barley, as were, often, tagliatelle. Bread from buckwheat or rye was treasured. Most villages had a communal brick oven which was lit once a week. "No meat, no wine," says one elderly interviewee.

The resourcefulness of that poverty is incessant and all by-products were scavenged: la *muraschera* was the worker who gathered up the *murüsca*, the offcasts from reeling silk. The *leità* was the bluey whey remains of butter- and cheese-making. "Back then it was an ugly life in the countryside, the day was never finished." It was even harder for women: one says they did exactly the same work as the men but without, they said, their strength. All, like the monks, got up in the dark hours to milk, spin, feed, weed and sow.

Lives were so broken that a *desmentioura* (a woman who helps you forget) would visit those in pain. And the community was so bonded in defending its orthodoxies that those who broke the unwritten laws (like breaking off an engagement) were subjected to the *ciabra*, a poignant, not always playful humiliation which drew attention to the transgression. Revelli describes the trail of ash that would lead from the church to the house of an abandoned bride or groom on the day of their beloved's wedding to another. The descriptions of life, and marriage, are utterly unromantic.

When post-war factories offered farm labourers work in the cities – often in the Michelin factory in Cuneo and in the Fiat complex in Torino – almost all decided to go. The comparison between a monthly salary and the annual uncertainty of farming was simple. "The worker gets their pay every month," one old man says to Revelli, "the farmer gets theirs once a year, after a whole year of watching the sun, waiting for the hazelnuts, the grapes... And the expenses are ever bigger. Nine months of winter, followed by three months of summer when you have to kill yourself with work between one prayer and another, and then the danger of hail..."

The more left, the fewer stayed. One man, born in 1913, says "youngsters able to do peasant labours don't exist anymore. Here we've given credence to motorisation." "Now everyone is rich," says one man with more wistfulness than envy. But they know what has been lost: "Once upon a time, the town square was full of hired hands and servants. Today the square is deserted."

There have been many attempts recently to reverse this emptying of mountain communities. Every year or two an Italian region comes up with an eye-catching strategy to attract people back to these abandoned villages. It often happens more in the south or centre of Italy, in Sicily, Calabria and Molise, but the enticements are offered in Emilia-Romagna and Piemonte, too. The financial incentives (like buying a house for one euro, or being paid a stipend in return for residency or opening a business) are so intriguing that the global media amplify the stories and some foreigners, and a few Italians, do end up moving to isolated villages. Sometimes those incomers have their own strategies – it's easier, for example, to obtain residency permits in areas that the authorities are trying to repopulate. But most come because they have jobs they can do remotely; or because they are retired and no longer need to work. From what I've seen of it, it's more long-term tourism than true rooting, and – outside the summer months – these villages are still picturesque husks of the pre-industrialised world. Actual villagers, integrated with the land as they work it alongside each other, following the same calendar of festivals and feasts which leavens the poverty, are very thin on the ground.

One of the oldest men interviewed by Revelli (born in 1888 and interviewed in 1971) did think that the exodus of youth to the factories would one day be reversed: "today's situation won't last," he said. "The world turns, and the day when we have to start from scratch will come. I won't see that day, but sooner or later it will arrive." Just over fifty years after those words, the day still hasn't arrived. But that old man's notion that society will "have to start from scratch" again one day seems convincing somehow. I'm not longing for that regression – it will surely only be enforced by desperation – but it's hard to imagine that we won't, one day, be forced back into hard labour in inhospitable terrains.

Perhaps because it's aquatic, there's an image about of the unnaturalness of modern life that I've often thought about. It comes at the conclusion of Thomas Hardy's *Tess of the D'Urbervilles*. In describing the disappearance of villages and village traditions, Hardy suggested that the explanation for rural populations migrating into large towns and cities was "really the tendency of water to flow uphill when forced by machinery". I've farmed a bit and know that agriculturalism is achingly tough and unpredictable. I don't romanticise the emotion and physical cost of bad weather, falling prices and loneliness. But trying to eradicate hardship and uncertainty has created, in part, the ecological crisis and unleashed a widespread existential malaise. In his book, *Tribe*, Sebastian Junger writes that "humans don't mind hardship, in fact they thrive on it; what they mind is not feeling necessary". But now, almost without exception, our most basic needs – water, food, shelter and clothing – are provided by others. We just have to buy them, and to do that must work to make the money. There's no immediacy to meeting our needs and those of others; there's always a monetary intermediary that gets fatter each year. And so it feels to me as if the river's redundancy is connected to our own. Its waters don't provide beaches and quenching freshness anymore. We don't visit it to launder clothes. A one-eighty-degree turn of the tap delivers our water uphill.

Now the hills either side of the Po valley are converging tightly. At Sanfront, the two valley roads on either side come together. The Po is three slim streams, each no more than a metre wide, which bend between the green-and-mauve of bushy buddleia.

It seems almost unreal that the river has come to this, that the vast, fearsome river is now little more than a mountain stream. At Paesana, it's barely two metres wide, bouncing over brown pebbles. It arcs off into low clouds, and I follow it along the village park. Soon the footpath disappears and you pull back up to that single road, past the trout farm and the little Monviso hydroelectric station with its pipes running down the side of the hill.

From here to the summit there's only one river and one road. The summit is Monviso, about 50 degrees above my sightline now. I've seen its triangular shape ever since Valenza, but now it's so close it keeps changing, the clouds like veils which uncover one side then the other. It's nicknamed "Re di Pietra", or Stone King, although its name, Monviso, obviously comes from the fact that its face is visible and identifiable from far away. Its point is at 3,841 metres, but other jagged peaks – Visolotto,

Punta Udine, Punta Roma, Punta Venezia – also mark the sharp boundary with France.

There's a legend about this Stone King: Vesulo was a monarch who was casting an eye over the other damsels of his kingdom (Vallanta e Soustra). Besimauda, his wife, wasn't happy, they argued and Vesulo banished her. She was so furious she disturbed the gods who punished the couple for the uproar by turning them to stone. Vesulo begged the gods one last wish: to raise himself and his wife so high that they could always look at each other and regret their argument. Besimauda is now in the Ligurian Alps (Bisalta) and Vesulo is Monviso.

The next time I see the Po it is mostly white, bouncing between boulders through dark, steep woodlands. These conifers have always been a symbol of the Po's source. One of the many explanations for the river being called "Padus" is that *pado* comes from the Gallic word for pines, found all around this approach to the source. Another local (Occitan) name for the Pian della Regina, the meadow just below the source, is "Pian Melzé", meaning "larch plain". Whether larch, spruce or pine, it's all softwoods, what they called (like *acqua dolce*) *legno dolce* – "sweet wood".

The valley is steep now, and although the villages either side – Ostana and Oncino – look adjacent to the river on a map they're actually a dozen or more hairpins above the water.

Once you're above the larch and elder, there's only Alpine tundra: thin, spongy topsoil on the rocks. It's the last day of July and the wildflowers are relaxing in this rare warmth. The bowed purples of Fairy's Thimble look strangely shy, their heads hooded. Alpine crowfoot looks like micro-fried eggs. Blue gentians have the flamboyancy of ballgowns.

There are so many Escher's blue butterflies that I often have to wave a foot at them before I place it. Sooty coppers and dragonflies flirt and compete around my knees. It's bare, here, but frantic, too.

Every patch of this scrub is dotted with specks and scents: there are the yellow splashes of mountain arnica and rock roses, the pink serrated petals of sweet williams, the buttery cinquefoils and the cabbagy-white domes of the laserworts. I watch the wind shake the seeds out of the rusty fluff of an Alpine anemone.

This area is famous for its rare Lanza's salamanders, but I don't see any, only the beasts that perhaps prey on them: a red-backed shrike is circling against the blue with its Zorro mask and eager claws. They say that the rusting, Second World War barbed wire up on the border is sometimes used by the shrike to skewer and store its grub. You've got to get what you can in this brief mountain summer.

The sounds are aggressive, too. These peaks are so steep that rocks constantly crack and slide. Every few hours you'll hear a deep rumble as the shattering mountain loses another stitch. The noise, echoing deeply against all these concave peaks, is like a sustained earthquake. Each time it happens a whinchat screams an alarm.

Every five minutes you see, in the midst of this peaty tundra, room-sized rocks from previous falls. The older ones are now patched with lichen and velvet moss, their first welcome to earth. Others have fissured further during winter freezes and now rest like cracked log ends.

According to the regional agency for environmental protection, there are two reasons why this mountain is crumbling. It is, in part, due to the "intense fracturing" of the notoriously fissile rock. But mainly, of course, it's due to warming temperatures and "the degradation of the permafrost which, where the amassed rocks are particularly fractured, acts as a cement through the presence of ice in the fissures".

The slow eradication of this Alpine cryosphere means that there have been spectacular landslides. For two weeks, in late June and early July of 1989, the temperature recorded in the Quintino Sella mountain refuge (at 2,640 metres) hadn't gone below 3 degrees. On 6 July, two mountaineers were spending a night in a bivouac in the Coolidge gully, hoping to reach the peak the next day. At 22.40, around 200,000 cubic metres of ice and rock detached from the mountain, shooting through the gulley and into the glacial lake, Lake Chiaretto, below.

The mountaineers survived, but the crash was so monumental that it was registered in the seismic station at Stroppo some 20 kilometres to the south. It was soon obvious what had happened: where ice had previously acted as a cement, now water had the opposite effect: "water lubricated the interface between ice and rocky substrate, enabling the glacier itself to detach." The lake is far smaller now, but still an ethereal colour. The grinding action of the glacier on the rock creates smaragdite dust which gives this water an almost cadaverous blue hue.

On Boxing Day 2019, something similar happened: once again, around 200,000 cubic metres suddenly detached from the Torione del Sucai. The boulders which rolled down the mountainside were huge: the largest were 200–250 cubic metres although previous landslides had dislodged immense blocks over 1,000 cubic metres. The energy of that landslide was such that the detritus covered an area of six and a half hectares. The fact that, this time, the slide had occurred in winter demonstrated the dangerous state of the crown of the "Stone King". It's increasingly common to read of these landslides in newspapers and see photographs of the grey dust rising around the peak.

The mountain, symbol of absolute strength, is caving in. That changing morphology is sometimes, like the river's promiscuity, a natural process. But often it's the accidental result of humanity running hot: our greed for speed is causing the Monviso to erode and I feel the same sense of foreboding as I did in the floodplains. There, however high the banks, you knew the river would one day wander again, because it always has. The more its arteries are constricted, the more the water backs up, especially as rainfall is now abnormally intense. And here, at the other extreme of the river, stones are giving in to gravity and drought. What had seemed eternal is proving impermanent and I grieve for the desiccation of this crumbling King. One month after I was there, the Quintino Sella refuge – the mountain's iconic *rifugio* since 1905 – closed due to lack of water.

As I approach Pian del Re, the river is pulled into white threads like a fuzzing wick. The double waterfall is only a drop of a dozen or so metres, but it's as if the Po is, finally, undressed. It's spread thinly over glassy rocks, flirting with the wind, almost vertical at last.

The river is glinting now: when you look east, through the mountains back towards the plain, its silvery ribbon curves and crashes between boulders. Even when it's calm, it catches the glaring sky, reflecting the rainclouds.

Above the falls, on the "King's Plain", it almost lazes again among the damp moss. And then, before you're really ready, it disappears into a crack in the rock, a hole between two vast, almost rectangular stones.

There's a painted sign proclaiming "Qui nasce il Po" – here the Po is born. The immense, dull, plodding, moody, Mexican Pianura Padana has finally come to this. I have an urge to tell the other tourists, taking photographs, that I've done the whole stretch, tell them about how long iIt's taken, and how my tramp has been oddly like the river: slow going. I got bogged down in the floodplains but there's a lightness now at last. The water is cold and tastes of nothing other than water.

But I can't stop without, if not reaching the mountain peak, at least completing the river's floodplain and touching the country's border. I've got to climb another 1,200 metres in altitude to get to where I want to end up. I keep climbing, enjoying the fact that the source is done, surpassed. It's behind and beneath.

You can feel the water cycle in your feet here. For somewhere so rocky, it's also boggy and squelchy. The dense mosses which cling to the tundra have absorbed last night's rain and now ooze precipitation into this cracking carapace, baptising the Po.

I'm zigzagging up the gravel face to the Buco di Viso. I don't know why I'm so fixated on that tunnel. It's not just the engineering feat of burrowing 100 metres through a rockface with fifteenth-century tools and skills. I like it because it's not a conclusive boundary but a passageway. Even though Monviso is an iconic example of a national boundary perfectly matching a topographical one, it has been drilled through. It offers not only an obstacle but also a telescope.

The clouds are far below now and the sun is hot on the shoulders. As I go above 2,500 metres, there are still puddles of unmelted hail from last night's storm. Smears of snow look car-park grey.

It's gravelly underfoot and so sheer it's hard not to slip. The path is less than shoulder-wide and often studded with angular boulders. When a horse is being led down, you have to lie on the steep gravel to let it, and its handlers, pass.

The path zeds up between brown coils of barbed wire and concrete forts. High above is a small horizontal patch with half a dozen people milling about by a black dot. That's the Buco.

I keep tacking up through the grey. Passers-by are now saying *bonjour* instead of *buongiorno*. Eventually I'm at the "pertuis". Painted on the wall to the right are, from top to bottom, the European, Italian and Piemontese flags. The rockface leans over the left of the aperture, which is uneven in all directions. But, like Staffarda Abbey, its jagged asymmetry is strangely ordered.

There's no illumination. Everything is black inside and it's suddenly cold in this dank emptiness. Somewhere, here, is the official boundary, the place where you leave Italy behind. It's lumpy underfoot and the sides of the tunnel nudge you to the right. It's an odd relief, after all this looking and searching, to see nothing at last. All I can do is feel my way to France.

Acknowledgements

I'm grateful to my editor, Neil Belton, at Head of Zeus and to all his colleagues for their wise guidance. My agent, Georgina Capel, and her crew – Rachel Conway, Simon Shaps and Irene Baldoni – have always offered unerring, and speedy, support.

Much of my journey was solitary, but occasionally friends or family accompanied me for a few days. I was always thankful for the company of Carlo Torinesi, Cecilia Rigattieri and the Gobbi boys.

Carlo Ferrari has provided me with a constant stream of books, and the librarians of Parma have been, as usual, impeccably efficient and helpful. It often seems as if every hamlet in Italy has a museum and I'm very grateful to all the curators that I disturbed. Many have done this journey before me and I acknowledge my predecessors, especially Guido Conti, Il Baffo and Linda Vukaj. Maria Cristina Bonati, Filippo Ziveri, Vittorio Sclaverani, Betta Salvini, Peter Robinson, Walter Donohue, Oliver Balch, James McConnachie, Claudio Belocchi, Franco Mortarotti, Clemente Pedrona, Paul Russell and Claudio Rinaldi all suggested approaches, places and leads, or lent me books and films.

For their teaching, translations, corrections and company, I'm very grateful to Patrick Francis, Paul Tout, Mike Beer, Andy and Marion Street, Daniel Green, Mary Massey, Paolo Mortarotti, Daniela Calebich, Laura Lenzi, Carlotta Pervilli, Francesco Pedrona, Alessandra Pasini Fusi, Lucia Sbravati and Robin Brown. The Calciatori Distrutti have kept me sane through tough times.

As always, my greatest debt is to Francesca Lenzi and to our children – Benedetta, Emma and Leonardo.

Any errors are, obviously, entirely mine.

Sources

ONE – *PIALASSA*

"mare purpureum": Virgilio, *Georgiche* (Garzanti, Milano, 2009).
"fluviorum rex": ibid.
"you need to understand the Po to understand Italy": Guido Ceronetti, *Un Viaggio in Italia* (Einaudi, Torino, 2004).
"the earth hoards its treasures... quick and fluid": Oliva Laing, *To the River* (Canongate, Edinburgh, 2017).
"It's as if there's an anarchic...": quoted in *I Segreti di Po Grande* (Repubblica Le Guide, 2021)
"personalities who are a bit strange..." ibid.
"an absurd and disordered overlap...": Corrado Govoni, *Uomini sul Delta* (Edizioni Ceschina, Milano, 1960).
"secchi ed ondosi calli...": Torquato Tasso, *L'Aminta e rime scelte* (Società tipografica dei Classici Italiani, Milano, 1824).
"dove 'l Po discende...": Canto V of Dante Alighieri, *La Divina Commedia. Inferno* (ed. Bianca, Garavelli) (Biblioteca Universale Rizzoli, Milano, 2015).
"you smelt the dead stench of swamps...": Renata Viganò, *L'Agnese va a morire* (Einaudi, Torino, 2014).

"we had been in Sicily and in Napoli...": quoted in Paolo Micalizzi, *Là dove scende il fiume. Il Po e il cinema* (Aska Edizioni, Montevarchi, 2010).
"e la città ch'in mezzo alle piscose...": Ludovico Ariosto, *Orlando Furioso* (Biblioteca Universale Rizzoli, Milano, 2012).
"And that fair town...": Ludovico Ariosto, *Orlando Furioso* (trans. William Stewart Rose) (Echo Library, Fairford, 2006).
"turn fields into lakes...": quoted in Aldo Tumiatti, *Il Taglio di Porto Viro: aspetti politico-diplomatici e territoriali di un intervento idraulico nel Delta del Po (1598–1648)* (Arti Grafiche Diemme, Taglio di Po, 2005).
"in just one hour...": ibid.
"If, when this river becomes murky...": ibid.
"is down there, always hidden...": quoted in Paolo Micalizzi, *Là dove scende il fiume. Il Po e il cinema* (Aska Edizioni, Montevarchi, 2010).
"a simplicity, a sincerity...": ibid.
"Tamisiana Repubblica di Bosgattia...": see Luigi Salvini, *Una tenda in riva al Po* (Marzocco, Firenze, 1957).

TWO – POLESINE

"To this very day...": Apollonio Rodio, *Le Argonautiche* (Rizzoli, Milano, 1986).

"madly he bears them down...": Virgilio, *Georgiche* (Garzanti, Milano, 2009).

"but by 1930 ... reduced by 50 per cent ...": Paolo Scorcinelli and Mihran Tchaprassian, *L'Alluvione. Il Polesine e l'Italia nel 1951* (Utet, Milano, 2011). Much of my reconstruction of the 1951 floods comes from this work.

"Che cor, duca di Sora, che consiglio...": Canto 36 in Ludovico Ariosto, *Orlando Furioso* (Biblioteca Universale Rizzoli, Milano, 2012).

"What counsel, Sora's duke...": Canto 36 in Ludovico Ariosto, *Orlando Furioso* (trans. William Stewart Rose) (Echo Library, Fairford, 2006).

"*inaudito esempio di barbara crudeltà*": Francesco Guicciardini, *Storia d'Italia* (Einaudi, Torino, 1971).

"the glory of our age": Mario Equicola, *De natura d'amore* (Cappelli, Bologna, 1989).

"Ebbe lungo spettacolo il fedele...": Ludovico Ariosto, *Orlando Furioso* (Biblioteca Universale Rizzoli, Milano, 2012).

"Your faithful people gazed on a long show...": Ludovico Ariosto, *Orlando Furioso* (trans. William Stewart Rose) (Echo Library, Fairford, 2006).

"many had harmed him...": Silvio Pellico, *Le mie prigioni* (Crescere, Schianno, 2019).

"violet ashes... lucid rays": Roberto Longhi, "Una favola del Dosso", in *Vita artistica*, 2 (May 1927), pp. 92-5.

"the oil in itself softens and sweetens...": Giorgio Vasari, *Vasari on Technique; Being the Introduction to the Three Arts of Design, Architecture, Sculpture and Painting, Prefixed to the Lives of the Most Excellent Painters, Sculptors and Architects* (Dent, London, 1907).

"narrating, imagining, rambling...": Mauro Lucco, "Fantasy, Wit, Delight: The Art of Dosso Dossi", in *Dosso Dossi: Court Painter in Renaissance Ferrara* (ed. Andrea Bayer) (The Metropolitan Museum of Art, New York, 1999).

"butterfly wings": Roberto Longhi, "Una favola del Dosso", *Vita artistica*, 2 (May 1927), pp. 92-5.

"squalid little city surrounded by marshes": quoted in Ermanno Rea, *Il Po si racconta: uomini, donne, paesi, città di una Padania sconosciuta* (Il Saggiatore, Milano, 1996).

"the lagunas spread their dead waters": Pietro Niccolini, *La questione agraria nella provincia di Ferrara: il versuro, la boaria, le partecipanze, i latifondi, gli scioperi, la disoccupazione* (Bresciani, Ferrara, 1907).

"magnificent, rich and admirable... narrow, poor and miserable": Galileo Galilei, *Considerazioni al Tasso di Galileo Galilei e discorso di Giuseppe Iseo sopra il poema di M. Torquato Tasso: per dimostrazione di alcuni luoghi in diversi autori da lui felicemente emulati* (Sebastiano Valle, Venezia, 1793).

"Re de gli altri superbo, altero fiume...": Torquato Tasso, *Opere* (Mursia, Milano, 1964).

"*scorza*": Francesco, Petrarca, *Le Rime* (Zanichelli, Bologna, 1963).

"... Così de gli altri fiumi il re tal volta...": Torquato Tasso, *Gerusalemme Liberata* (Mondadori, Milano, 1979).

"... So when his banks the prince of rivers, Po...": Torquato Tasso, *Jerusalem Delivered, a Poem* (translated Edward Fairfax) (Routledge, London, 1890).

"rosea", "rossastro", "rosseggiare":
Giorgio Bassani, *Cinque storie
ferraresi* (Einaudi, Torino, 1956).
"barren lands of the reclamation... the
hair of an old nag": Giorgio Bassani,
L'Airone (Feltrinelli, Milano, 2013).
"deserted beauty... the bare stones":
Gabriele D'Annunzio, *Laudi del
cielo del mare della terra e degli eroi*
(Treves, Milano, 1903).
"laziness which is essentially
sensuality...": Ermanno Rea, *Il Po
si racconta: uomini, donne, paesi,
città di una Padania sconosciuta* (Il
Saggiatore, Milano, 1996).
"maestosa languidezza...": Giorgio
Bassani, *Cinque storie ferraresi*
(Einaudi, Torino, 1956).
"luminous dust": ibid.

"as flat as asphalt": dir. Michelangelo
Antonioni, *Gente del Po* (Artisti
Associati, ICET, 1947).
"sullen... the brown god...": from *The
Dry Salvages*, in T. S. Eliot, *Collected
Poems 1909-1962* (Faber, London,
1963).
"shuddering the spade underwater":
from "Crepuscolo di Sabbiatori", in
Cesare Pavese, *Poesie* (Mondadori,
Milano, 1966).
"the Bassa is pure sex...": quoted in
Guido Conti, *Il Grande fiume Po*
(Mondadori, Milano, 2012).
"going beyond the banks of the
river...": quoted in Paolo Micalizzi,
*Là dove scende il fiume. Il Po e il
cinema* (Aska Edizioni, Montevarchi,
2010).

THREE - IL MANTOVANO

"We're on the edges of the
provinces...": Guido Conti, *Il
Grande fiume Po* (Mondadori,
Milano, 2012).
"was almost always empty...": Gianni
Celati, *Verso la foce* (Feltrinelli,
Milano, 1989).
"beehives on boats...": Plinio il
Vecchio, *Storie naturali* (Biblioteca
Universale Rizzoli, Milano, 2011).
"Non molto ha corso, chel trova
una lama...": Canto XX in Dante
Alighieri, *La Divina Commedia*.

Inferno (ed. Bianca Garavelli)
(Biblioteca Universale Rizzoli,
Milano, 2015).
"Before that confluence it finds a
level...": Ciaran Carson, *The Inferno
of Dante Aligheri* (Granta, London,
2002).
"became madmen, they killed the
Mantovani for fun...": Carlo
Botta, *Storia d'Italia continuata da
quella del Guicciardini sino al 1789*
(Elvetica, Mendrisio, 1832-3).

FOUR - LA BASSA REGGIANA

"I'll be reprimanded once again...":
Cesare Zavattini and Gianni Gardin,
Un Paese vent'anni dopo (Einaudi,
Torino, 1976).
"It's unique and it's not the usual
absence of noise...": from Zavattini's
Introduction to Enzo Sermasi,
*Padania: Il Fiume cerca il mare. Il
Po nel Delta* (Calderini, Bologna,
1975).

"one wears the Po like a suit": quoted
in Paolo Micalizzi, *Là dove scende
il fiume. Il Po e il cinema* (Aska
Edizioni, Montevarchi, 2010).
"banks of the mad...": Alberto
Bevilacqua, *Viaggio al principio del
giorno* (Einaudi, Torino, 2001)
"the painter who doesn't put animals in
his pictures isn't a painter": quoted
by Fabio Carnaghi in his notes to

the exhibition "Antonio Ligabue. L'arte difficile di un pittore senza regola" (Palazzo Reale, Milano, 2008) and frequently quoted in other exhibitions.

"the string-puppeteer believes man is perfect...": Italo Ferrari, quoted in notes at Il Castello dei Burattini (Museo Giordano Ferrari), Parma.

"the puppet has to be rustic...": quoted in Fulvio De Nigris, *Italo Sarzi: burattinaio annunciato* (Pàtron, Bologna, 1986).

"in the shack of the puppets the soul of the people sings": in Italo Ferrari and Francesca Castellino, *Baracca e burattini* (Società Editrice Internazionale, Torino, 1936)

"For us, the puppets are...": quoted in Fulvio De Nigris, *Italo Sarzi: burattinaio annunciato* (Pàtron, Bologna, 1986)

"within the Emilian territory...": ibid.

"To see people gripped by a puppet...": ibid.

"In 1865, forty people had asked for a passport...": Carmelo Lanzafame, *Socialismo a passo di valzer: storia dei violinisti braccianti di Santa Vittoria* (Libreria Musicale Italiana, Lucca, 2006).

"marshy and low-lying places...": ibid.

"15 per cent of all arable land": Guido Crainz, *Padania: il mondo dei braccianti dall'Ottocento alla fuga dalle campagne* (Donzelli, Roma, 1994).

"53,000 tonnes... 94,414 tonnes...": ibid.

"from almost a quarter of a million in 1870 to 145,000 in 1910": Luciano

Segre, *Agricoltura e costruzione di un sistema idraulico nella pianura piemontese: 1800–1880* (Banca Commerciale Italiana, Milano, 1983).

"there was a funeral every day": dir. Nico Guidetti, *La vera o presunta storia dei violini di Santa Vittoria* (2016).

"26 per cent of the vote in Emilia...": Guido Crainz, *Padania: il mondo dei braccianti dall"Ottocento alla fuga dalle campagne* (Donzelli, Roma, 1994).

"an extreme case of this tendency towards popular associationism": Giuseppe Catellani, *Santa Vittoria dei braccianti: l'organizzazione cooperativistica in un villaggio rurale della bassa reggiana (1890–1915)* (La Nuova Tipolito, Felina, 2000).

"twenty-three affiliated cooperatives... 171 hectares...": ibid.

"the 350-hectare estate was purchased for 715,000 lire...": ibid.

"my mother, who is from Fanano...": Giuseppe Pederiali, *L'Osteria della fola* (Garzanti, Milano, 2002).

"a dark stain moving in front of the bottle...": ibid.

"Whoever imagines the mafias as only violent or murderous organisations...": Enzo Ciconte, *Mafia, Camorra e 'ndrangheta in Emilia-Romagna* (Panozzo, Rimini, 1998)

"he's very kind, very calm, very composed and polite": see www.cortocircuito.re.it/dichiarazioni-sindaco-brescello/

FIVE – BASSA PARMIGIANA

"a kind of 'meeting house' for noble women of easy virtue...": Gigliola Fragnito, *La Sanseverino. Giochi erotici e congiure nell'Italia della*

Controriforma (Il Mulino, Bologna, 2020).

"It was an unrestrained, socialite's life...": ibid.

"we do nothing other than dance night and day": quoted in Roberto Navarrini, *La corrispondenza di Vincenzo Gonzaga con Barbara Sanseverino, contessa di Sala*, in "Proposte. Rivista delle Associazioni culturali della Bassa Parmense e della Sezione 'Italia Nostra' di Fidenza", I, 1973, 3, pp. 10–11.

"There's no benefit to being a woman, nor a lady, nowadays": letter to Cardinal Francesco Sforza di Santa Fiora, Colorno 13 January 1596, quoted in Amadio Ronchini, *Vita di Barbara Sanseverini: contessa di Sala e marchesa di Colorno* (Vincenzi, Modena, 1865).

"has a bizarre quality about it...": Eric Newby, in *The Times'* "Four Corners" travel supplement, 1998.

"Closed within her humid bastions...": Bruno Barilli, *Il Paese del melodramma* (Adelphi, Milano, 2000).

"air, air... there's no air": Paolo Rumiz, *Morimondo* (Feltrinelli, Milano, 2003).

"light exploding in undoing... clay-marl soil": Gianni Celati, "Condizioni di Luce sulla Via Emilia", in *Romanzi, cronache e racconti* (Mondadori, Milano, 2016).

"drab... wanton tears... don don di campane": "Nebbia", in Giovanni Pascoli, *Poesie* (Zanichelli, Bologna, 1929).

"the ancestors of the Coltaresi...": Luca Goldoni, *Giornale dell'Emilia* (1950).

"*le preci*... therein made their fire": *Raccolta generale delle leggi per gli stati di Parma, Piacenza e Guastalla, Anno 1820* (Tipografia Ducale, Parma, 1821).

"the Po's watershed surface diminished from 6 to 43 per cent....": Pierluigi Viaroli et al. "Space and time variations of watershed N and P budgets and their relationships with reactive N and P loadings in a heavily impacted river basin (Po river, Northern Italy)", *Science of the Total Environment*, Vol. 639 (2018), pp. 1574–87.

"have increased by 47 and 102 per cent respectively": ibid.

"1.24 million pigs... 6.71 million": ibid.

"was estimated at 300,000 tonnes per year": ibid.

"an exhausted land...a horror of vacuity": Paolo Rumiz, *Morimondo* (Feltrinelli, Milano, 2003).

"2,642 kilograms of zinc... 243 of arsenic": Ermanno Rea, *Il Po si racconta: uomini, donne, paesi, citta di una Padania sconosciuta* (Il Saggiatore, Milano, 1996).

"*il muggito*"... the innards of the earth": Guido Conti, *Il Grande fiume Po* (Mondadori, Milano, 2012).

"the only respectable river... like men who walk on their hands": Giovannino Guareschi, *Piccolo Mondo: Don Camillo* (Rizzoli, Milano, 1948).

"vast, deserted... is slow": Giovannino Guareschi, *Tutto Don Camillo: Mondo Piccolo* (Rizzoli, Milano, 1998).

"Seven food outlets... 6,000 volumes": Margherita Becchetti, *L'Utopia della Concretezza: vita di Giovanni Fabaroli socialista e cooperatore* (Clueb, Bologna, 2012).

"I lived for two years as a prisoner...": Guido Conti, *Giovannino Guareschi: biografia di uno scrittore* (Rizzoli, Milano, 2008).

"a Monarchist in a Republic... not a free man but a subversive": ibid.

"the clear and honest face": Giovannino Guareschi, in *Candido*, no. 7, 1953.

"at the end, the two enemies... thin trench of trills": Giovannino Guareschi, *Tutto Don Camillo: Mondo Piccolo* (Rizzoli, Milano, 1998).

"the great river sometimes arranges these quirks": ibid.

"actually more things happen here...": Giovannino Guareschi, *Don Camillo e il suo gregge* (Rizzoli, Milano, 1970).

"the beating sun makes people sleep in the day...": Giovannino Guareschi, *Mondo Candido 1948–1951* (Biblioteca Universale Rizzoli, Milano, 1997).

"a hot and dusty wind...": Guido Conti, *Giovannino Guareschi: biografia di uno scrittore* (Rizzoli, Milano, 2008).

"the only true enemy...": ibid.

"humour... is the acid with which...": ibid.

"our unhappiness comes from the freneticism... our anxiety": from *La Rabbia* (1963), dir. Pasolini/Guareschi.

"the earth does not betray... gnaw on the nut": Guido Conti, *Giovannino Guareschi: biografia di uno scrittore* (Rizzoli, Milano, 2008).

"when the waters of the Po were drinkable... the great cesspit of Padania": from typed pages on display in the Museo della Civiltà Contadina G. Riccardi (Zibello).

"makes it clear that the terramare...": Maria Bernabò Brea and Mauro Cremaschi, *Acqua e civiltà nelle terramare: la vasca votiva di Noceto* (Skira, Milano, 2009).

"the hostelries were always full of shouts and songs... positive convulsion which is thoroughly Italian": Bruno Barilli, *Il Paese del melodramma* (Adelphi, Milano, 2000).

"my heart beats faster...": letter on display at Museo Casa Barezzi (Busseto).

"look for example... at our sunsets...": Guido Conti, *Il Grande fiume Po* (Mondadori, Milano, 2012).

"it is better to say 'I am suffering'...": Simone Weil, *Gravity and Grace* (Routledge, London, 1963).

"Sl'è grand al Po...": Cesare Zavattini, *Stricarm' in d'na parola: (stringermi in una parola): 50 poesie in dialetto* (Pesce d'Oro, Milano, 1973).

SIX – CREMONA, PIACENZA, PAVIA AND LOMELLINA

"a whirling rotational motion...": Valerio Ferrari et al., *La Golena Padana e il Fenomeno dei Bodri* (Fantigrafica, Cremona, 2008).

"In the 1723 land census there were 130... only about thirty left": ibid.

"based on theft and deceit..." and following quotations: Rosellina Gosi, *Il socialismo utopistico: Giovanni Rossi e la colonia anarchica Cecilia* (Moizzi, Milano, 1977).

"they are experiments from which...": ibid.

"desertion in the face of the enemy...": Errico Malatesta, writing in *Rivendicazione* (Forlì, 1891).

"between 1975 and 1985, almost 12 million cubic metres...": P. Viaroli et al., "Variazioni recenti dello stato trofico delle acque costiere dell'Emilia-Romagna in relazione alle pressioni antropiche e ai carichi dei nutrienti nel bacino del Po", in *Biologia Marina Mediterrranea* 25 (2018), pp. 2–18.

SOURCES

"Go and say to the river...": quoted in
Guido Conti, *Il Grande fiume Po*
(Mondadori, Milano, 2012).
"strong brown god...": from *The Dry
Salvages* in T. S. Eliot, *Collected
Poems 1909-1962* (Faber, London,
1963).
"the 'arimannie'... the income from
fishing and salt-flats...": Arrigo
Solmi, *Le diete imperiali di
Roncaglia e la navigazione fluviale
del Po presso Piacenza* (Archivio
storico delle province Parmensi,
1910).
"although we should and could...
without our interdiction...":
G. Raccagni, "The teaching of
rhetoric and the Magna Carta of
the Lombard cities: the Peace of
Constance, the Empire and the
Papacy in the works of Guido
Faba and his leading contemporary
colleagues", *Journal of Medieval
History*, 39 (2013), pp. 61-79.
"It isn't really a river...": Gianni
Brera, "Quel Terribile, Affascinante
Fiume", in *Quaderni di Famiglia
Cristiana*, 25/4/1984.
"it stretches out like a python...": ibid.
"Padre Po... evil bellyful": Gianni
Brera, in *Tempo*, 22/5/1971.
"the current smacks... makes rich":
Gianni Brera, "Quel Terribile,
Affascinante Fiume", in *Quaderni di
Famiglia Cristiana*, 25/4/1984.

"riverside life is characterised by
precariousness": ibid.
"cantankerous common father... having
their bread removed": Gianni Brera,
in *Tempo*, 22/5/1971.
"there's the red-gold to the wheat...
the blue-green of the paddy
fields...": Renata Viganò, *Mondine*
(supplement to no. 4 of *Guida del
Lavoratore Agricolo*, 1952).
"in little more than a century...":
Salvatore Pugliese, "Produzione,
salari e redditi in una regione risicola
italiana", in *Annali di economia*, III,
1927, p. 17.
"O cara Mamma... I'm exploited":
Franco Castelli et al., *Senti le rane
che cantano: canzoni e vissuti
popolari della risaia* (Donzelli,
Roma, 2004).
"On one side is hunger...": Viganò
Renata, *Mondine* (supplement to no.
4 of *Guida del Lavoratore Agricolo*,
1952).
"develop institutions to manage...":
Giulio Boccaletti, *Water: A
Biography* (Pantheon, London,
2021).
"samboira": Gian Vittorio Avondo,
*C'era una volta il Po. Tradizioni e
cultura popolare sulle rive del grande
fiume in Piemonte* (Capricorno,
Torino, 2014).

SEVEN – MONFERRATO AND TORINO

"14.5 metres... 30 centimetres...":
Anon., *Storia Mineraria di Coniolo*
(Nuova Operaia, Casale Monferrato,
2004).
"By 1911, many of the villagers...":
Anon., *Le Miniere di marna di
Coniolo* (Nuova Operaia, Casale
Monferrato, 2015).
"Two miners, a fifty-one-year-old...
three more in 1933": Anon., *Storia

Mineraria di Coniolo* (Nuova
Operaia, Casale Monferrato, 2004).
"as early as 1493... there were only
190": Franco Crosio and Bruno
Ferraroti, *Due Secoli di Vita
Forestale nel Bosco delle Sorti della
Partecipanza di Trino* (AGS, Trino,
2019).

"agnostic attitude... goes against the current": Nuto Revelli, *Il Mondo dei vinti* (Einaudi, Torino, 1977).

"in 2018, 220 kilograms...": "Manta River Project: Le microplastiche nel fiume Po" (Autorità di Bacino Distrettuale del Fiume Po, November 2020).

"One 2020 study revealed...": ibid.

"unsanitary, inconvenient and dangerous sites": Torino city council meeting 10/5/1860, quoted in Barbara Fioravanti et al., *Bertolla* (Servizi Grafici, Chivasso, 2006).

"they stopped, then took off again...": P. Morini et al., *Aspetti della storia di Barca Bertolla – Regio Parco – Barriera di Milano* (VI Circoscrizione Amministrativa, Torino, 1990).

"on 29 September 1703...": Geoffrey Symcox, *Victor Amadeus II: Absolutism in the Savoyard State, 1675–1730* (Thames & Hudson, London, 1983).

"by August 1706, the 44,000 French troops...": Guido Amoretti, *La Verità storica su Pietro Micca* (Associazione Amici del Museo Pietro Micca, Torino, undated).

"The consequences of the battle of Torino": Geoffrey Symcox, *Victor Amadeus II: Absolutism in the Savoyard State, 1675–1730* (Thames & Hudson, London, 1983).

"by a profound irony": ibid.

EIGHT – TOWARDS SALUZZO

"The earliest records of hemp in Carmagnola...": Carlo Poni and Silvio Fronzoni, *Una fibra versatile: la canapa in Italia dal Medioevo al Novecento* (Clueb, Bologna, 2005).

"eighteen cord-makers in Carmagnola...": information from Ecomuseo della Cultura della Lavorazione della Canapa (Carmagnola).

"Rinaldo Comba's studies of medieval Piemonte...": see Rinaldo Comba, *Contadini, signori e mercanti nel Piemonte medievale* (Laterza, Roma, 1988).

"in 1882, the town had sixty-six... 25 tonnes of rope...": information from Ecomuseo della Cultura della Lavorazione della Canapa (Carmagnola).

"by the 1920s, there were seventy distilleries...": information from Museo della Menta (Pancalieri).

"Hildegard of Bingen...": Hildegard of Bingen and Oliver Davies, *Selected Writings* (Penguin, London, 2001).

"In Staffarda one feels at ease...": Carlo Peano, *I Segreti solari di una abbazia Cistercense* (Gribaudo, Cavallermaggiore, 1999).

"a logos which makes water... a suffering, living Word": Guido Ceronetti, *Un Viaggio in Italia* (Einaudi, Torino, 2004).

"ma nessuna di grazia armonìa tacque...": Silvio Pellico, *Poesie e lettere inedite di Silvio Pellico* (Tipografia della Camera dei Deputati, Roma, 1898).

"celle eaue que est si clere...qui'il ne croit": Marvin J. Ward, *A Critical Edition of Thomas III., Marquis of Saluzzo's Le livre du Chevalier Errant* (UMI, Ann Arbor, 1988).

"my Lord, do with me as you think best... unless it pleases you...": Giovanni Boccaccio, *Il Decamerone* (BUR, Milano, 2004).

"*savissima/o*... punched and pierced you": ibid.

"a man so truly wise... kind and prudent beyond measure": Girolamo

Parabosco, *I Diporti* (Tommaso Masi, Livorno, 1795).

"entertain my spirit... worthy of four words": ibid.

"Gasparo, your boldness... contentment and delight... here is the fruit of thy seed... with fury and force": ibid.

"Ludovico II and his second wife...": Rinaldo Comba (ed.), *Ludovico II Marchese di Saluzzo: Condottiero, Uomo di Stato e Mecenate (1475–1504)* (Società per gli studi storici, archeologici ed artistici della provincia di Cuneo, Cuneo, 2005).

"The provident prince observed...": Gianni Guadalupi (ed.), *I Signori del Po*, Vol. I: *Dal Monviso a Cremona* (Franco Maria Ricci, Parma, 2002).

"12,000-florin costs... 10,600...": Rinaldo Comba (ed.), *Ludovico II Marchese di Saluzzo: Condottiero, Uomo di Stato e Mecenate (1475–1504)* (Società per gli studi storici, archeologici ed artistici della provincia di Cuneo, Cuneo, 2005).

"a haughty and fearsome woman...": Gianni Guadalupi (ed.), *I Signori del Po*, Vol. I: *Dal Monviso a Cremona* (Franco Maria Ricci, Parma, 2002).

"Tutrix and Curatrix": Aldo Mola and Anna Faloppa, *Monete dei marchesi di Saluzzo* (Bodoni, Saluzzo 1990).

NINE – STONE KING

"creusa": Corinna Praga, *Andar per creuse a Genova e qualcosa di più* (Sagep, Genova, 1997).

"comital taxes, levies on meat... béals, canaux et conduits": Alex Berton et al., *Lous Escartoun* (Associazione Culturale La Valaddo/Alzani, Pinerolo, 2002).

"4,000 gold ducats a year... €9 a head per annum": Walter Ferrari and Daniele Pepito, *Escartoun: La Federazione della Libertà: itinerari di autonomia, eresia e resistenza nelle alpi occidentali* (Tabor, Valsusa, 2013).

"each Escarton... is therefore a grouping of communities...": Alex Berton et al., *Lous Escartoun* (Associazione Culturale La Valaddo/Alzani, Pinerolo, 2002).

"a sparkling air of freedom...": Walter Ferrari and Daniele Pepito, *Escartoun: La Federazione della Libertà: itinerari di autonomia, eresia e resistenza nelle alpi occidentali* (Tabor, Valsusa, 2013).

"se uno di noi cade": ibid.

"In the Escartons... inquests and trials": ibid.

"a pogrom": Giorgio Tourn, *I Valdesi: la singolare vicenda di un popolo-chiesa: 1170–1999* (Claudiana, Torino, 1999).

"massacred, dismembered, hanged... done to death": Prescot Stephens, *The Waldensian Story: A Study in Faith, Intolerance and Survival* (Claudiana, Torino, 2015).

"the fired houses which are yet smoking...": ibid.

"Avenge, O Lord...": John Milton, (eds Stephen Orgel and Jonathan Goldberg), *A Critical Edition of the Major Works* (OUP, Oxford, 1991).

"£38,097": Prescot Stephens, *The Waldensian Story: A Study in Faith, Intolerance and Survival* (Claudiana, Torino, 2015).

"the first duty... families in need": Giorgio Tourn, *I Valdesi: la singolare vicenda di un popolo-chiesa: 1170–1999* (Claudiana, Torino, 1999).

"today the enemy's force... fight for his cause": ibid.

"not a religious hypothesis...": ibid.

"as the bedraggled refugees...": Prescot Stephens, *The Waldensian Story: A Study in Faith, Intolerance and Survival* (Claudiana, Torino, 2015).

"a little Switzerland... a chill at every turn": Edmondo De Amicis, *Alle Porte d'Italia* (Sommaruga, Roma, 1884).

"our little Canaan... have not prevailed against me": Henri Arnaud, *Il Glorioso rimpatrio dei Valdesi* (Claudiana, Torino, 2001).

"Of all the people that ever have been...": Peter Boyer, *A History of the Vaudois* (Mory, London, 1692).

"Little by little... Lilliputian state": Alex Berton et al., *Lous Escartoun* (Associazione Culturale La Valaddo/ Alzani, Pinerolo, 2002).

"Ami, nosti parlà soun touti dous rouman...": Frédéric Mistral, *Mirèio: Pouèmo Prouvençau* (Roumanille, Avignon, 1859); see also *La Valaddo*, N.32, 1981, pp. 3-4.

"paura maire... sens aiga": see www. chambradoc.it/giacomoBellone/ occitania-1.page

"In the Maira, Varaita and Po valleys... isolation grows day after day": Nuto Revelli, *Il Mondo dei vinti* (Einaudi, Torino, 1977).

"we came up from zero... lice make lice... no meat, no wine... the day was never finished...": ibid.

"the worker gets their pay... danger of hail... youngest able to do peasant labours... the square is deserted": ibid.

"today's situation won't last... sooner or later it will arrive": ibid.

"really the tendency of water...": Thomas Hardy, *Tess of the D'Urbervilles* (OUP, Oxford, 1998).

"humans don't mind hardship...": Sebastian Junger, *Tribe* (4th Estate, London, 2016).

"at around 22.40, 200,000 cubic metres...": see www.alpidicuneo. it/discover/cultura/il-crollo-del-ghiacciaio-coolidge-e-il-miracolo-del-bivacco

"water lubricated the interface...": see http://webgis.arpa.piemonte.it/ Web22/sifrap/iii_livelli/Monviso-Sucai.pdf

"on Boxing Day 2019...": ibid.

Index